With a Pasty in my Pocket

by

Jack Ingrey

&

Malcolm McCarthy

Published by: Bodmin Town Museum,
Mount Folly, Bodmin, Cornwall, PL31 2HQ

Acknowledgements

I would like to thank several people for their help over the last few years with my collecting of images and information which has culminated with the illustration of Jack's book.

Firstly I would like to thank Margaret Ingrey, her enthusiasm and assistance has been unstinting, secondly I would like to thank Bill and Janet Johnson for their assistance with technical problems, sorting the text and getting it ready for publication.

I am deeply indebted to Ian and Anita Rutherford for use of Anita's family photographs and the time she has taken providing names and information. Rex Trenouth and Esther Leverton have also been very helpful giving of their time freely to help me identify people.

Over the years many people have encouraged and helped me, either by passing pictures on to me or by helping by supplying information to bring the pictures to life. I thank you all and hope that if the collection continues to grow I will be able to produce something else.

Cover design by W H Johnson based on a photograph of 'Packhorse Bridge, Trescore' by Malcolm McCarthy.

Published by:
Bodmin Town Museum, Mount Folly, Bodmin, Cornwall, PL31 2HQ.
Manuscript prepared for publication by W H & J M Johnson, the publishing team.

ISBN: 978-0-9549913-4-0

Printed by MPG Books Ltd, Bodmin, Cornwall

Forward

Jack was my best friend, although I was only half Jack's age our interests were so similar that we got on like a house on fire. There was nothing I liked more than visiting Jack for what seemed a few minutes only to realise that a couple of hours had past. This book was written before I knew Jack and shelved awaiting a publisher. He showed it to me one day, and after reading it I told him it had to be published. He asked me to supply photographs to illustrate it, and other images to make it a more complete record of the Parish of St Merryn. I agreed to do this and he insisted we went on the cover as co-authors, hence my name is on the cover after Jack's, though I hasten to point out that this is Jack's book.

Jack had a good life being born on the 23rd September 1915 and brought up in the Parish of St Merryn which he so loved. He was an only child, born of a loving family and as this book will illustrate he had great fun and fond childhood memories which stayed with him until his dying day. Sadly Jack died on 27th May 2005 and he now rests in St Merryn churchyard.

Jack will be well remembered in the village for the excellent pantomimes that he wrote and produced for the St Merryn Musical Society. I have included quite a lot of photographs of these pantomimes as I felt that Jack's book would be an appropriate place to preserve them and hopefully provide a little hilarity and nostalgia to the local readers.

Jack married Margaret Lockett in October 1966 and they lived together in Polmorla a bungalow they had built on the Harlyn Road adjacent to the meadow that Jack so loved. The Padstow Institute owes Margaret a great deal of gratitude, as I asked her if we could publish this book with all proceeds from the sale of the book going to the Padstow Institute 'Restoration Fund', Margaret readily agreed and I reciprocated. Jack would have approved of this civic use of his hard work and I as Chairman of the Institute I was delighted to be able to use my collection of photographs to illustrate Jack's vivid childhood memories and to raise some money for a worthy cause in the town I love so much.

Jack would love to have seen this book in print, and he nearly did, as we had a publisher who had taken on the project, unfortunately we had a disagreement over royalties and we pulled out of the deal. This obviously played on Jack's mind as shortly before he died he asked me if I thought we had done the right thing.

I must at this time take the trouble to thank Bill and Janet Johnson who are the publishers of this book. They are receiving no payment whatsoever for all their work, allowing us to raise more money for the restoration fund.

The Institute, a well known grade two listed red brick building in the Market in Padstow, was opened on Monday, 19th November 1883, this book is being published as a celebration of its 125th anniversary. It was built on the site of the old London Inn to provide a place where the men of the town could read, play cards, billiards and snooker. The Institute was well used in the days before television; these days the reading room and library have gone, only one snooker table being available to the members, a second table being hidden beneath the museum exhibits. Today the rooms are used as public rooms downstairs and the temporary home of the town museum upstairs. The Institute was bought by the members in 1938 when the Prideaux Brune Estate sold off a number of properties by Auction. In recent years the income to the Institute has dwindled and the building has fallen into disrepair. The present Committee have been working very hard, and the outside of the building has had a facelift over the last two years. Pete Bennett and Jeremy Grubb have kindly performed a temporary repair to the roof, which has kept the building dry this winter, previous winters we have had to use buckets and jugs to catch the water. Despite this temporary repair we will need a new roof on the building in the not to distant future. Easy as it is to hide our heads in the sand we must try and raise vast sums of money to replace the existing roof, the problem is so serious that we have actually advertised one of the downstairs rooms for commercial let. This is a route that regrettably we are having to consider for the long term well being of the building.

I am delighted to say that now the building is starting to look better due to its recent facelift, we are getting support from local people. I recently wrote a little article for the Padstow Echo and had a very positive response and a welcome flurry of cheques from well wishers.

I hope that this book provides enjoyment to a lot of people, I am sure that it will bring back memories of times past to the older generation, providing an insight into times not that too distant past for the younger generation, but most of all I hope this raises a lot of money for the Restoration Fund and helps the fine old building in some small way.

I would like this book dedicated to the memory of a true Cornishman, Jack Ingrey, a man I am proud to have called my best friend.

Malcolm McCarthy
Chairman and Trustee of the Padstow Institute
March 2008

4

Contents

Jack's father Herbert Ingrey as he was dressed when Jack first set eyes on him.

Two photographs of Jack's mother
Mildred Ingrey

Part One: Halcyon Days

1

Trehemborne - A Stranger Returns

I looked up, and the man peered down at me. We stared at each other as he stood with one arm around my Mother; then he reached down and lifted me from my cot. We continued staring as he held me up at arm's length.

The man was dressed in a brown coat and odd-shaped trousers; his legs were wrapped with brown bandages, and the badge on his hat glittered in the lamplight.

I reached out a hand to Mother; she did not move, and I was about to yell for my grandmother when suddenly the man drew me tight against him. My night-shirt caught in the brass buckle of his belt and he could not disentangle us. He kissed my forehead which was beginning to pucker. Mother separated us, and they both began to laugh.

The man said, "He isn't shy, but he isn't talking."

"He will, but he doesn't know you yet", replied Mother.

We sat by the fire, and I perched awkwardly on the man's knees, my bare toes growing uncomfortably hot. Mother said: "Jack, this is your Dad - he's home for good. Be a good boy and give him a kiss."

My toes tickled; I curled them up, leaned backwards and planted a reluctant kiss on the man's face, at the same time wriggling aggressively, and he lowered me to the floor. I ran to Mother, who lifted me up, and I put my arms around her neck. The man smiled at us as Mother rocked me to and fro.

It was Xmas Week 1918, and World War I had recently ended. I was three years and three months old, and this was the first time I had seen my Father who had been drafted into the Army before I was born, and now he was home on demobilization leave having spent a considerable time in German East Africa.

This scene was enacted in the kitchen of Rose Cottage in the hamlet of Trehemborne, North Cornwall, and I remember it as though it was yesterday.

A few weeks later my Father obtained work as a farm labourer at Porthcothan, and with the job went two rooms in the farmhouse. My Mother who had lived with my grandparents and her unmarried sister during the war years uprooted herself and joined him. I remained behind while they furnished their new home, and at the end of January 1919, I joined them.

Two years later, I started school, and it was decided that it would be more convenient for me to stay with my grandparents at Rose Cottage during each school term from Monday to Friday. I enjoyed this happy compromise until I was old enough to travel alone on the long road from Porthcothan to

Trehemborne. After a year we moved into a recently vacated cottage at Trevorrick Lane End a quarter of a mile away, and thereafter I stayed at Rose cottage on odd occasions only.

At the age of twelve years we left Trevorrick Lane End when my Father gave up farm labouring to drive a lorry, and we settled down in the village of Shop in the centre of the parish where I have remained to this day except for World War II when, like my Father before me, I joined the territorial Army and was soon whisked away for five long years.

Rose Cottage as it is now. The scene of many an exploit from Jack's youth.

2

Rose Cottage

Rose Cottage hasn't changed much since I lived there nearly ninety years ago. Standing four-square against the narrow road and the meadow fronting Trehemborne farmhouse. The slate roof and front windows are unchanged except that the windows which were always painted white are now bright red and incongruous against the pointed stonework which, when I lived there were covered in ivy. Gone is the pine tree which stood in the front garden and never flourished, carrying only a few anaemic branches at eaves level. The little pitched-roofed porch with small-pane windows and matching door has not changed, neither have the two minute gardens on either side enclosed by wide, sloping stone built buttresses upon which I would lie stretched out on summer evenings with eyes closed, listening to the Bray's gramophone, which they played in their garden at Trevear a quarter of a mile away. The intoxicating strains of The Laughing Policeman wafted across the meadows, intertwined with the laughing voices of the three Bray sisters.

How I would laugh, and my Aunt Gladys and Gran would come out to listen, and soon we were all laughing uncontrollably. Mrs Bray must have heard us, for sometimes she played that record a second and third time.

The old lean-to bicycle shed by the stream shows its age and has lost its front and rear doors; the wooden side wall bulges, but it was built long before my time and has probably seen the passage of eighty years or more - a remarkable life for a flimsy structure of wood and galvanized iron.

The elder trees growing between the wall and the stream are now more gnarled, but still grow red-brown Jews Ear fungus on their trunks. The once swift-flowing stream is now sluggish and shallow. Steps leading down to the water have crumbled away, and the two culverts passing under the road seem so much smaller now. The iron safety bar above the culverts upon which I loved to swing and perform acrobatics, has been replaced, and the height seems so much less than it was on the day my hands slipped and I crashed down into the stream, loosening two front teeth and gathering a crop of gravel rash.

When I lived at Rose Cottage a passage ran from the front porch past the straight flight of pitch-pine stairs to the kitchen at the rear. On the left of the stairs was the sitting-room with alcoves on each side of the iron grate.

On the right hand side of the passage was the front-kitchen, with glass-fronted cupboards instead of alcoves, and a smaller iron grate. Below the glass doors were two solid doors, and in these lower cupboards my toys and books accumulated to bursting point.

The kitchen was open-beamed, and at the far end stood a black Cornish range manufactured by local iron founders Oatey and Martyn. On the left of the stove was a built-in food cupboard, and below it was a space where sooty black saucepans and a boiler were housed. Near the back door was a range of open shelves on which stood our everyday china; below the shelves stood our spare boots and shoes and a large square biscuit tin held Cherry Blossom boot polish, brushes and cloths.

The larder cupboard with three shelves was under the staircase and beneath the shelves stood a large wooden tub or kieve which held for most months of the year, pieces of salted pork from the last pig-killing.

An open-ended lean-to with galvanized iron roof and whitewashed wooden walls protected the backdoor. Here was fixed a wide wooden shelf upon which stood enamel bowls, a soap dish, face flannels and a cracked and discoloured mirror which reflected only parts of our heads when we combed our hair after washing. Beneath this shelf stood an earthenware pitcher containing hen's eggs pickled in water-glass. A large galvanized bath for use on washing-day, and for the occasional bath in front of the kitchen stove. Two buckets of water for drinking, cooking and general use completed the ensemble.

The kitchen overlooked the vegetable garden and orchard. With the pump cistern, a wooden item encased in wood, with a rusty iron handle, and a lead spout which dripped water into a granite trough beneath. A huge, thick blue Cataclew stone, hewn from a local quarry of that name, covered the mouth of a deep well which never dried up.

Two bedrooms of identical size, formed the main accommodation of Rose cottage, together with a small lean-to room over the kitchen which was occupied by my Aunt and I when Gran took in visitors, then our temporary camp beds were put up amidst the long-standing junk, books and bric-a-brac, we were so cramped together that we often fell over each other. The slate roof still retained the heat of the sun, making the air humid when we went to bed, for the only ventilation was a small iron skylight which was so rusted that we were afraid to open it more than one inch in case it fell down on us. But as compensation

10

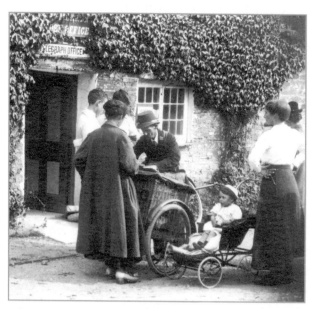

Postman Joe Brown with his wicker post cart outside the post office that was later to become Jack's home at Shop.

there were nights when I caught a glimpse of the moon or a single star through its murky glass and watched them until they moved out sight.

Gran loved her white front porch with its white slatted shelves filled with pelargonium geraniums, and a Christmas cactus, from the roof a maidenhair fern in a wire basket hung from a short chain. Many folk were entertained within the narrow confines of the porch, Joe Brown the diminutive postman when he delivered letters, mainly from Gran's eldest daughter Mary who had moved to West Cornwall. Sometimes Joe brought catalogues from the London firms of Barkers, Gamages, Derry & Toms, Whitely and Selfridges.

Gypsies made frequent calls, and one glib old lady named Selina always assumed that she was entitled to be entertained with tea and buns for at least an hour. Gran was afraid to refuse her and would bring out one of the best sitting-room chairs and Selina would soon be firmly ensconced within its ample arms in the doorway, with her back towards the road.

Selina hawked hand-made clothes pegs, lace edging, reels of cotton, pins, needles and safety pins, all of which were contained in a large wicker basket which she placed in front of her on the porch floor, bringing them forth, one by one as she sampled and commented on Gran's tea. I have seen Gran go back and forth to the kitchen three times to satisfy the old harridan's pernickety tastes. "Just a drop more milk me dear, a little more hot water, do 'ee think I could 'ave a spoonful of sugar?"

Sometimes Selina's piercing black eyes squinted at me through the folds of her brown wrinkled face, and she would point a be-ringed finger complete with dirty nail at me and say, "You've got a lucky face me boy. You'll grow up to be a clever one," and seeing my disbelief, would nod her head vigorously making her golden sovereign earrings flash and the rows of glass beads around her neck tinkle like tiny bells.

Having satisfied the old gypsy's latest whim, Gran would have now unwittingly purchased a dozen clothes pegs and filled up a proffered tin can which had been brought out surreptitiously from beneath the lace.

"Just a drop more tay for the road, me dear, and 'ave 'ee got any old clothes to give away?" "Nothing for the moment, Selina."

"Well, 'ave 'ee got any rabbit skins for sale? Your man's doin' a lot of trapping, I 'ear."

Aunt Gladys, who was usually present at these sessions, would come to Gran's rescue. "Father sells them all to Mr Hawke when he collects the rabbits. We haven't one skin in the place, and if we had, we couldn't sell it because it's not ours to sell."

Gran would look anxiously at her daughter, afraid that she would be ill-wished by the gypsy if she failed to carry out her demands. Selina knew she couldn't push her luck with Gladys, so brushing crumbs from her rusty black frock she would pick up her basket, move aside to allow the chair to be taken back to the sitting-room and make for the roadway.

"You'll be blessed with good fortune for 'elping a poor gypsy woman on 'er way," were Selina's parting words as she waddled away to seek another victim.

If Gran and Aunt Gladys drank tea with Selina, she always insisted in reading their tea cups. This ritual involved the throwing out of any excess liquid onto the path, standing the cup, mouth down into the saucer, turning it around clockwise three times, and tapping the base with one grubby finger. Selina then held the cup at arm's length and squinted at the pattern of tea-leaves inside.

"There be a journey comin' soon me dear, and good news from far away," she would inform Gran.

"A tall man with a red face and fair 'air will be callin' on you, me Girl" she would tell Aunt Gladys.

Selina couldn't go wrong because she knew Gran often went to Newquay to visit relations, and Aunt Mary's weekly letter would soon arrive. Aunt Gladys had a tall, fair haired rosy cheeked boyfriend who called on her twice each week. All these details Selina gleaned from snippets of conversation obtained at various times in the porch.

During the 1920s Gran took in paying guests. Among them was Miss Dorothy Richardson who spent several weeks in the sitting-room writing one of her massive novels. Miss Richardson worked at the round table which was draped with a dark green velvet cloth. Sometimes the black coal scuttle was filled with screwed-up balls of paper and the floor beside it littered with balls that had missed their target. She smoked continuously, and her fingers were stained with nicotine. Her ashtray overflowed and sometimes the grey dust filtered through the cloth onto the polished surface of the table. When she went for a walk Gran moved in, cleared away the paper debris and sighed as she took up the tablecloth to shake in the garden.

Miss Richardson wore gold rimmed spectacles part way down her nose and would peer over the top of them with a quizzical look when I wandered into the room. She told Gran that she did not object to my company provided I did not talk when she was writing. I enjoyed watching her expressions as she scribbled and screwed up the balls of paper. One day I said, "Miss, your hair is changing colour." She got up and looked in the mirror which hung over the fireplace.

"Why Jack, you are quite right, it must be the smoke from my cigarettes," she said as she ran a hand through wisps of nicotine-laden hair which had changed from blonde to a mousy brown colour.

Miss Richardson entertained many visitors and I circulated freely among them. I did not know their names at the time, but Aunt told me about them when I grew older. Among those people was John Davys Beresford the novelist who owned the front part of Porthcothan Farm where I once lived for a short time; Alec Waugh, Naomi Jacobs, Storm Jameson, and a Mr Aitken. One day a little man with a squeaky voice sat me at the table and taught me how to draw airships, little did I know that I was being entertained by H.G. Wells.

When Dorothy Richardson left, Gran gave a tremendous spring-clean to the sitting-room for tobacco smoke had permeated everything. The starched cream curtains were stained brown and were so rotted that they fell to pieces when taken down, and the table cloth spent several days on the clothes-line until ash and nicotine fumes had dispersed.

Dorothy Richardson returned on several occasions once to introduce her new husband, Alan Odie the well known Punch cartoonist. To me he seemed an odd sort of man. I saw him once at the Post Office, a gaunt spectre under a wide-brim trilby-style hat. A shapeless mackintosh draped his shoulders, and his shoes were worn and muddy. He was buying postage stamps, and when he came to pick them up, his long, talon-like finger nails could not grip them, so he had to scoop them along the edge of the counter with the palm of one hand and catch them in the other.

Years later, after World War II, I met Dorothy Richardson again. Now widowed, and a celebrity in the literary world she had retired to a ground floor flat not far from my home. I called on her one day, and she remembered me. Now her hair was grey, with a few strands of the original blonde colour - or was it nicotine? We talked mainly on current affairs for she seemed reluctant to discuss those days when she was writing at Trehemborne. "I'm getting absent minded," she said, and certainly proved it when she brought in the coffee. Unfortunately she had confused the sugar bowl with the salt pourer and too late, I shook it into my cup. I suffered salted agony, but somehow managed to conceal my discomfort - she drank hers neat! That was the last time I saw her, for she died a few months later.

The rear of Rose Cottage was pleasantly quiet. A variegated ivy climbed the stone wall, and each spring a yellow jasmine bush sprouted yellow flowers by the washhouse. Inside the washhouse a step-ladder led up to a dark loft where ivy tendrils pale and ghostly, had grown in above the wall plates and spread over Grandfather's seed potatoes stored on the uneven floor. One day I found a bunch of dusty old envelopes containing receipted bills impaled on a spike pushed in where floor and roof intersected. I amused myself by pulling off the black and the brown stamps and sticking them with my spit, in patterns, on the kitchen window. Gran soon put a stop to this and consigned stamps and envelopes to the kitchen stove. Years later, I realized that I had been playing with Victorian Penny Blacks and early Browns and wondered if a small fortune had been destroyed.

A Veronica hedge ran parallel to the rear path with a large Hebe bush at the far end. A grit and ashes path divided the potato patch on the left side from the mixed vegetables and gooseberry bushes on the right side.

A large rainwater butt stood in a corner outside the back porch. We dipped into its inky depths with a galvanized washing bowl, and many a gnat larva was plucked out before ablutions were begun. If the barrel was full, I could just see the top of the water, and sometimes when it was half empty I would get out a small milking stool and stand precariously balanced on its three rickety legs to bend over into its depths. I loved to ripple my hands through the velvet softness of the water and its wriggling occupants. One day I bent further and further into the barrel until my elbows were wet, so it was not surprising that I over-reached. My feet left the stool and I hung screaming with my face within inches of the black, menacing water and the smelly algae-encrusted sides. My Aunt rushed to release me, and a severe smacking effectively deterred any further explorations of the barrel; especially as she graphically explained that I could have drowned head downward had I toppled over the rim of the barrel.

It was not my only watery experience. If the weather was fine on a Monday, Gran did the family washing on the flat even surface of the stone well-cover. She brought the galvanized bath from the lean-to and placed it with the bottom rim protruding slightly over the top of a large stool. From the washhouse copper which had been lit earlier, she brought buckets of hot water until the bath was half full, adding a jug of pump water if it was too hot. All the dirty linen was piled on the well-cover, and a wicker flasket stood waiting to accept the carefully washed and wrung-out articles. Gran would then peg them onto the long wire clothesline which was supported in the centre by a twisted apple tree branch.

One morning during the summer of Miss Dorothy Richardson's stay, I was happily sailing a small boat in the pump trough. Gran had filled the bath with dirty washing and was busily rubbing it on the whitewood washboard. Little glassy soap bubbles floated up to the surface and popped in the warm air as she scrubbed and lathered with a chunk of yellow Puritan soap.

Suddenly my Aunt called loudly from within the cottage, "Mother, Blind Charlie's here, and he wants to know how many packets of tea you want this week?"

14

Gran mumbled something under her breath, wiped her soapy arms in her apron and went indoors. I sat alone in the bright sunshine, blowing my little home-made cork boat with white paper sail around the trough. A thought passed through my mind: How lovely my boat would look floating on those bubbly waves! I plucked it from the trough, making sure that Gran wasn't coming, and dropped it in the bath, but I miscalculated for it landed on a bed sheet which emerged like a white island in the centre of the sea of bubbles. I leaned over to move my boat, it was just an inch away from my eager fingers. I leaned further towards it and my fingers grazed the sail. The iron rim of the bath cut across my stomach as I strained to clutch the sail. At that moment I heard Gran's approaching footsteps. I jerked backwards and straightened up, but my feet slipped and I crashed down onto the well-stone pulling bath and its contents upon me. An enveloping deluge of hot soapy water descended; I spat out suds and steam, and was shrouded in sheets, shirts and sundry intimate articles of clothing. The bath was upturned above me, and the stool had fallen across my legs. Above the sound of gurgling water I could hear Gran's voice, loud and clear, and rising steadily to crescendo. "Oh! You little Devil! I can't turn my back for one moment without you getting into mischief! Gladys, come quickly and see what he's done!"

Gran lifted off the bath, and I struggled through the layers of sheets and clothing as Aunt detached them from my dripping body. I stood speechless; the enormity of my folly slowly dawning as I saw earth and dirt clinging to the washing, and soapy water flowing in all directions.

Quivering with embarrassment, and looking like a drowned rat, my Aunt, with scant ceremony, stripped me completely naked.

"Don't you dare move an inch until I come back," she stormed, and I was left blushing in the sunshine with my hands crossed over my private parts, my feet making wet patterns on the one dry corner of the well-stone.

Gran glared, but said nothing as she straightened up the stool, reaffixed the bath, refilled it and plunged all the washing into it. Aunt returned with a towel and dry clothing accompanied by Miss Richardson and two lady friends to witness the results of my escapade. I could have killed them all as they stood there laughing, their eyes focused (or so I imagined) on my private parts as Aunt said, "Put your arms up and let me wipe you dry."

"I won't, I won't!" I screamed, and hung on to my John Thomas until she forced my hands away. I burned with shame and humiliation before these strangers. No-one was going to see my body except my family! But to no avail, I was jerked, shoved, mauled and dried until I glowed. My privacy had been violated, and to crown my discomfort I saw Thea, an old maid who lived next door peeping through the hedge with a grin like a Cheshire cat on her ugly face, as she surveyed my nakedness.

Tall plum trees lined the riverside bank of the garden, producing dancing cascades of white blossom in spring and sweet, juicy plums in the autumn. Beneath their branches grew a line of currant bushes which stretched as far as the orchard.

The orchard contained some twenty apple trees, and its grassy floor was my Paradise where I played, thumbed through my picture-books and practiced writing on a slate when I started School. Bullfinches and chaffinches nested in lichen-crusted branches, and blue tits popped in and out of a hole in the trunk of a gnarled old elder tree. I learned the names of the various apples from Gramfer: one tree which bore large and lovely yellow fruit, which could be reached by climbing on the roof of the pigs' house, was called Hollow core, and there were Streakies, Winter Reds and Quarantines, all of which were probably local names for I have never found them in any reference books.

In spring, blue and white violets grew in clumps around the tree roots and scented the air, together with a scattering of primroses and wild daffodils. In summer, bees droned continuously on the blue heads of catmint growing on the edge of the stream.

Adjacent to the pigs' house was the straw house, so named because straw was stacked there for the comfort of the pig. Gramfer's gardening tools stood in line against one wall; shovel, fork, rake, hoe, billhook wheelbarrow, others with unusual names and uses; hacker, biddix, zye and visgey.

Tucked snugly between the pigs' house and straw shed was the wooden closet, dark, smelly and small when compared with the three-seater closet I used when I went to my weekend home at Porthcothan. My Aunt re-decorated the closet annually with scraps of wallpaper, and sometimes there were three different patterns on the walls. But it had its advantages, for one could sit unobserved, with the door open and enjoy the view of the orchard, and listen to the grunting of the pig.

A ramshackle hen house in the furthest corner of the orchard was hidden behind a cluster of hawthorn bushes, and beside it, overgrown with stinging nettles was the rubbish heap. I scavenged this treasure area from time to time, for there was always something of interest to be salvaged. I could transform an empty cocoa tin into a boat by punching a hole in the lid, inserting a stick for the mast and adding a square of newspaper for the sail. The tin was partly filled with water to keep it upright during its precarious journey downstream, through the culvert and into the reed-fringed millpond beyond, where it would bob aimlessly among the ducks until it foundered.

The stream formed the boundary with the two adjacent properties, one of which contained a carthouse-cum-stable from whose open half-door an ancient horse named Diamond surveyed his personal haystack by the stream and continually neighed for sustenance. Diamond's owner was an elderly man with pink cheeks partly obscured by a long white beard, and the straggly white hair on his head was topped with a trilby hat. He was short in stature but very upright.

He often carried a walking stick and spent considerable time in his well-kept vegetable and flower gardens situated on the high ground behind his house which was once a chapel. His wife looked like an aged Queen Victoria, and was usually dressed in black; she had borne him a family of three sons and two daughters.

The eldest son lived next door to his parents in a cottage which was rapidly deteriorating externally, and bursting at the seams internally through his robust sexuality which had produced four sons and four daughters, all of whom lived under that roof. His wife was a gentle, pale shadow of a woman who appeared to live in a state of submissive drudgery through ministering to the needs of her husband and their fast-growing brood.

Sometimes when we were in bed, the stillness of the night was broken by the slamming of doors, shouting, swearing and screaming as our neighbours rushed from their cottage into the darkness. We would jump out of bed and listen at the landing window to the uproar which would gradually die away to little sobbing noises down by the stream.

"He's come home drunk again and turned them all out," Gran would say, shaking her head sadly. "But he'll meet his match one day, and I hope it's soon."

The start of this mass exodus was the moment when the father undid his leather belt and lashed out at whoever was nearest to him. Gran's wish came true, for some weeks later there was a repeat performance. The eldest son retaliated, thrashed his father with his own belt and left him all night with black eyes and bruises in their orchard. Shortly afterwards that son left home for good, but never again was there a disturbance, for we heard that he had told his father that he would be back in an instant if there was any trouble.

Jack's Gran Beatrice Carne pictured far right, outside her home at Rose Cottage.

Two photographs of the back of Porthcothan Farmhouse, where Jack lived near his beloved Valley.

3

Porthcothan

Soon after Father was demobilized he obtained a work as a labourer at Porthcothan Farm. With the job went free accommodation: a living-room which overlooked the farmyard, and a large bedroom facing west into a walled garden and lawn with a magnificent view of the distant bay. The domestic area was built on two levels with high walls. Very little light filtered through the window which faced the blank stone wall of an outhouse and even when the oil lamp was lit the ceiling seemed remote and mysterious to me.

My memories of those fleeting months of our stay at Porthcothan are blurred except for three; a closet, a hacksaw blade, and a friendly artist.

A part of the outhouse building which ran parallel with the roadway contained our closet, a narrow room with a box-like contraption surmounted by a flat board which contained three holes, each of a different size. Their purpose reminded me of the story of the three bears and the three sizes around which their lives revolved. Circular wooden covers crowned each hole; the boarded front was scarred by the contact of many heels and bleached to the colour of honey from scrubbing over many years. The pitched roof was slate covered, with open beams where generations of spiders had spun their webs. The unplastered walls displayed the shapes of the stonework through countless coats of whitewash; the rickety door painted green on the outside and brown on the inside contained a small pane of glass which let in very little light. Above the door frame were two rows of slanting wood boards which gave ventilation. A rusty thumb latch which I could not reach, and an even rustier bolt ensured privacy. A wad of torn newspaper, each sheet measuring about six inches by four inches hung on a string from a rusty nail in the centre of the door. The uneven earth floor was a home for woodlice that processed across its cold surface before disappearing into the cracks where it joined the closet framing. A bucket of earth stood in one corner and beside it a small shovel. A peculiar smell always pervaded this building and I was ignorant of its origin.

"What is it. Mother? Where is it coming from?"

"From down there." She pointed vaguely to one of the holes. "It's in the earth." And that was all I learned.

I was conversant with the basic calls of Nature, which were referred to as 'Number One', and 'Number Two'; the latter function, I was told, must always be carried out in this building.

"Don't ever go to the closet alone, Jack."

"Why, Mum?"

"You might sit on the wrong hole and fall through."

"Would I go where the smell is?"

"Yes, and you would die."

"Would I be an angel then, Mum?"

"…I don't think so, not in the state you would be in."

"Would I smell…" Mother cut me short. "That's enough! You'll find out one day."

So when Number Two was imminent, I reported to Mother, and she accompanied me. Sometimes I went with Father and together we sat in splendour until, as Father put it, 'the spirit moved', and we laughed at the noises we made.

One day when Gramfer visited us, I went with him, and during proceedings he taught me a rhyme which horrified Mother when I recited it.

If you want to poop with ease,

Place your elbows on your knees,

Put your chin between your thumbs,

Give a squeeze - and out it comes.

My cot, with sides of vertical iron bars stood in a corner of our bedroom, near my parent's double bed, and a small dressing table and wardrobe occupied the remainder of the sparsely furnished room. One summer evening Mother put me to bed at the usual hour of seven o'clock. Strong sunlight seeped through the drawn curtains and I didn't feel sleepy. For some unknown reason I knelt up on the bed and pushed my head through those vertical bars. I felt my ears squeeze flat, and to my horror I couldn't pull my head back. The bars caressed my neck as I moved my head back and forth. "Mum! Mum! Come up! I want you!" I yelled, but she didn't answer my cries. I screamed loudly and then became frightened and wept. Still Mother did not come to my aid, so I lay down on my stomach, my eyes pointing to the floor and sobbed until I was exhausted.

It seemed like an hour before Mother came to see if I was asleep. The sun had gone from the window, but it was still daylight.

"Mum! Mum! I can't move!" I wailed.

Mother took one look at my predicament, dashed away and fetched Father who knelt before me on the floor, patted my trapped head and tried to lever apart the two bars which held me fast, but they did not move. Father left the room and returned with a large file which he rubbed against one of the half-inch thick bars which he hoped to sever and pull apart. His efforts seemed endless, and my neck was sore. Mother comforted me with a drink of warm milk and put a small pillow under my chin to ease my discomfort.

"I must get a hacksaw. 'Tis the only way to get him free," said Father and went next door to the farmer who said that he had no such tool. Then Father went down to the Mill to get the farmer's son, who also was unable to help. Twilight was deepening and I started another bout of sobbing. Mother said that I

20

would soon be free, but I could sense her fear; my neck was growing more painful by the minute and Father was desperate.

"I'm going to cycle to Trehemborne, Art Brenton has a hacksaw, I've seen it hanging on his workshop wall." (Arthur was the local carpenter and undertaker) Father collected the hacksaw and called at Rose Cottage to inform my grandparents of my plight. Gramfer insisted on cycling back with Father, and Gran, panicking at this news, set out on foot. By the time they arrived, I was gone past caring.

Mother lit two candles, and holding one in each hand, leaned over me in order that Father could see what he was doing. I felt the vibration of saw and bar as he continued cutting, and I cried out, for it increased the pain in my neck. Zig-zig-zig rasped the blade, and particles of iron filings dropped to the floor. Gramfer stroked my hair and whispered: "It won't be long now. Jack boy you're nearly free." As Father increased his efforts, Mother, whose arms were now aching through holding the candles at such an awkward angle, suddenly moved away leaving Father in near darkness. The hacksaw blade slipped from the groove and grazed my cheek. I howled with fright, and louder still as dollops of hot candle grease dripped over my naked legs. Gramfer quickly took charge of the candles and Father resumed his cutting.

Gran arrived like a spent tornado, pushed her way into the room and fell on her knees beside Father. She began to kiss me, exclaiming loudly: "The poor boy is feverish! Milly get a cold flannel for me to put on his forehead!"

Father became angry for Gran's ministrations were hindering his efforts. The saw blade squealed and grated; suddenly I thought I was going to die for it broke through the metal and the little teeth rubbed my neck.

"Ohh! Ohhhhh! My throat's cut!" I yelled.

Father withdrew the blade and bent the severed bar apart. Blessed relief - I was free! I withdrew my head and stood up in the cot, my face swollen and tear stained. Red weal's on my neck showed where the bars had chafed and where the saw blade had touched, but had not broken the skin.

Gran lifted me out. I broke free and made a frantic dash for my enamel chamber pot which was under the big bed, but too late - my pent up water and emotion flowed unchecked. I wetted the floor and Gramfer's trouser leg. No one chastised me and I was taken down to the kitchen, washed, fed, cosseted, and that night I slept with my parents in their bed.

Next day I heard Father telling Mother that I could have been released without any cutting, for each bar was threaded through holes of the top and bottom framework of the cot, and was secured by nuts which, when unscrewed had only to be lifted up and out.

That incident, my own personal agony, and the details related many times by my family, remain imprinted in my mind, for whenever I see a cot, with metal sides I always experience an uncomfortable feeling around my neck.

I was allowed to play in the walled front garden, and there I met a grey haired middle aged man, an artist, who lived in rented rooms in the front part of the house. At first I watched him through the large sliding sash window which came almost down to floor level, as I played with my toys on the lawn. He stood for hours at his easel, painting on large canvases. On sunny days he left his room and came out carrying an attaché case which held his equipment; under his arm was a small white canvas; on his back a rucksack containing food and drink. When he returned during late afternoon, there was always a partly completed picture on the canvas, and this he straightaway copied onto a larger canvas which was waiting on the easel.

One day as he passed me in the garden, he turned, stopped, and said, "You watch me painting through the window, don't you?" I nodded, being very shy in those days. "You can come inside and have a closer look. Would you like that?" I found my voice. "Yes. Yes please."

"Then I'll ask your Mother if she will allow you to come."

The man kept his word, and next morning I was sitting comfortably in an easy chair in the room he called his studio. Framed pictures covered the walls; unframed glowing canvases were propped against every piece of furniture; and on the easel was a large, half completed picture of a scene which I recognised as Golden Burn beach and the Arch Rock.

This kindly man told me his name was Henry Bishop. He enjoyed painting the Cornish cliffs and the sea. In my child's eyes his pictures were wonderful masses of black, grey and brown rocks filled with sinister caves and crevices, towering over beaches of glowing ochre and yellow sand; vivid green cliff tops blazing with wild flowers; white seagulls skimming over translucent green and blue waves; pebbles glinting around the base of smaller rocks, and lines of curling white foam.

I had seen the cliffs on Sundays when Father was free from work and we walked with Mother to the beach and along the narrow paths enclosed by gorse and thorn to Rowan, and Minnows. Sometimes my legs became tired and Father would hoist me high and set me down on his shoulders with my legs astride his head. From this perch I watched the waves and rocks lying far below, and although I was not aware of the dangers they presented, I loved these excursions, so when Mr Bishop invited me into his studio, I absorbed all the beauty of his paintings, for they portrayed cliffs and waves like the real ones I had seen.

As I sat enthralled, he talked, but all the while his eyes were on the canvas. He described the colours that flowed from tubes onto his palette and how they mixed together as I watched him plunge a blue brushful of colour into a yellow daub on the palette, and with a swirl of the brush change it miraculously into green. He named the seabirds that flew over his scenes; he showed me the black and white plumage of oystercatchers, their orange bills and pink legs; the black backs of the large gulls, and the white backs of the smaller gulls. He showed me how he painted ripples in the sand, and how to make grass wave in the wind; he recited the names of many wild flowers, but the quivering sea pink was the only one I remembered. I enjoyed my sessions with Mr Bishop which were usually two or three times a week. One morning my friend said: "I am going up to London to hold an exhibition of my pictures. My work here is finished, but one day I hope to come back again."

He collected all the paintings together, sorted and packed them into tea chests and crates. That same evening he knocked on our living room door, thanked Mother for the cleaning and bed making she had done for him, and handed her a sealed envelope. He said he had enjoyed my company, and hoped I would be an artist when I grew up. As he went, he shook our hands, and into mine he pressed a coin, smiling as he did it.

Mother was beside herself with joy, for the envelope contained a crisp five pound note, which to her, in those days was a fortune. I too was rich with my shiny half-crown piece.

Next day his studio was bare, and I felt sad. But lying on the table was a small, well worn black paint box containing a few partly used tubes of oil paint, a palette, a few brushes and a note which read: You can practice with these, and one day I may come and see your pictures.

We never saw or heard of Henry Bishop again. I used those paints until the little tubes were flat and empty, and the hairs wore thin on the brushes. My pictures, daubed on white kitchen paper were meaningless to my parents, but to me they were rocks and sea and sky; and I believe they were the first stirrings in my young mind which led to my love of the cliffs and shores of this Cornish coast throughout the coming years.

A view of Porthcothan from the Beach

Beach Cottage, Porthcothan

The Valley looking towards Trescore from Porthcothan.

4

Lane End

From Porthcothan Farm we moved a quarter of a mile inland to a small semi-detached cottage known as Lane End situated at the head of a cul-de-sac which ended at the hamlet of Trevorrick.

The cottage was very basic and comprised one large bedroom, sitting room, kitchen and a minute scullery. It was stone built and the roof sagged in the middle making the slates ripple like waves of the sea. The sliding sash windows were tiny, and the front and back doors were so low that anyone who was taller than five feet nine inches cracked their heads on the lintels if they were not careful. The sitting room had low, widely spaced beams and open ceiling; floral wallpaper bulged and crinkled over the roughly plastered walls. The slate paved floor was so uneven that the legs of furniture had to be trigged up, and in damp weather the floor sweated under its covering of linoleum and coconut matting which became sodden and smelly.

A narrow staircase with a door at each end led straight into the bedroom. Once when I annoyed Father beyond his endurance, he chased me with a slipper shouting, "I'll tan your arse, you little bugger!" and I fled up the stairs. Father followed, cracked his forehead on the crossbeam and fell down as though pole-axed. I thought I had killed him, and frightened, I crept down to the bottom stair where I howled like a Banshee. Mother, tired of my squalling, smacked both my ears and, small though she was, she dragged Father to his feet and dumped him in an armchair where he groaned, shook his head, then after what seemed an age opened his eyes and glared at me. I rushed to his side, and, through floods of tears, apologized. The incident was never again mentioned; neither did Father ever beat me with slipper or belt, although I received several well deserved flat-hand smacks on the head.

My iron-sided cot was discarded when we moved from Porthcothan and I now slept in a small camp bed in a corner of the bedroom.

Our bedroom ceiling was unique, being formed from white calico material tacked to the roof slopes and the cross beams of the principal rafters. It had been fixed many years before our arrival and was now aged to the colour of old ivory; lime pointing from the undersides of the slates had dropped onto it and caused the fabric to billow down into the room like an inverted ship's sail.

One Saturday evening in early spring. Father decided to whitewash this ceiling, and having no pair of steps, he stood on the bed, bucket in one hand, brush in the other and started to apply the whitewash, wobbling as he worked. Unfortunately his vigorous brushing split the calico asunder for the fibres were worn out and he was enveloped in a cloud of lime dust, a shroud of decayed material and blobs of whitewash. The bed was a tragic sight, and Mother verged on hysterics when she saw it. Father gathered up the mess of bedding, ceiling and whitewash and dumped it in the back garden. As he cleaned himself, he told Mother to make up a temporary bed for themselves on the floor, and also to move my bed because there was more ceiling to come down. Father then set off on his bicycle to buy calico and tacks for a new ceiling, leaving us to clean up the mess.

The replacement ceiling took Father several evenings to fix and, as an improvement, he nailed the calico up against the rafters and slates, leaving the principal beams exposed, which made the room seem less claustrophobic.

Despite the lack of daylight downstairs, we were very comfortable, for my parents had been to several furniture sales and bought a quantity of essential furniture for our new home. We had two large leather armchairs and a sofa, all of which were stuffed with horsehair, four straight-back dining chairs and a round mahogany table. A black fender stood around the base of the iron fireplace with Mother's prized brass poker, fire shovel and tongs. Sepia prints of Constable's 'Haywain' and Romney's 'Cherub Choir' adorned the walls, in company with Father's 'Honourable Discharge Certificate' from the Royal Garrison Artillery.

The kitchen was lit by a tiny window, and a chipped brown fireclay sink anchored on two large brackets stood beneath it. From its base a lead waste pipe passed through the wall and discharged into an open drain which attracted flies in summer and the occasional rat. Beside the sink stood two galvanized buckets which contained the day's water supply for washing, cooking and drinking.

Our water supply was from a shallow, communal well two hundred yards down the lane. The well, only four feet deep, was set in a wall with a lintel over the top and with a large blue slate slab fixed vertically across its opening; despite its shallowness it never dried up. Mother usually fetched the water and, weighed down by the heavy buckets, she made slow progress as they slopped water over her legs and shoes. Sometimes I went with her and when she wasn't looking, I would throw a small pebble into the well, and lean over the stonewall to watch the reflection of my face wiggle and waggle in the ripples.

Our cooking was done on a black Cornish stove, and as the oven was small, vegetables were usually cooked on a paraffin-oil stove whose temperamental flame sputtered and guttered when one passed by.

A high stone wall separated our cottage from the lane and our next door neighbour, and was joined to the field hedge which bounded our back garden.

The front courtyard was paved with slate stones. Behind them, against the walls, were raised flower beds fronted with large beach pebbles. A cherry tree grew by the front door, devoid of branches until it reached the roof. Each spring it produced masses of white flowers, but to my disappointment it never bore fruit. On winter nights when a gale was blowing, I would listen fearfully to the eerie scratching of its branches on the slates as I lay in bed and I conjured up fearful visions of a horrible monster who was trying to get in.

Four bushes thrived in the courtyard - a purple lilac, a sweet smelling syringa, a veronica with sticky leaves and a pink, flowering currant. A host of orange marigolds, multi-coloured asters, nasturtiums and poppies, all raised from penny seed packets overflowed the beds. A brown pottery rabbit from Woolworth's sat at the foot of the right hand door jamb, while a small iron gate in the south wall kept the outside world at bay from this little haven.

But it was not always so idyllic. One Friday night in November 1923, a tremendous rainstorm started just as my parents came up to bed. The scraping of the cherry branches and the noise of the torrential rain was appalling, but after a while I fell asleep despite the non-stop thumping, drumming and hissing sounds.

Suddenly I was wide awake. The bedroom was bathed in lamplight. It was still raining. Mother was sitting up in bed shouting loudly: "Wake up! Wake up! There's something making a noise downstairs!" Father stirred, grumbled under his breath, and sat up.

"What are you making such a fuss about, Milly?" he asked.

"Listen! There it is again!" cried Mother, and I heard a dull, thudding sound from down below. Father leaped out of bed, his shirt tail flapping around his thighs (pyjamas were unheard of) and rushed down the stairs. Mother followed in her nightgown, like a pale, fluttering wraith.

"God Almighty! We're flooded out!" yelled Father rushing back into the bedroom. "Get dressed, you two, and light a candle!"

He pulled on his long pants and trousers, rolling the legs of both up above his knees. Mother looked stricken as we both dressed. I lit a candle and followed Father down the stairs, and in the guttering yellow light I saw an amazing sight.

Our sitting room was flooded to a depth of almost two feet, for the water had reached the fourth tread of the stairs. The bumping noise we had heard was the sound of Mother's large galvanized bath, half filled with clean washing, floating around in a small current caused by water oozing through the front door. The easy chairs and sofa were half submerged, and the door mat was floating.

I held the candle high as Father plunged through the flood to light the oil-lamp which was kept on the mantelpiece with a box of matches by its side in case of emergency. Father's breath hissed as the coldness of the water, and the stone floor struck his legs and feet as he fumbled with the matches.

Mother, now fully dressed, came down the stairs and sat with me above the rising tide. She took one glance at the devastation, and wept bitterly. I put my arms around her, she was trembling. Father waded to the kitchen to fetch a hurricane lantern then made his way back to the front door. We watched him unlock it and, as he pulled it open, he was almost bowled over by a surge of water. As he pushed his way into the courtyard Father shouted: "There's no stopping it! It's right up to my waist now, and there's more coming from the road. I've got to do something to let it out!"

The bath continued its bumping, and the chairs which were set around the table fell over and floated. Mother stopped crying now, pulled up her skirt, tucked it inside her knickers and stepped down into the water. I could have laughed; she looked so funny, but so pathetic.

"Don't move Jack! What ever you do, don't move or you'll fall in and drown!" she called, her teeth chattering as she waded through the flood, gathering everything up which was still above water and putting it onto the table.

Father returned with a crowbar from the tool shed.

"Milly, come and hold the lantern, I've got to make a hole in the wall. It's the only way to get the water out," he shouted.

Mother pushed her way against the flow and joined him. I went upstairs, drew back the curtain and looked out. Mother was standing on top of a flower bed with water up to her knees, holding the lantern high. Father was hitting the courtyard wall with the crowbar low down under the water. His arms moved mechanically and he seemed tireless as he worked the crowbar deeper into the wall. Mother's face was a blank, staring mask.

Suddenly there was a sucking noise and Father yelled: "'Tis through! 'Tis through! Hold the light closer, Milly!" I saw for a second, the water form a vortex around the hole.

Father took the lantern from Mother. "Stay where you are, and don't fall, I'm going outside to make the hole bigger." From the roadway I could hear him hacking away at the hole.

I dashed down the stairs and saw that the water level was slowly dropping, and after what seemed an age, it went down to about a foot in depth. Father returned carrying an old bass broom, and Mother joined me on the stairs; together we watched him broom the water towards the doorway. The rain had ceased, but the night was pitch black. The flood water continued to recede, and beneath a coating of mud the floor appeared. The bath grounded by the doorway like Noah's ark; the mats and linoleum flattened, and a dark, uneven tide-mark appeared on the wallpaper.

The kitchen stove which was usually kept alight at night had long since been doused by the flood, so Mother boiled a kettle on the oil stove and made a pot of tea. We took it upstairs, and never did a cup taste so good as in those dark hours.

"There's nothing more we can do until morning, and then we'll move everything out into the garden to dry off - if 'tisn't raining," said Father.

Mother was clearly unhappy. "I think the chairs and sofa are ruined, and I don't know what we shall do with the lino, 'tis sure to crack into pieces", she wailed.

"Well, it may not be so bad, after all. Let's get some sleep," replied Father as he shed his sodden clothing, wiped the mud and sweat from his body and took a clean shirt from the cupboard. Mother did likewise, put on her nightgown, reached up, turned out the hanging lamp and slowly climbed into bed.

"Blow out the candle. Jack, I don't know what we're going to find tomorrow morning!"

Sleep we did, but fitfully, and once I thought I heard Mother weeping, but I couldn't be sure. Daybreak was slow in coming and held back by lowering clouds, but the extent of the flooding was obvious, even in the dim light.

Wherever we looked, there was mud. A brown film almost three feet high plastered the walls; the linoleum was slippery, the matting caked, every piece of furniture oozed slime; the courtyard paving was brown, most of the earth in the flower beds was gone and the rocks were dislodged.

Being Saturday, there was no school, so I helped my parents as best I could. Together we carried out the linoleum, rugs and matting and draped them on the clothes line. Father broomed the slime from the courtyard and carried out the furniture to dry. Fortunately the sun came out; the weekend stayed fine and our furniture slowly dried out.

There were casualties in the chicken run. Five hens died with their heads stuck through the mesh of the wire netting, having panicked during the storm, and for days thereafter we had chicken with everything. Our next-door neighbour lost her old tomcat, and spent days calling in vain: "Mutty! Mutty! Mutty-Mow me Dear! Where are 'ee? Come 'ome to Mother!" Father got so annoyed at her continued outpourings that he said, "If old Mary don't shut up soon I shall clout her one in the ear hole." But he was only joking. A week later he brought her a kitten from a recent litter born at the farm, and Mary was happy again.

Mother relit the kitchen stove and the sitting room fire; the cottage began to exude a clinging musty damp smell; wallpaper came unstuck; plaster fell off in lumps; the two armchairs and sofa survived but, as Mother had predicted, the linoleum disintegrated. We were left with cold stone floors, and lived in discomfort for many weeks for drying-out was terribly slow. When spring came our landlord called in a mason, who made good the plastering and Mother repapered the walls and bought new linoleum.

Trevorrick comprised a farmhouse occupied by a very old man and his elderly son and daughter who were both unmarried. Of the other four cottages, one was occupied by 'Mazed' Jim and his sister; another by their relatives who, at holiday time catered for a family of four visitors. When this cottage became vacant the visitors bought it and returned regularly for many years. Next door to them lived a family of five - husband and wife, two young daughters and their brother; at the end of the lane lived the Bennett's and their children.

Our flooding was not the only major happening, for each month as the moon grew to fullness, so did Jim's personality change. We called him 'Mazed Jim' for he became a temporary religious maniac shouting and roaring his praises of The Almighty; holding long sermons to invisible audiences, and interspersing them with snatches of hymn singing. Sometimes he was taken to Bodmin Asylum to cool off, but he was kind, gentle, and would never hurt a fly whether sane or insane, and I often went into his cottage and chatted with him when he was alone.

Jim's brother who lived nearby was taken ill, and one morning in delirium he jumped out of his bedroom window, clad only in his shirt, and ran through the lanes to the beach and away over the cliffs. He was spotted by the postman who raised the alarm and a hue and cry ensued. Father joined in the chase and the poor sufferer was seen crossing a field whose boundary ended at the two hundred feet high Rowan cliffs. As he raced towards the cliff edge, one of the runners caught up with him and grabbed his shirt, but too late, the poor sufferer broke free and jumped to his death. The party climbed down the zig-zag path to the foot of the cove and found that he was still alive, but the fall had crushed his body, and he died before they could carry him to the cliff top.

I joined the children of the hamlet in communal games in the overgrown orchard which belonged to the farm. Here we made houses from purloined walking sticks covered with old sacks obtained from the barn, then in the semi-darkness we took turns in acting out the roles of mothers and fathers. We made beautiful mud pies garnished with stalks and flower heads and commented on each others 'cooking'.

When we played doctors and patients we turned the house into a surgery, where all the childish complaints we knew of were diagnosed, discussed, and examinations made with a stethoscope contrived from empty cotton reels and wire. Inevitably sex reared her innocent head and considerable experimenting and discussion ensued regarding the differences between male and female genitalia. We touched, smelled, licked, giggled and played with each others bodies in all innocence. One day our activities came to an abrupt end when one of the girls said she wanted to pee standing up like I did. She was about to begin when there was a shout and her mother appeared. Threats, clouts, smacks and admonitions were delivered; our parents were informed of the filthy deed. From that day onward sex was a forbidden subject, and nobody told us what we had done wrong, or why.

How ignorant we were compared with the children of today. Apart from the flood, we were comfortable at Lane End and, during the years we lived there, I became interested in Nature. Someone gave Mother a battered copy of Gilbert White's 'Natural History of Selborne' and two small illustrated companion books entitled 'Birds', and 'Nests and Eggs' shown to the Children, which they thought might be of interest to me. I read them avidly from cover to cover, and the lanes, hedges, ditches, verges and fields began to reveal their secrets. Soon I knew the name of every bush on the road between our cottage and Porthcothan Farm. In spring they contained few nests that were not known to me. I thrilled at my first sight of a clutch of blue-green hedge sparrow eggs, and the feeling on my fingertips of a cluster of minute eggs as I carefully probed the interior of a wren's nest. There were starlings' nests in holes in the walls of old farm buildings, and telltale grasses and feathers overflowed from other holes where sparrows were nesting. I knew where pied wagtails and yellowhammers nested on the road to Trehemborne. I gathered newts, tadpoles and water snails from stagnant ponds in corners of fields, brought them home in jam jars and placed them on the slate sill of our kitchen window. Sometimes they lived; more often than not the sun heated the water and they died. I also obtained a small book on wild flowers, and botany came to the fore as I attempted to identify the many species which I collected, pressed and mounted in a scrapbook.

Then came my brief friendship with a boy named Oliver; my excursions with him to the cliffs with memories of Mr Bishop and his paintings still fresh in my mind, and my discovery of Trescore Valley and its delights where I spent scores of happy hours until we moved further inland to another part of the parish.

The back of the cottage where Jack lived at Trevorrick Lane End, the cherry tree that use to scratch his window can clearly be seen.

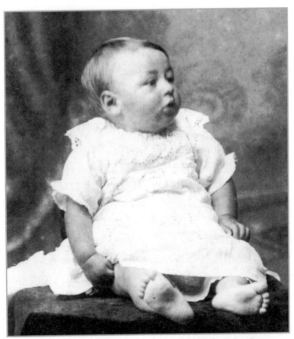

Jack's baby photograph that his Mother
showed to him after his likeness was taken.

Jack on his mothers knee having his
likeness taken by Mr Buxton at
Lower Trevorgus.

Jack standing on a leopard skin
beside his mother posing for
Mr. Buxton.

5

My Likeness is Taken

I was playing with old Floss when Mother appeared and, taking me by the arm, she examined me closely from top to toe.

"You can't be 'taken' in those clothes!"

"Taken where?" I said. But Mother had gone indoors. I continued to throw stones for the dog to fetch, and a few minutes later Mother shouted, "Come in and be washed."

Mystified, I went indoors and Mother immediately stripped off my clothing and thoroughly washed my face, arms and legs. Then we went upstairs to the bedroom where my best Sunday suit was laid out on the bed. Mother helped me into the brown velvet coat with mother-of-pearl buttons and cream coloured crocheted collar and cuffs. My matching velvet shorts and cotton underpants were suspended by a small pair of braces, and my ensemble was completed with short cream socks (which would not stay up) and a pair of brown shoes.

"Why am I being changed? It isn't Sunday. Are we going to Padstow?"

"Just you wait and see," smiled Mother as she carefully parted and combed my pudding-basin styled hair down over my forehead.

Mother had changed into a striped floral blouse, a brown woollen skirt, and shoes with stand-up tongues which flapped as she walked. Gran inspected us, nodded her approval, and Mother brought out my pushchair. I was about to sit in it. "No! You musn't ride in it now, not until you're tired!" said Mother, pulling me away.

The mystery deepened when we passed Mrs Old's shop near the crossroads and reached the hamlet of Cottages where Mother stopped to chat with Ethel, a pleasant, stoutly built lady who clasped me to her, and planted a wet kiss on my forehead as my face sank into her rolling bosom. From their conversation I gathered we were heading for Lower Trevorgus, a farmhouse further along the road.

We rounded a bend and turned into a narrow, rutted lane still muddy from yesterday's summer shower. Mother told me to climb into the pushchair in order that my shoes would not be soiled.

A large stone built house came into view, with deep windows which looked onto a lawn with a tall monkey-puzzle tree in the centre. Mrs Leadville, the farmer's wife was standing by the front porch and greeted Mother on our arrival. I gathered that whatever was going to happen would happen soon when she said;" You're the first to arrive, there are several more coming to have their likeness taken. Mr Buxton will be with you in a minute; he's getting his camera ready." The lady then brought a chair and a leopard-skin rug from the porch and placed it clear of the tree.

"Make yourselves comfortable," she said, and went into the house. I dismounted, and followed Mother to the chair which gave a protesting creak as she sat down.

I pestered Mother with questions.

"Mum, what is a likeness? Why do they take it from you? Does it hurt?"

"A likeness is a photo."

"What is a photo?"

"It is a picture of you which comes out of a camera on a piece of paper."

"What is a camera?"

"A kind of box on a stand."

"Why do we have our likeness taken?"

"Because I want a picture of you as you are now before you go to School and start growing up. Your Gran wants one to be framed and hung up in the sitting-room."

I was still confused, but Mother was saved from further questioning by voices issuing from the porch.

"Yes, I can manage. I can carry it all. Thank you."

A tall, red-faced man wearing a straw boater hat, striped blazer and white flannel trousers emerged carrying a three-legged stand upon which was mounted a sort of box with bellows, from which protruded a glass eye which glistened in the sunlight; attached to the back was a length of black velvet cloth.

Mrs Leadville fussed around and introduced us to Mr Buxton who said, "Ah, Mrs Ingrey! We've met before." Mother nodded. "Yes, about four years ago."

"How the boy has grown! Wouldn't have recognised him."

Mrs Bennett looked surprised and went indoors again. Mr Buxton opened up the legs and, taking hold of the black cloth, threw it over his head and for a while fiddled with the staring glass eye, at the same time holding the contraption as he walked slowly backwards. At last he emerged from beneath the black draping, and appeared to be satisfied as he walked towards us.

"Now, Mrs Ingrey we must get the pose right. Just turn sideways a little; move the right foot back...further. That's fine."

Mother wriggled and twisted, and the chair creaked loudly in protest.

"Now young man, you sit on your Mother's knee, and tell me when you are comfortable."

I did as I was told, and promptly fell off.

"Sit more upright, Mrs Ingrey, and hold the boy closer. Ah! That's got it. Don't move, and when I say smile, smile!'"

He rushed back to the box, put his head under the cloth again and twiddled the eye. Then he grabbed a long rubber tube with a ball on the end, shouted, "Smile!" and squeezed the ball. We smiled and I felt myself slipping off

34

Mother's knee again. Twice more we got settled and the performance was repeated.

Then Mr Buxton said: "Once more Mrs Ingrey, in a different pose with the boy standing beside you. Young man, hold your Mother's hand." I obliged, standing close to Mother and gazing expectantly at the camera.

"Oh! Excellent! Excellent!" came Mr Buxton's voice from beneath the cloth, as his hands moved the bellows and the eye. As he was about to squeeze the rubber ball, my attention was diverted.

A large black dog ran past us, sniffed at the stand, then promptly cocked one hind leg, missed the stand and shot a yellow stream over Mr Buxton's legs. A loud yell came from beneath the cloth, as the camera and Mr Buxton teetered to the ground - a jumbled mass of limbs and equipment.

The dog ran out of sight. I screamed with laughter. Mother gave me a black look, a hard slap on the wrist and rushed to help Mr Buxton who was slowly disentangling himself. He said: "There's always a first time. I've got four more clients this afternoon, and if that darned dog comes back I shall be really soaked." He picked up the equipment and examined it carefully. "Thank goodness everything is intact. I was afraid the glass plates might have smashed."

Our session ended on a happy note with Mr Buxton saying, "My wife will be highly amused when I tell her what happened." Mother replied, "She won't be when she has to wash your flannels."

I looked at my red wrist but said nothing, and sat in the pushchair. Mother pushed me all the way back to Rose Cottage and forgot that I should have walked part of the way.

"Now I know what taking my likeness is. Mum," I said, "but what happens next?"

"You'll know in about a week's time," she replied. The family were anxious to hear full details of our visit, and when Mother mentioned the dog she pointed at me. "That boy screamed like a whitneck (Cornish word for weasel) when the old dog did his job, and I gave him a good smack. I could have killed him!" A week later the postman delivered a large envelope. "This is the result of having your likeness taken," said Mother as she withdrew two brown pictures. I was thrilled at what I saw; there was I sitting on Mother's lap, and another picture of me standing beside her.

"These are photographs," explained Mother, "but only rough copies. Mr Buxton will make proper large ones when I tell him how many we require."

Mother decided to have three copies of each picture, and was very pleased when the final results arrived printed on thick black mounts. I too was delighted to see how smart I looked in my best suit.

Then Mother showed me a picture of a chubby baby dressed in a white frock. "Mr Buxton took that when you were nine months old," she said. "You kept crawling all over the floor and wouldn't keep still for one moment."

But the photograph I really would have liked would have been one taken at the moment when the dog cocked his leg and Mr Buxton and his camera fell to the ground.

The opening of the St Merryn Institute 29th September 1907

6

Saturday Night Shopping

Father was paid for his week's work at five o'clock every Saturday afternoon. After tea and a quick change of clothing, in rain or shine, the three of us walked to the village for Mother to do her weekly shopping and for Father to meet his friends at the Institute or public house.

For this expedition I was dressed according to the weather. In winter I wore boots, woollen stockings which ended in elasticated tops above my knees, corduroy shorts, Luvisca underwear, shirt, jersey, cap and wool mittens; if it rained, a black oilskin coat and hat completed my ensemble. In summer I wore white shirts, khaki shorts and sandshoes, and Mother's copious shopping bag contained a woollen jersey to slip on if it turned cold.

Frosty winter nights were magic when a thin sickle moon hung amid a sprinkling of flickering stars on a velvet black sky. A fortnight later, among those same glittering stars, the moon, now full, rode high over the landscape like a great orange coloured pumpkin.

Sometimes there were shooting stars, and Mother would point skyward calling excitedly: "Look! Look! A new child is being born!" For a while I believed her until I heard that babies were brought by storks. But there were no storks in Cornwall, only herons, and when I asked if herons also brought babies, she said, "No!" I said, "Well, who does bring them?" I was very confused, and so was Mother when I persisted in asking for more explicit details.

Sometimes as we walked between the dark, high hedges of the lane, the screech of a barn owl would send thrilling shudders down my spine. I would grasp Father's hand tightly as the dark silhouette of the bird skimmed overhead into the fields beyond.

Father could name several of the stars and constellations, showing us the Plough, with the North Star gleaming coldly beyond and in line with the two stars at the end of the ploughshare he showed us the Heavenly Twins, the faintly glimmering Seven Sisters, and several others, but he couldn't remember their proper names which were, he said, too long and foreign sounding.

Sometimes Father's hob-nailed boots touched a stray spar stone and a bright yellow spark flashed for an instant. My boots had little nails in the soles and I would drag my feet on the road in an attempt to produce similar sparks, but nothing happened except a rebuke from Mother, "Jack! for goodness sake lift your feet up and stop that silly game!" The thorn-filled hedges, interspersed with ivy bushes gave shelter to roosting birds. When there was no moon, Father lit our way with a carbide gas lamp which he shone at random into the hedges where its beam pinpointed huddled blackbirds, thrushes, and robins. In a few years time I would see similar birds being cruelly killed in the beams of that same lamp when I would take part in a bird-beating expedition.

At Trehemborne we always called at Rose Cottage for a quick word with Gran who would be sitting comfortably with her feet on a stool reading the *Family Journal* or *Christian Herald*; on daylight evenings she would be sitting in the window seat with one eye on the text and the other on the roadway. My Aunt usually joined us, and away we went, four sets of feet clitter-clattering up the hill past Trevear turning.

Dwellings were few until we reached the School where light streamed through chinks in the long curtains of the adjacent School House. The tinkling sound of the Headmaster's piano were the only signs of life until we reached the Men's Institute. This odd looking structure was a gutted railway carriage minus its wheels, set up on blocks on waste ground by the roadside. Oil lamps swung from the curved ceiling, and in this mellow, smoke laden shack men played darts, while others sat at tables concentrating on games of draughts and dominoes. Sometimes through the uncurtained windows, a line of green-baize covered tables indicated that a whist drive was imminent.

"I'll be waiting for you on the cross-roads at nine o'clock, so don't be late." was Father's usual parting instruction as he went to join his friends.

"And don't you drink too much beer if you go to the pub," was Mother's rejoinder as we went on our way.

Laughter and muffled conversation filtered through the small shuttered windows of the Farmers Arms Inn as we reached the crossroads. In the shadow of the old semi-derelict ivy clad cottage on the corner, the glow of cigarette ends and occasional giggles indicated that young men had congregated to exchange the week's gossip before going to the Institute, and the older ones to the public house.

Nearby, behind the window of his little single-storey cobbler's shop, sat Charlie Rabey, his spectacles gleaming in the soft yellow flame of a single candle; his head bent over his last, his hammer bumping rhythmically on the heavy leather boot which he was repairing. On this occasion Mother called to collect a pair of shoes which he had re-soled. She opened the stable-type door and I followed her into the tiny room where three old men were sitting on a bench seat talking to Charlie. Their conversation ceased abruptly as we entered.

Cobwebs festooned the window panes, and larger ones hung from the open beams. A rusty oil stove oozed warmth and paraffin fumes which mingled with the strong smell of leather. I dug the toes of my shoes into the earth floor and made little channels and scratchings which I covered in as soon as I had made them. The old men watched my performance saying nothing, and their glassy stares made me feel uncomfortable. Charlie took down Mother's shoes from a shelf which held several other pairs awaiting collection, and wrapped them in a sheet of newspaper.

"That'll be one and six pence, Mrs Ingrey, and I bet your new bottoms'll last longer than the tops." Charlie's face wrinkled into a smile.

As we closed the door I heard one of the old men say, "Bert Ingrey's boy isn't very big, is he? I bet he won't be as good a footballer as his Father." That old man's remark buried itself in my subconscious mind for I grew up to dislike football and when I was forced to play, I always felt as though I had two left legs!

A few yards beyond the cobbler's shop was our Saturday night goal Mrs Old's shop. Large square bay windows, capped with slated lean-to roofs glowed with light from the interior, and the overhead bell to the recessed door between them jangled harshly as we entered. Warm air tinged with all manner of smells welcomed us into a world of counters piled high with groceries; shelves packed with biscuit tins and sweet bottles, and a jumbled area of ironmongery. A high stool stood beside the newspaper counter which divided the groceries from the ironmongery, and if it was vacant. Mother would say, "Sit up there and amuse yourself while I do the shopping." From this vantage point my eyes and mind scanned and absorbed the variety of goods on view every Saturday night for several years.

What pleasure there was in sniffing and savouring the smells of tobacco, smoked bacon, kippers, coffee and cheese, slightly marred sometimes by a whiff of paraffin. The laundry section contained *Rinso*, *Soako*, *Persil*, *Robin Starch*, *Reckett's Blue*, *Lux*, *Puritan* soap and washing soda. Beside them were *Cuticura*, *Pears* and *Palmolive* soaps - more refined products for personal hygiene; These were followed by tins of *Nugget* and *Kiwi* boot polish, bars of salt for curing pork, and blacklead for smartening up the fronts of kitchen stoves. Cigarettes were stacked by brands in packets of ten and twenty, many of which today are but memories: *De Reszke*, *Kensitas*, *Star*, *Robin*, *Black Cat*, *Players Navy Cut*, *Goldflake* and ever popular *Woodbines* in paper packets of five for tuppence.

Two counters were placed at right angles in the grocery department, and on them sat three sets of scales, the largest was a magnificent object with two brass pans suspended by brass chains from a bar pivoted on the central stem. By its side stood a collection of brass weights varying from fourteen pounds down to one ounce. Sugar, currants, raisins, butter, lard, cheese, rashers of bacon and slab cake were weighed on this scale.

The second scale was much smaller, with one detachable pan and a flat platform for the weights, and was used only for weighing sweets from large glass bottles. Oh! the pleasure of their delectable contents! Striped humbugs, sherbet-lemons, gob-stoppers, toffees, pear drops, jelly babies and liquorice allsorts, to mention but a few. Large gob-stoppers were four a penny, and my favourite sweets because they lasted longer. I would roll one around in my mouth, transferring it from cheek to cheek, then removing the sticky object to see if it had changed colour because, like the cross section of a tree, gob-stoppers were formed of layer rings each a different colour.

The third scale was similar to the sweet scale but with additional quarter and half ounce weights for weighing twist tobacco which, in addition to being smoked, was chewed extensively by many of the older men who had the disgusting habit of spitting it out in unexpected places.

Dozens of *Peek Frean* and *MacFarlane Lang* biscuit tins and packets breakfast cereals completely filled one wall. Another section held all kinds of cake, bun and sponge mixtures; yeast, green sticks of angelica, glacé cherries and tiny bottles of cochineal and vanilla essence.

Cheeses wrapped in butter-muslin shrouds stood on the floor next to tins of *Fray Bentos* corned beef, red salmon, herrings and pilchard.

A bacon slicer proudly displayed a notice that it could cut individual requirements into any one of fourteen different thicknesses.

Away from the groceries were several shelves filled with library books, offering at tuppence per volume worlds of adventure, love, fantasy, travel and morality. Over the years I graduated from Hans Anderson's and Grimm's Fairy Tales to *Treasure Island*, *The Old Curiosity Shop*, the *'William'* books, and the then popular adult Cornish authors Silas and Joseph Hocking. Mother and my Aunt steeped themselves in romances by Elinor Glynn, Ouida and Marie Corelli.

Newspapers and periodicals were stacked on the counter by my high stool, and Mrs Old allowed me to thumb through them provided I did not disarrange the pages. In those early days I read *'Playbox'*, *'Rainbow'*, *'Bubbles'* and *'Tiger Tim's Weekly'*. As I grew older they were superseded by *'Children's Newspaper'*, *'My Magazine'* and *'The Champion'*. Later when pocket money permitted, I bought *'The Magnet'* and enjoyed the hilarious Greyfriars School adventures of hero Bob Cherry and the fat villain. Billy Bunter. Mother and my Aunt bought *'Peg's Paper'* and *'Poppy's Paper'* respectively. Gran was content with *'The Family Journal'* and *'The Christian Herald'*. Mother took *'The Daily Sketch'* and Gran took *'The Daily Chronicle'* (both papers now long defunct) and when read, an exchange was made of both weekly and daily papers between us.

The ironmongery department was a jumble of buckets, baths, washboards, tea- and dinner-sets. Chamber pots hobnobbed with vases, egg-cups, oil table lamps, coir mats and sweeping brushes. During the Spring-cleaning season the floor was piled with bundles of wallpaper, packets of paste, tins of paint and buckets of distemper. A large stand of vegetable and flower seeds from Messrs Toogood also appeared and from them Father made his selection for our small garden. It was almost impossible to walk through this part of the shop without knocking something over, and the window was equally crammed from top to bottom with a jumble of goods.

At Christmas-tide this window was stripped of its ironmongery and transformed into a glory of tinsel, paper chains, Christmas stockings of various sizes, glass balls, and a beautifully decorated fir tree. Mrs Old's drawing-room behind the shop was also stripped of most of its furniture. Trestle tables were erected against the walls and down the centre of the room. Display shelves made from empty orange boxes and tea chests were placed on them then camouflaged with coloured crepe paper. The walls were draped with paper chains and tinsel. A vast display of seasonal gifts crowded the impromptu shelves. Gloves, ties, shirts, shoes and shaving soap for the men; blouses, head scarves and perfumes for the ladies - all of which were displayed in colourful cardboard boxes.

A wonderland of toys catering for all pockets was spread out for the children. German clockwork mice with eyes that gave off sparks made from brimstone when wound up; clowns that performed acrobatics on bicycles; humming tops that played tunes and hummed in different keys; wooden monkeys that climbed up and down sticks; a whole range of lead farmyard animals, birds and buildings, trees and fences; Meccano sets and Hornby trains. Some toys cost as little as six pence. Today they are collectors' pieces - the new antiques.

Mother spent freely at Christmas, because each week during the year she paid whatever money that could be spared into the Christmas Club. Sometimes I knew she was secretly saving up to buy something special for me, and I cherish the memory of opening a large brown paper parcel one Christmas morning and finding inside a magnificent nickel-plated Number Three Meccano set. Over the years it was gradually updated and added to until it was equivalent to a Number Six set. I was then able to make the complete range of cranes, engines, industrial machinery and buildings from the lavishly illustrated instruction manual, with the nickel-plated parts replaced by brightly coloured enamelled pieces.

Father Christmas was in attendance on the Saturday before Christmas, and always on Christmas Eve if it didn't fall on a Saturday. Draped in a red cloak, bobble hat, and with beard a little lop-sided, he smiled benignly at young and old from a far corner of the room. Beside him was a gaily decorated tea chest into whose depths children up to the age of twelve years were invited to grope for a free lucky-dip present, none of them worth much - an orange, a bag of sweets, a small box of crayons and a wire puzzle which I never managed to take apart. Father Christmas was, in fact, played by two persons; big Percy with his benign smile and non-stop jaws which chewed quid's of twist tobacco, the juice of which trickled out and stained his beard. Buckle, a little Father Christmas, was a sailor, a relative home on Christmas leave. He had a faraway look in his eyes but sometimes he would shrivel one with a gimlet gaze. He had a nasty habit of treading with his heavy, highly polished boots on the toes of any child who attempted to take two presents out of the dip.

The shop had developed from small beginnings, being run as a family business. Once a week a member of the staff called 'for orders' at the homes of customers in the more remote parts of the parish, and was given a list of requirements, for there were no telephones. Goods were delivered by van on the following day. Paraffin and methylated spirits were in great demand, as many houses possessed a Primus stove and a new-fangled Aladdin lamp, for as yet there was no electric light.

Olds' remained unchanged during the thirties, World War II and the restrictions of rationing. Then in 1952 a great upheaval took place. The whole of the shop, storage space and ground floor accommodation was completely gutted and refurbished as a self service grocery, the second to be opened in the whole of Cornwall.

A new shop front with large plate glass windows was installed, and in place of the wonderful, odorous mish-mash so long housed on wooden shelves and counters, the goods were now transferred to large gondolas clad with the recently invented Formica plastic. Organised chaos was ousted for clinical, methodical display and the old, between the wars, atmosphere evaporated overnight.

It took many of the older generation months, even years, to adjust to this new method of self service. Mrs Old's cumbersome but efficient Kalamazoo system of accounting and production of weekly bills gave way to a special pay-desk with cash register attached, and shopping became almost impersonal. Even now, forty years on, I still happily visualise those yellow, lamp-lit Saturday nights sitting, watching, smelling, and absorbing the uniqueness of a village shop as I stand on the same spot in today's queue with my wire basket under the unblinking glare of white fluorescent strip lights.

Harry Parsons, Leslie Hawken, Cyril Ball & Herbert Ingrey outside Old's Shop at Shop.

7

Around the Houses

Mother's bicycle was her work-horse, an old machine which accumulated rust in winter for Father to scrape off in spring and repaint with black enamel. It was a mongrel machine, assembled from a frame, handlebars and driving wheel, salvaged from a rubbish dump. During reconstruction it was kept under an equally rusted canopy of corrugated iron sheeting in the back garden. Gradually as his pocket could afford, Father brought the ancient vehicle to life with a leather seat, two new pedals and a chain. Then came brake blocks, wheels one at a time, a small paraffin oil lamp which sat proudly on its bracket, and finally a wide carrier which was secured to the rear of the frame. These renovations to the carcase were carried out on Sunday mornings when he was free from farm work.

One evening Father said, "I've finished your bike Milly." He propped it against the courtyard wall. Mother and I came out to inspect his handiwork, glinting in the evening sunshine.

"I'll try her out first Milly, and if she's all right you can start riding now," he said.

I stood in the lane with Mother agog with excitement as Father mounted the bicycle and pedalled away to Trevorrick. I could see that Mother was getting agitated for in a few minutes she would be mounted on this monster and trying to balance herself.

Father reappeared around the bend smiling and excited as he dismounted and lovingly eyed his handiwork.

"She's a beauty! Goes like a train! You won't have any trouble with her. Come on, Jack, get on the carrier. We'll see how she goes with two up!"

I could not lift my leg high enough to clear the top of the carrier, so Mother lifted me on. Father got astride the frame and held the handlebars firmly.

"Now, away we go!" he called, as his feet engaged the pedals and he lifted himself onto the seat. I put both arms around his waist and pressed my face firmly against his backside which was moving to and fro.

"I can't see anything!" I yelled.

"Well move back a little, and turn your head sideways." Father replied.

Suddenly, a hedge sailed by, then the gateway to the orchard, then in a few moments we swerved through the entrance to the farmyard, circled it, and headed back through the lane. Mother watched us dismount. Father forgetting I was on the carrier, being accustomed to riding a man's bicycle, dismounted by lifting his right leg high, and swinging it in an arc he caught me full in the face.

My nose began to bleed, but I was too thrilled with my brief ride to cause a scene as Mother handed me her handkerchief to wipe my face.

Mother's first riding lesson was about to begin.

"Now Milly, you get on and steer. I'll hold on to the back of the seat so that you can get used to balancing," said Father.

"Oh! Oh! Do you think I'll be all right?" called Mother, now poised gingerly on the seat, her legs dangling.

"Put your feet on the pedals! Jack, keep out of the way! You'll put your Mother off," exhorted Father. I couldn't have done this because I was too busy attending to my bleeding nose.

"Now, off we go!" said Father, and they moved away withal wobbling of handlebars, and excited cries from Mother.

I could see that Mother was doing very well; she was steering straight, and her feet were gently moving the pedals. Up and down the lane they trundled, with Mother steadily gaining confidence. I trotted on behind, interested in her every movement, and noticed now, that sometimes Father removed his hand from the seat and, unbeknown to Mother, let the bicycle run free.

Father was now two paces behind Mother, and I couldn't contain myself for excitement. I shouted: "Mum! Mum! You're balancing all on your own!"

Mother heard me, turned around, saw Father well behind her, screamed loudly, immediately lost her balance and plunged headlong through a bank of cow parsley, and vanished into a deep ditch. We quickly rescued Mother who was unhurt. The bicycle was intact except for a slight twist in the handlebars which Father corrected, and insisted that Mother remount and have one more ride.

"If you don't Milly, you'll lose your nerve; so up you get!"

Mother reluctantly remounted and they went down the lane once more, Father holding the seat to restore her confidence. My nose had now stopped bleeding, and when they returned Father put the bicycle away and we went indoors for supper.

Mother's lessons continued daily; she learned how to mount, dismount and most importantly, how to use the brakes, an operation which she found difficult, for she frequently mistook the front brake for the back brake, and in doing so she flew over the handlebars several times. Her nervousness vanished completely following a solo trip to Trehemborne and back. Father and I waited anxiously and it was near darkness when she arrived. On the carrier was tied a large vegetable marrow which Gramfer had given her. Mother's only complaint was that she carried no matches, so she was unable to light the oil lamp. I was now eager to travel as pillion passenger to Trehemborne, so a few days later, we successfully wobbled our way to Rose Cottage.

Further refinements were gradually added to Mother's bicycle; a wicker basket hung over the handlebars; a new rear mudguard was fitted, the lower edges of which were perforated with tiny holes, and a fanlike arrangement of coloured cord was threaded through them to a perforated plate at the wheel hub. This was a dress guard, for on a windy day Mother's skirt could catch in the back wheel and either bring her to an unexpected halt or plaster the hem of the garment with mud if it rained.

Gran's connections with the literary world brought Mother into contact with the owners of some of the seaside houses which were occupied only during their holidays. She would act as caretaker, open up the windows and give the rooms an airing. For this service, Mother was paid a fee of two shillings and six pence (12.5p) per house, per visit. Fortunately two of the houses were close to each other, so she dealt with them simultaneously. This extra money was a bonus, as Father's wage was only about one pound per week, plus fringe benefits of free milk, and the occasional turnip and flatpoll cabbage.

There were less than a dozen dwellings in the whole of Constantine; undulating sand dunes covered with wiry marram grass stretched for a quarter of a mile from the beach to the inshore fields; through them wound a rough metalled road to the beachhead. Somewhere beneath the desolation lay a village, buried long ago by the shifting sands, the only visible remains being the lonely ruins of a church and a holy well, both over a thousand years old.

Mother visited two houses: Treglos, and Lacey's Cottage. Treglos was a small, stone built house near the road junction to Treyarnon. Today, after several changes of ownership, extensive additions, and renovations, it has become the largest hotel in the area.

The children of the then owners were well provided for with a library of books, many of which I read from cover to cover during our frequent visits. The wonderful tales of Hans Anderson, the brothers Grimm, and Maurice Maeterlink transported me into a fantasy world of princes and princesses, mermaids, tinder boxes, witches, snow queens blue birds and swallows. There were also books about butterflies, birds, trains, ships, and wonders of the world. On fine days I sat in a revolving summerhouse on the lawn, absorbing all the fairy stories and knowledge at my temporary disposal. If it rained I sat by one of the fires which Mother always lit to help air the house.

Mother's employers had now discovered that she was an excellent cook, and persuaded her to help their staff cooks whenever she was available, which was usually three times a week. I was allowed to join her, and I played games with their children, sometime riding around the countryside with them in a huge chauffeur-driven *Mercedes-Benz* car.

A new owner whose wife was a concert pianist added a large music room to house her grand piano. On two occasions concerts of chamber music were held in the music room. Mother helped to prepare refreshments for the guests, who were mostly visitors, local dignitaries and music lovers. In my best brown suit, I sat tucked away in a far corner of the room enthralled by musicians Melsa and Moiseiwitch, whose eminence in the music world was completely unknown to me.

Lacey's Cottage, a delightful, unobtrusive building, was perched near the cliff edge, overlooking the curve of the bay. Mother continued as caretaker there for several years after finishing at Treglos which was now a small hotel. I was in my middle teenage years.

Here I played Bing Crosby records on a portable gramophone, enthralled by *'When the blue of the night..'* and many other songs crooned by that inimitable voice which is still singing on tapes and compact discs today - a far cry from the tinny reproduction and hissing of those old speed 78 records.

I thumbed through many scrapbooks of photographs, newspaper and society magazine cuttings collected by Mother's employers. I followed their progress through debutante balls, theatre visits, race meetings, skiing, boating, and hobnobbing with the rich and famous and various foreign royalty.

Here I read Dame Daphne Du Maurier's first novel *'The Loving Spirit'*, Ethel Mannin's *'Ragged Banners'*, Michael Arlen's *'The Green Hat'* and many thrillers by Edgar Wallace.

During this period I too had learned to ride, and was now the proud possessor of my own bicycle which I rode alongside Mother, who had also acquired a replacement for Father's homemade bicycle which had finally clapped out. During the winter months, Lacey's Cottage generated a wonderful atmosphere as the light began to fail early in the afternoon. Mother lit the oil lamps as she busied herself in various rooms. I sat in the bay window and looked across the sweep of the bay at the procession of waves, hills and valleys of water, rising and crashing down, hissing out their final moments at the foot of the dunes. Often a chill northerly wind flattened the acres of marram grass, and flung spatters of sand against the window panes; the tamarisk bushes on the hedges rattled, moaned and protested.

Then Mother would douse the inglenook fire, visit each room to check that the windows were closed and secure and, turning out the lamps, we would gather up the remnants of our meals, struggle into our mackintoshes, lock the front door and walk across the small garden in the near darkness to our bicycles. With eyes smarting from the blast, and faces stung by flying sand, we mounted our bicycles and wobbled precariously across the cliff top, past the spot where we held our picnics during those halcyon summers of my childhood. From the headland, the red beam of the lighthouse suddenly swung its arc across the empty seascape. We struggled a little harder against the gale, hoping to be home before darkness was complete, for the road was winding, and we had we had no lights on our bicycles.

8

Clifftop and Seashore

My young days were greatly influenced by cliff-top excursions with my parents; by Mr Bishop's colourful paintings, and his descriptions of flowers, birds, rocks and waves; but a teenage boy who sometimes came to stay with his relatives at Treburrick in the adjacent parish influenced me most of all.

Oliver was tall, lean, angular, suntanned, with unruly fair hair, and a pinched brown face made vibrant with luminous grey eyes. He had little regard for dress and wore a nondescript shirt which once was white; his grey trousers were marked by earth and oil stains, and held up by a leather Scout belt to which a sheath knife was attached. He did not wear stockings, and his toes showed through holes in his sandshoes. His home was somewhere in West Cornwall and his visits were usually during school holidays.

I first met Oliver one April morning in a small quarry named Peacock's Roost when I was looking for birds' nests. He was doing the same thing, so we continued our searching together and, as a result of this meeting, we became friends.

Oliver was a loner who enjoyed the open fields and the cliffs. He invited me to his Aunt's house where he kept a collection of bird's eggs, and a small library of books on Natural History, several of which he lent me. I read them avidly in the evenings until my eyes were strained in our dim lamplight.

Oliver called regularly at our cottage and, although Mother was not impressed by his appearance, she had no objection to our friendship as he was polite and well-spoken. One morning Oliver offered to take me to Porthcothan and Porthmear, and assured Mother that he would take good care of me. A momentary doubt clouded her face, but she was too polite to object.

"Wait a minute, you must take something to eat," she said, and went into our back-kitchen. She returned with two large pasties which she wrapped, and put into my school satchel.

"I don't get pasties very often at home, and I dearly like them," said Oliver. "I'll carry that," he said, reaching for the satchel, "It'll be easier for Jack."

"Oh, you haven't anything to drink!" said Mother. "I'll..."

"Don't worry, there's spring water where we're going to, and we'll drink it like this," he laughed, cupping his hands and putting them to his mouth.

"Be sure and come back by half past four," said Mother, "otherwise I shall be worried."

"We will. Mother, because we'll be starving by then," I said, and away we went, walking, talking and running as the mood took us, to Porthcothan Bay.

It was low tide, and Oliver showed me caves into whose dim interiors huge globules of water dripped from roofs lost in darkness. Unaccustomed to such exercise, I slipped and slithered over rocks, and grazed both knees in doing so.

"That's nothing. Splash them with sea water!" laughed Oliver. The sharp sting made me wince, but it stopped the trickles of blood which were beginning to show.

We climbed some of the smaller rocks, and Oliver showed me where to look for footholds; how to grip the rocks, and how to assess the easiest way to the top before starting to climb.

From an overhanging ledge, we gazed into the green, sunless depths of the narrow Horsepool and I could just distinguish the form of a crab crawling over the sandy bottom. My legs were hanging out over, and I suddenly realised that I might not be able to get back. I shivered with fear. Oliver sensed this, for I felt his hands tighten around my waist, and he said softly, "Don't look down. You're quite safe. Lift up your legs and lean back," and he drew me slowly backwards, out of sight of the water. I felt embarrassed at this incident, but he assured me it was nothing to be ashamed of, as he too was once frightened of heights.

"You'll be climbing steeper places than this, when I've finished teaching you. Come on, we'll have a look at Wills' Rock."

We climbed half way up the huge detached rock to a wide ledge, and sat watching a flutter of gulls on the sand.

"Do you know how this rock got its name, Oliver?" I asked.

"I've no idea. Do you?"

"Well, Father told me there was an Excise Officer named Thomas Wills who lived at Trevorrick, and he kept watch for smugglers, here on this rock."

"You mean they landed their stuff around here?"

"Yes, and they carried it up the valley to the Vugga."

Oliver's grey eyes widened. "I don't know anything about smuggling up here, but down West where I come from, they did terrible things. What's this Vugga?"

"'Tis a cave. I don't know where it is, but I'll ask Father."

"Then we'll be able to go up the valley and find it!"

"The smugglers caught old Wills one night, tied him up and threw him into the sea," I said, relishing the drama of the situation.

"And he was drowned?"

"No, he floated, the waves carried him in and left him high and dry on the beach. Next morning someone found him and untied him."

Oliver was really impressed, and suggested that I find out more about the smuggling.

The Fogue in Porthcothan Valley, now hidden by undergrowth.

We clambered down from Wills' Rock, raced along the tide line, through the rugged opening of the Arch Rock, and up the short winding path from Golden Burn beach to the cliff top which led to Porthmear.

The rugged rocks forming Trescore Islands glittered in the Spring sunshine. "I'll take you over there one day. I know the places where the crabs hide, and I can borrow Uncle's crab hook. We might even catch a lobster," Oliver said.

I was thrilled at the prospect of taking home a large crab, for Father had done this once then, after boiling it, he cracked it to pieces with a hammer on our front doorstep, and we ate it with our fingers.

We reached rock-filled Porthmear cove with its narrow foreshore of grey and black sand, and green valley with winding stream leading into it. A huge cliff towered above the cove on the far side, and cast a wide, dark shadow over the sand.

Oliver was in his element as he ushered me around the rock pools, pointing out small fish, shrimps, anemones and crabs among the swaying weed forests. From a hole in the side of a deep pool I saw the protruding head of a conger eel. We searched for cowrie shells, squeezed fronds of bladder wrack and made them pop.

Seabirds were nesting. I followed Oliver up the cliff slopes through wiry turf and budding sea pinks to a series of ledges from which a spurt of angry gulls took flight, diving and shrieking at our intrusion. Clusters of mottled brown and black eggs lay precariously on sparse nests of stalks and weeds, and Oliver picked up two fluffy chicks who squawked in distress.

"Here, you hold them," he said, and my hands were filled with squirming, downy flesh as I teetered uncertainly on the ledge as the mother gull swooped and dived at my head. Oliver laughed at my discomfort, took the chicks and returned them to their nest.

As we clambered down, Oliver pointed out holes in the cliff face where jackdaws were nesting, and when we passed the entrance to a cave he said, "Clap your hands, Hard!" I did this, and a flock of pigeons flapped noisily over our heads and vanished above the cliff top.

The morning seemed to have flown by, when Oliver said, "We'll eat now, and there's drink over there." pointing to a thin stream of water which trickled from a green bank at the beach head.

We sat down and munched our way through the pasties; Oliver ate ravenously and said, "I've been up since six o'clock helping Uncle with the cattle, and I only had time for a piece of cake before coming over to you. But your Mother's pasty has made up for that." He laughed, licking his lips.

We sat happily in the sunshine and watched turnstones foraging among bladder wrack and pebbles. A rock pipit flitted anxiously to and fro with its beak full of dried grass stalks.

"If we sat here long enough we should see where the nest was being built," said Oliver, "but we haven't time, so lets have a drink and move on."

The gushing water was ice-cold, with a slightly earthy taste. Then, replete and refreshed, we climbed up banks of dead brown bracken, with new green fronds breaking through, and thickets of spiked yellow gorse which gave out a sweet smell which reminded me of coconut.

We reached a high plateau of fields and tussock wilderness, following the ill-defined cliff path for a while, before leaving it as we headed towards distant Park Head. Suddenly, Oliver pushed me sharply aside. "Look out! We nearly had that one!" and peering down I saw that our feet were within inches of four large mottled brown and greenish eggs with their pointed ends lying together. Oliver picked up an egg and held it gently as though weighing it.

"What sort is it?" I asked. "Curlew. They don't often nest around here; they move back to the moors for breeding. This egg is heavy; it'll hatch soon." Oliver carefully placed it with the others in the scanty nest formed from a few dried grasses. Park Head seemed a long way off as I stumbled through clumps of budding sea pinks, large exposed flints, and over an ancient, crumbling stone hedge crowned with windswept tamarisk bushes. But it was worth all the sweat and gasping to stand at the end of the headland and take in the tremendous rock panorama of Bedruthan, Newquay, and away down past St Agnes to St Ives and the faint outline of Cape Cornwall. Below us on the rocks, cormorants, like dwarf scarecrows, were drying their outstretched wings in the sun. Several stonechats, perched on the highest branches of the gorse bushes, flicked their wings and tails as they watched us suspiciously, and uttered soft chirring calls as they flew to viewpoints further away as we approached. Oliver thought we might find nests, but after a long search, we were unlucky.

Neither of us possessed a watch, and Oliver said, "I think we'd better turn back now, otherwise we'll be late, and you won't be allowed to come again."

That was the last thing I wanted to happen, for in no way would I upset Mother, and today I had seen and done so many wonderful things. I told Oliver how much I enjoyed his company, and everything he showed me, and I couldn't wait to go on another trip. We made our way back to Porthmear, and I found my legs were beginning to drag a little, but I said nothing. Oliver seemed as sprightly as ever. By the time we reached Golden Burn and Porthcothan, the tide was in and we kept to the cliff path. I was now several paces behind him, and he turned and laughed.

"Don't worry Jack, I'm five years older than you. You'll toughen up, and I'm here for another three weeks so we can go off again."

We had reached the roadway, and he handed me my satchel. "I'm off now, Uncle'll be wanting me to help him get the cows in for milking. I'll call at your place as soon as I can."

Oliver almost ran up Trevethan Hill, turning and waving as he went. Then he vanished around the bend, and I walked slowly over the bridge, stopping several times to catch my breath and ease my aching legs before I reached Porthcothan Farm and the level quarter of a mile walk back to Trevorrick Lane End. The clock showed fifteen minutes past four; I was in good time, and Mother was pleased to see me.

I slumped into our biggest armchair and related in detail the day's events, except, of course, my cliff climbing experiences.

True to his word, Oliver took me cliff-roaming again. On these excursions he showed me how to distinguish between the different cloud formations; the wild flowers that were now abundant; I learned how to skin a mole, and how to mount a butterfly so that the pin was almost invisible.

The following Spring, he brought for one of our jaunts, a hammer, a small iron bar with pointed end, and also a short length of rope which had a shaped metal eye at one end. We went to Minnows Cove where he hammered the bar into the ground near the cliff edge, then knotted one end of the long rope to it. He tied the short rope to his middle, threaded the eye through the long rope, and pushed the remainder over the edge.

"Cheerio, I shan't be long," he said, and holding the long rope in both hands, he stepped back over the cliff edge and disappeared from view. I lay flat on my stomach and peered down in amazement. There he was, spidering towards a ledge on which a few guillemots were perched like black sentinels. They flew off as he landed and, bending over, with one hand he grasped an egg which he promptly put into his mouth. He then climbed up the cliff face arm over arm, his body lying almost at right angles as he heaved himself upwards. As his head appeared, he made grimacing motions for me to remove the egg. The narrow pointed end was in his mouth and the bulbous end protruded like a small deflated balloon. I reached over and removed it. Oliver flung himself up onto the grass.

"I've done this twice this year, and each time I've busted the egg. You've got to have someone at the top to take it. Now, how about you having a go?"

"No! No! I'm not used to doing things like that. Father would kill me if he found out!" I sputtered. I'm sure Oliver thought I was a coward, but he only grinned and said nothing. However, during the following week I experimented under his supervision on a cliff about twenty feet high, and found the exercise exhilarating. Then under his gentle persuasion, I tackled a real cliff in Pepper Cove, and brought up a gull's egg in a small pouch which hung from my neck. My ascent was a failure, for bits of cliff dislodged above me and gave me a bleeding ear. I bruised my knees; the egg broke and squashed through the pouch all over my shirt. The sandy beach and rocks below beckoned, and I felt dizzy. I knew I mustn't look down again. My arms ached, it seemed an age before I reached the cliff top and thankfully wriggled my body onto the welcoming turf. Oliver was delighted.

"It's having the nerve to go over the top, and not to be afraid to look down. And you've done it. An old egg doesn't matter. You can always go down and get another one."

"Not again today," I said, "look at my shirt! Look at this!" I opened the pouch and there among the slime was a downy chick almost ready to be hatched.

For three years I enjoyed Oliver's company; then came the summer holiday when he did not appear. How I missed him; his knowledge, his guidance and his companionship. His Aunt and Uncle told me he had joined the Merchant Navy, our paths never crossed again. Both seemed reluctant to give me further information, and a few months later, they too left the area.

Thereafter, I was on my own, but Oliver had, during those expeditions, kindled in me a great love of the sea, and the beautiful but sometimes terrifying coast which fringes my homeland parish.

When I merged into my teenage years, I continued to walk these airy cliffs, and clambered down their tortuous zig-zag paths into less frequented coves with local friends, and helped them bring up planks, pit props, and all manner of jetsam. We found cases of undamaged tins of peaches, and on one occasion, twelve-inch long tallow candles strewn along the beaches at the high water mark. Less pleasant finds were bloated bodies of dead animals which had either fallen over the cliffs, or washed from the deck of some passing cattle boat.

There was also competition: at Constantine Bay an elderly lady was Number One beachcomber. Throughout the year, whatever the weather, she trudged from her house near the beach, and walked along the curved tide line.

With her head down, her plump little body enveloped in a stained old mackintosh, her hair and face shrouded by a scarf knotted under her chin, she looked like a bizarre bundle of living jetsam. A pair of fierce eyes peered out from what could be seen of her leathery, withered face. She quickly gathered her treasures, placed them in a heap above high water mark in the shadow of the sand dunes, and made several journeys between shore and house with this daily harvest. Her tongue was like a rasp; her temper matched it, and woe betide anyone who dared to approach her booty when she was in the vicinity. Sometimes at low water she scavenged for steam coal which emerged onto the shifting sands over the site of a turn-of-the-century wreck. This coal, now rounded into black pebbles from countless tides, was often collected by other local people for their sitting-room grates, where it crackled, split, and sometimes flew glowing and dangerous onto rugs and carpets.

With six golden beaches, all within fifteen minutes of each other by car, it was only natural that my parish was discovered by an ever-increasing flow of holidaymakers. Many of these visitors were confident that they knew everything about our Cornish sea, and its moods, because they had swum the length of their municipal swimming pool a few times.

The narrow width of Treyarnon produces some of the finest surf in Cornwall at full tide, but as it recedes it also creates a death-trap for the unwary. A strong under-current sweeps across the mouth of the bay and carries everything with it towards Trevose Head. Consequently several drownings took place and the District Council placed large WARNING notices, lifebelts and lifelines at all potentially dangerous beaches. Often the warnings went unheeded and, myself and school friends who now spent many summer hours sunbathing, would watch these foolhardy, low tide swimmers, often far out beyond the rocks of Trethias Island. We have rushed into the sea, waving and yelling at them to come back. We have stood chest-high in raging surf only to be told, "Why can't you mind your own bloody business!" or other such derogatory phrase from an arrogant male swimmer.

Women were equally objectionable, and one supercilious female told us that she was a swimming instructress, and was quite conversant with the state of the tides and currents. Later that afternoon we had the dubious pleasure of watching her being helped exhausted from swiftly receding breakers. She was one of the lucky ones! One old lady, unnoticed, sailed far out to sea on a Lilo mattress, and was quite oblivious that she was heading for America when, still half asleep she was hauled ignominiously aboard a boat by an angry farmer who had been called away from his harvesting to go to her aid.

Saddest of all was the tragedy which befell a young university student who had the face and figure of a Greek God, and he knew it, as each day he pranced and posed in the surf with a bevy of young ladies. With strong over arm strokes he would swim out beyond the breakers, as though showing off his swimming skill to his admirers. We warned him of the danger of low tide swimming, and he thanked us courteously, but we sensed arrogance beneath his patronizing smile.

Late one afternoon in September there were slow breakers and a fierce undertow. Adonis, as usual, was far out beyond them. Suddenly he shouted; his arms waved wildly, and in seconds he disappeared. Again the farmer was summoned and, with a makeshift crew, negotiated his boat through the breakers with difficulty, and searched the area in vain for an hour or more. Meanwhile the police had been notified, and a sad assembly of relatives, girl friends and others, including myself, gave evidence of what we had seen. After the crowd had dispersed we told our Constable the facts, and he wrote them down mumbling, "There's always one silly bugger, every year."

The local press carried headlines on the drowning, and twelve days later, a startled bass fisherman hooked a body which was floating under an overhanging rock in Mackerel Cove. The naked, bloated, headless torso was identified by a birthmark as the missing student. Coastguards and police wrapped the sad remains in a tarpaulin and they were then conveyed to a mortuary.

I was one of a mixed gang of local bathers when board surfing became popular. We graduated from cheap, half-inch thick, deal boards with one rounded end, to gaily painted, streamlined, five-ply boards with shaped turned-up ends. Finally, a few of us obtained some wide pieces of balsa wood which we shaped into boards on which we sometimes managed to stand and wobble our precarious way to the shore, long before Malibou boards appeared.

Now the beaches are used all year round by wetsuit clad Malibou boarders, belly boarders, windsurfers and canoeists. New techniques are used which were never dreamed of in my youth. Surfing is a highly skilful, thrilling sport, calling for intense concentration, and beautiful to watch. Most beaches have summer lifeguards, life saving equipment, flags to indicate the state of the sea, and emergency telephones, all funded by the Local Authority. Inshore rescue groups do sterling voluntary work; and rescue helicopters and air ambulances clatter down from the sky within a few minutes of an emergency call. But the Cornish sea is omnipresent, omnipotent, unchanging, and Man is but a small speck of flotsam who will never master it, despite modern techniques and appliances.

Nude bathing took place on one of our beaches long before it became popular elsewhere.

Jocelyn, a teenage friend of mine, was the proud possessor of a pair of ancient, battered, high-powered binoculars.

One Saturday morning in late May we were sitting on the cliff top at Treyarnon, taking turns in scanning the rocks and deserted beach. Suddenly Jocelyn's fingers furiously twiddled the focussing screw.

"Hey! Look what's coming down the path!" he almost yelled, passing me the binoculars.

I quickly refocused, and looked in the direction in which he was pointing. A woman wrapped in a bathing towel, and three naked children were descending into the cove. When they reached the sand, the woman dropped her towel before our uninitiated, disbelieving eyes. She stood like a goddess with lithe, suntanned body, large firm uplifted breasts, and a black triangle of pubic hair. She clapped her hands and the quartette ran like deer across the beach and into the sea. I passed the binoculars to Jocelyn, who was getting excited, he had a look, passed them back and then we kept passing them to and fro as the little group jumped up and down in the waves.

"The big girl's got tits like lemons!"

"Look at Mother's arse wobbling!"

"Have you seen many like this before?"

"Dozens!"

"You haven't, you're lying!"

"I have...Well...my sister..."

"She's only a kid..."

Our bickering continued until the family returned to the cove and lay face down on the sand to sunbathe under our magnified, distant gaze, which stirred up, and aroused our adolescent minds - and other things, during that May morning.

I mentioned the bathing party to Father, and he told me a story, which I wish I could say was true.

"That lady has been doing it for years," he said. "I was out wrecking one day, and there she was, lying on the sand, naked as she was born. She picked up an old saucepan which had washed in, and held it in front of her.

' "Good morning, Ma'am, lovely day," I said.

She replied: "I'm not embarrassed. And I can read your thoughts."

"I'm not embarrassed either," I said. "And I can read your thoughts also. You think there's a bottom in that saucepan, don't you? Well, Ma'am, there isn't." And I walked away.'

I have lived almost ninety years beside these beaches which fringe this Atlantic coast, with only a break of six years during World War II. Here I have watched the changing seasons on cliff and seashore, and I have changed with them. But my thoughts invariably turn back to those joyous, unfettered days of my childhood and early youth when my ears and my eyes absorbed the slow, low, sighs of summer seas in the crescent curve of Constantine Bay; when I first heard the cadence of singing waters, and the pealing thunder of winter breakers merging with the chorus of windblown seagull cries on Harlyn Bay; and the humid days when the moaning foghorn, pierced a pearl-grey mist which crept down from Trevose Head, and formed dewy globules on late-flowering sea-pinks; and from the trumpets of pink sand dune convolvulus, I listened to the soft droning of bees.

My thoughts wander back through a tremble of light points on summer waves, falling exhausted on pillowing sand-rippled foreshores; and my feet move through furrows, undulations, swirls and curves of sand patterns, created by the constant movement of the tides.

Sometimes I see a boy, from those long-ago teenage years, sitting on an old wooden seat on top of a darkened cliff watching reflections of a crescent moon rippling a silver path to the horizon. Here he listened to unseen curlew voices, calling in the autumn sky. Here he found peace that only lovers of the sea can find and understand, and that peace has remained with him to this day.

Then I see him, satiated by sight and sound, walking back to a shadowy tamarisk-hung stone hedge where his bicycle is parked, and I watch him pedal slowly homewards, absorbed in the voices of the waves, the whispering night breeze, the moon path, and the calls of the birds; all of which remain fresh in his memory today.

Beach Cottage, Porthcothan

9

The Valley

I was a gangling ten year old when I first set foot in Trescore Valley which was about a mile from our cottage. On most Saturday mornings I accompanied Mother down to the Mill to buy cream from the farmer's wife who always had a pot of tea ready. After drinking mine and getting bored by their small talk, I would excuse myself and walk down to the mowhay where the ancient waterwheel creaked and groaned as the chattering stream of water flowed into its wooden buckets and away through the leat to join the larger stream in the Valley. One morning as I stood beside it, my eyes wandered to the Valley, and I hoped that one day I would explore it. My wish was soon fulfilled, for on the following Saturday, Mother had to open up a house at Constantine for the absent owners who had suddenly decided to take an early holiday.

"Mum, if I fetch the cream today, can I go into the Valley? I promise I won't go too far."

At first Mother was dubious, but I persisted, and she gave in to my request. She made me a pasty and filled a flask with tea which I put into my school satchel, together with my well thumbed book on Natural History.

"Keep away from the river. Don't climb trees. Tell Mrs Hawken I'll pay for the cream next week, and be sure you are back by tea time," admonished Mother.

At half past nine on that Spring morning I hurried along the road, and within a few minutes stood by the signpost which pointed to Trescore Valley. A moorhen eyed me suspiciously from the reed fringed duck pond as I hastened down the steep cobbled track where snow-white blackthorn cascaded over the ditches. I wanted my flask of tea to last all day so I stopped at the shallow thorn-embraced well on the left side from whose arch of stonework grew bunches of Harts tongue fern. I kneeled down, cupped my hands, dipped them into the crystal clear, ice cold water which immediately produced a sharp, short numbing pain in my temples as I gulped down several mouthfuls.

The hamlet came into view; three houses only, the Mill at the bottom and, over-shadowing it, a tall gaunt house, reputedly haunted; next to it was a cottage with small-pane windows which looked out onto a lawn sprinkled with apple trees. An imposing entrance gate flanked with high granite posts topped with egg-shaped ornaments overlooked a wide gravel path which curved to the front door.

Opposite the gateway was a low stile which led into a small meadow and from it a footpath ran parallel to the right-hand hedge. Joyfully I clambered over

Two photos of Trescore Mill in the valley at Porthcothan. Jack had many a happy hour here living just above the Mill House in the back of Porthcothan Farmhouse. The photo looking down the hill shows the mill house, the one looking up the hill shows the mill which is far older than the mill house, the wheel can clearly be seen. The road use to go down past the mill to Trescore packhorse-bridge and the road then led up over the hill towards Trevethan Farm. At the time the pack horse bridge was the main route through Trescore there was no road, as there is now, around and over the bridge at Porthcothan.

the stile, and sped down the path where another stile guarded the entrance to the Valley. Here I sat for a while, gazing for the first time into what was to be my secret, wonderful world.

Elm trees clustered the stile, their leaves a delicate translucent green through which the sunshine filtered, and from their branches came the 'pink pink' call of a chaffinch. Lamb's tail catkins hung fresh and yellow, and at the end of the path an ancient humpback stone bridge about four feet wide straddled the stream. I approached it in wonderment, absorbed every detail of the curving arch and the lichen covered stones. There were no protecting side walls and I wobbled as I walked over the hump. Water eddied around small rocks near the foot of the bridge, and on one of them I saw a small robin-like bird with a white breast bobbing up and down. Amazed, I watched it take off, dive, and proceed to walk down stream under the water. I quickly thumbed through the bird section of my book and discovered that I had seen my first Dipper.

I plunged through the knee-high green spikes of an iris bed to the stream edge and saw a brown-spotted trout dart swiftly out of sight. A vole peeped out through the leaves of water forget-me-not on the opposite bank and seeing me, plopped into the water where the morning sun sent silver darts of light across the ripples of its wake as it swam downstream.

Trescore Cottage

I followed a winding cow path along the foot of the Valley whose side sloped steeply away through a wilderness of old bracken. Shining green bluebell leaves pushed upwards through the dead brown fronds; I knelt down to examine them and saw tight bud spikes forming within the clusters of leaves, and I knew I would soon return again to enjoy their blue glory.

High up in a hawthorn tree I spotted a magpie's nest, and forgetting my promise, I mounted the overgrown hedge upon which the tree was rooted, and began to climb. It seemed easy at first, because I was thin and could wriggle my way up through the lower branches. Alas, soon my hair was entangled, and a shooting pain in my knee told me that I had contacted a thorn. Undeterred, I finally reached the domed nest of spiked twigs. The female magpie had long since flown out, and with her mate chattered angrily nearby. With thorns sticking into me from every angle, I managed to turn around and find the entrance to the nest. Inside, upon the mud and grass lining lay seven mottled grey-green eggs.

Gingerly I pushed my right hand through the opening, my fingers touched the tops of the warm eggs. The magpies chattered furiously as they hopped to a nearer branch, their eyes baleful, their feathers glinting green and purple in the sunlight. My fingers fumbled over the eggs until I grasped the nearest one. Slowly I withdrew my hand and had drawn it clear of the nest when an enormous thorn gouged into my middle finger and broke off. Red lights danced before my eyes; more thorns pricked my back and legs; I could not move upwards, neither could I climb down. Blood from the wound formed a sticky mess on the egg shell. I hung there for what seemed an age, feeling guilty at having disobeyed my Mother. A silly verse flashed through my mind:

When you're up, up, up,
You're up, up, up,
And when you're down, you're down.
And when you're in the middle of a hill
You're neither up nor down!

But I was stuck in the middle of a tree and suffering intense pain. The ridiculous words and my precarious situation suddenly made me laugh and gather my senses together. I forced my feet to find holds on the trunk and branches. With knees grazed and bleeding; with threads of wool from my jersey pulling tightly from the branches, I inched myself down to the top of the hedge, one hand gripped the egg, the other disentangled my clothing, and somehow I managed to slide down to the ground. Trembling and sweating I sat down by my satchel and plucked leaves and broken twigs from my hair.

The thorn was large and deeply embedded in my finger. I tried to pluck it out with my teeth, but could not get a grip. I tried to pinch it between thumb and first finger nail, and was partly successful as I pulled and eased it upward. But it broke in half; a quarter of an inch stuck to my thumb nail, the remainder lay embedded and immovable in my finger. Mother magpie returned to the nest, and her mate watched me balefully from the top of the tree.

I gathered up my satchel and precious egg and walked to the river bank where I sat with my legs dangling over the edge, a few inches above the water. The morning sun was strong and, despite the nagging pain in my finger, I lay back amidst the sedge and weeds. I closed my eyes as sunlight, warm and diffused pink, filtered through my eyelids.

60

I don't know how long I dozed, but I awoke to the mewing of a buzzard which hovered directly overhead. I watched its beautiful outstretched wings as it circled effortlessly, paused, and plummeted down into the grass beyond the stream where it remained out of sight for a few moments. Then it rose and glided away with a mouse in its talons.

I began to feel hungry. My pasty, well wrapped in newspaper and tucked inside a discarded sugar bag, was still warm. I bit off the top, savoured the thick pastry crust, the juicy peppered chunks of potato and meat, ate one half, and washed it down with tea from the screw-on cup of my flask which was so hot that I could hardly bear to hold it. Replete now, I read my book, noting plants, trees and insects which I might expect to find, and so the hours sped by.

I followed the cow path up to a point where it was joined by another path which led away through a maze of willows. Here I came upon a crude wooden footbridge, but as it was now well into mid-afternoon I crossed over it, turned back and followed the other path on the opposite side of the stream. When the Mill came into view I ate the remainder of my pasty, took off my jersey and carefully pushed back all the strands of wool which had been plucked out, for I knew that I wouldn't be allowed to come here again if my clothing was damaged. Then I decided to blow the egg, and soon found a long thin thorn with which I proceeded to prick each end of the egg. This was not easy for the shell was thick and the thorn was rather blunt. However, I managed to form two holes and pierce the membrane within. I blew hard into the egg but produced only a small bubble of fluid. I puffed harder, the shell broke and my mouth and hands were filled with a mass of blood and embryo magpie. Thoroughly disgusted, I threw the remains into the stream, watched them float away, and rinsed my hands. All I had to show for my efforts was a throbbing blood stained finger.

When I reached the last bend, and the humpback bridge came into view, I realised that here the stream was much wider and deeper. This did not deter me from crossing so I took off my boots, stuffed my stocking into them, tied the laces together, slung them around my neck and lowered myself into the water. The coldness, despite the hot sunshine, made me gasp and I almost dropped my satchel. As I stepped over pebbles and reached the middle of the stream, water lapped my calves then, without warning I struck a patch of mud near the opposite bank and sank down until the bottom of my shorts were touching the surface of the water. As I moved my legs up and down, my feet sank deeper into the silt and the water crept up past my thighs to my bottom. I managed to throw my boots and satchel onto the bank, but prising myself out of the water was not easy, for as I pressed my hands on the grassy edge, lumps fell into the stream and splashed my now well-wetted torso. A few yards downstream I noticed a small fallen tree trunk and by careful side-stepping I reached it and, balancing myself across it, hoisted myself to the bank. I collected my boots and satchel, took off my shorts and underpants, laid them out to dry and stretched out my wet legs and thighs in the sunshine. The tail of my shirt was wet so I turned onto my stomach, closed my eyes and daydreamed.

"Hey, Boy! What be doin' there with yer arse turned up?"

I awoke with a start, turned over and pulled down my shirt to cover my nakedness. Above me stood a stocky unshaven youth with a grinning, wide-open mouth from which a few discoloured uneven teeth protruded. As he laughed at my discomfiture I noticed that he was slightly cross-eyed and I had an immediate feeling that he wasn't quite normal. He was leading a cart horse whose shaggy body seemed to be in dire need of a currycomb.

"I got wet crossing the stream and I'm drying my clothes."

"Aw, why didn't 'e jump across? 'Tis easy!"

"I never thought of that, and it's too wide," I said, hoping that he would go away.

"I'll show 'e. You 'old the mare a minute," and he thrust the reins into my hands as I stood feeling stupid in my short shirt.

"You got to take a run," and the youth turned and sprinted away from the bank. He stood for a moment, his brown eyes gleaming, his mouth set in a lockjaw grin.

"Now - you say: One, two, free. Go!"

I shouted his instruction and with a, "Wheeee!" He took off and sailed over the stream, landing a good three feet beyond the far bank.

"See, Boy, 'tis easy!" he shouted. "Now I be comin' back! You tell me again when to go."

I repeated the formula, and with a tremendous, "Wheeeeeee!" he took off, missed his footing and fell flat into the water. At that moment the mare whinnied, and shook her head. The reins slipped through my fingers and she cantered away down the Valley.

"You silly young bugger, you've made me git wet to the skin, and you've let Mary loose. I...I wen't shaw you 'ow to jump river never no more!" and climbing out, he shook himself like a dog and ran down the Valley shouting: "Mary! Mary! Mary! You wait fer me, I be all wet and unkumfertuble!"

I dressed quickly for my clothing was now almost dry, picked up my satchel and walked slowly along the cow path to the humpback bridge. I could hear a faraway voice, somewhere down near the beach, shouting, "Mary you old bugger, you wait 'till I catch up with 'e ... Mary ...!"

I hurried back to Lane End thinking I was late, and was surprised when Mother greeted me with: "You're early, dear. I didn't expect you yet. You've got the cream, and how was Mrs Hawken?"

Horrified, I stammered: "I thought I was late Mum, I ran all the way home. I've forgotten it!"

"Now it will have to wait until tomorrow. And your Father won't be very pleased to have his tart without cream!"

62

I rushed past Mother, almost knocking her over. "I'm going back for it!" I shouted, and was gone before she could say another word.

I arrived at the Mill panting and bathed in sweat.

"Whatever have you been doing Jack, you're all of a lather?" said Mrs Hawken as she opened the dairy door. I told her that Mother had been away; that I had spent the day in the Valley, and had forgotten to call for the cream so I'd run all the way back. She gave me the cream in one of her own glass dishes, for in my hurry I had forgotten to take Mother's dish from my satchel.

"Now you go home slowly, and don't spill one little drop. I've put a bit extra in for you when you get your breath back," said Mrs Hawken. "and by the way, did you see Charlie when you were over there?" She pointed to the Valley. "He was supposed to bring a horse down from Trevathya for my husband."

"I met a man with a horse called Mary. He showed me how to jump across the stream, and he fell in, and the horse ran away. He's probably down on the bay now."

"That's him! He's a bit -" Mrs Hawken tapped her head with a finger, "lacking up there, but he's harmless. Came from an orphan's Home, I believe. Lives with the Benny's. He'll turn up sometime."

I thanked Mrs Hawken, and as I trudged up the hill I saw Charlie coming out of the lower lane, mounted on Mary. He didn't see me, and having recovered my breath, I ran the remainder of the way.

Mother was in a better mood now and wanted to know how I had spent the day. I was surprised that she made no inspection of my clothing, and I kept

Postman Brown at Trescore Bridge

63

my swollen finger out of sight. I told her what I had seen and done with the exception of the robbing of the magpie's nest and my wetting in the stream. She knew of Charlie, but wasn't very happy when I told her that Mrs Hawken had said that he was a bit simple, but harmless. I asked if I could go again next Saturday. She promised to ask Father, he in turn raised no objection.

Some days later my finger had festered to such an extent, that fearful of blood poisoning, I was compelled to show it to my astonished parents.

"You've been bird nesting again. You don't find thorns that size in bushes. You've been climbing, haven't you?" said Father sternly. Reluctantly I told him the whole story as he poked and prodded with a darning needle, making me wince with pain. Eventually he dislodged it, and to this day I can show the mark it left on my finger.

For two years I continued to visit the Valley, mostly on Saturdays, and from the lengthening days of Spring into late Autumn I made frequent evening visits after school. I began to know each side intimately; each small meadow and hedge; each bend in the stream as far up as Lewidden bridge. I watched gorse flame and die high on the slopes where the Valley joined the fields, and Gramfer told me that below Trevathya the area was known as Fiery Mountain.

Among the gorse and bracken were adders, slow-worms and lizards. When I came upon my first adder I was petrified and wondered what I would do if it attacked me and I was poisoned, but it slithered away into the undergrowth, and I breathed again. Later I learned that adders only attacked if disturbed.

I trapped lizards in my butterfly net, brought them home in a jam jar and turned them loose in our garden hedge.

From my nature book I identified the various trees and bushes - the ash, oak, willow, elm, horse chestnut, blackthorn and wild rose; I was already very familiar with the hawthorn! Often I would lie hidden among the beds of wild flowers, half stupefied by their scent and the warmth of the sun as I listened to the songs of reed warblers, whitethroats and twittering wrens. My eyes wandered to the droning bees and butterflies as they sipped nectar from the flowers. Stretched out there with my book, I felt that I too was sipping from a wondrous cup which Nature was holding out to me.

Once I was stirred from my lethargy by ants which were scurrying wildly over my naked legs, and I found that I was lying on their nest. I stood up, prodded it with my boots and watched the furious activity as hundreds more emerged. I wondered how their tiny minds were reacting to the vast disturbance I had caused to their little world.

Sometimes I would sense that I too was being watched, and turning around would see a herd of young bullocks advancing slowly. Holding their limpid, brown-eyed gaze in mine, I listened to their ponderous breathing and the buzz of flies on their dusty backs as they scattered them with a flick of tail. Then I would stand up, clap my hands and away they would run, only to return again as

I continued my nature watch.

On summer evenings I loved to walk along the southern rim of the Valley and watch the sun sink down into its bed of burnished clouds. I marvelled at these cloud patterns, and visualized them as sky gods, elemental shapes, towering peaks and castles, all conglomerating and quickening around the dying sun. Then as the velvety twilight crept down, I felt the touch of dew and shivered slightly as I waited, and listened for the creatures of the night to appear.

A tawny owl had a favourite perch on a twisted elm branch, I sometimes watched it as it slumbered, oblivious of the smaller birds that mobbed it. Then as the twilight deepened, it sailed through it like a shadow and quickened the Valley with its haunting call.

On another evening I watched the entrance of a badger sett and, after what seemed an age, Brock emerged, sniffed the night air and like a white-nosed ghost, lumbered down the fern-filled slope, quite unaware of my presence. Then there was the time when I could have touched a dog fox which slunk past me down to the water meadows where a flock of roosting geese immediately set up an uneasy hissing as it passed by.

During those two years I watched the Valley change from the blossoming of spring, through the fullness of summer, to autumn's ripening and winter's nakedness. I saw the first primroses at the beginning of blustering March, then as the days lengthened, those green acres of bluebell leaves (which I saw on my first visit) pushed their tight buds through last year's wizened bracken fronds until a carpet of blue haze covered the slopes. The image of this beauty imprinted itself upon my mind and, like Wordsworth's daffodils, it remains as a joyous memory of those halcyon days.

All through the year I listened to the voices of the trees. In winter my eyes followed the twisting starkness of their leafless tracery as the north-west wind blew through the Valley. I imagined their conversation as they talked to each other. "Hold fast," said the oaks, the elms and the ash to their tight-clothed buds containing next year's leaf, "spring will come, the wind cannot blow for ever." Then the leaves burst open and the Valley stirred as they whispered, sang and quivered in the sunlight as the air was filled with bird song.

I was totally absorbed in all these changes, and lived in a world of fantasy whenever I crossed the little bridge. The stream chuckled between its earthy banks, as I watched damselflies floating languidly over the reeds, their wings shot green and gold by sun shafts. One morning I caught a dragonfly and, holding its body with earth stained fingers, I listened to the whirr of its captured wings, marvelled at its multiple eyes and cruel jaws; then I let it fly having second thoughts that the place for such a beautiful creature was in the air, not on a board in my butterfly collection with a pin stuck through it.

Wild ducks probed the shallows of the higher reaches of the stream, their flat beaks sucking up microscopic life, and a mallard would stand for hours on one leg, quite oblivious that I was watching him only an arm's length away.

Half way up the Valley, in an offshoot on the right hand side, was a long-disused quarry with perpendicular ivy clad sides. High up on its rim stood the roofless ruins of a cottage with only a few stone walls remaining, gaping holes indicated where once doors and windows stood. Over the years Nature had gradually encroached and filled the parlour, kitchen and bedrooms with a tangled growth of weeds and bushes. On the lonely wall tops a mat of white saxifrage spread like tiny stars.

Many times I entered this derelict place and looked through the parlour window opening which scanned the winding Valley down past the mill to the beach and restless sea. I mused over the onetime occupants: was it the quarry owner and his family?; was it a temporary home for the quarry workers?; what did they look like?; what did they see and hear from this window - the flicker of bobbing lanterns?; the lowered voices of smugglers as they made their way to the Vugga Hole across the Valley with contraband from some schooner lying off the bay?; and were they themselves involved? My reverie was broken by the flapping of an annoyed jackdaw from the ruined chimney, so I wormed my way out through the jungle of foliage and followed the narrow path down to the quarry once more.

On the lush greenness of the quarry floor ferns poked their way up through the half-light, for the sun only shone there when it had cleared the quarry face long after mid-day had passed. In autumn the light was thin and fleeting, and in winter, I suspected only twilight, for it was too far away for me to venture in those shortened days, and the pathways would be deep in mud.

Several apple trees, lichen-covered and long since unpruned, still formed the nucleus of a once pleasant orchard near the quarry. Here amid grass and twisted trunks I sat listening to bird song and breezes soughing through the branches. Sometimes when silence descended I felt that I was tapping some echo from the past, did I really hear the clink of pick, the fall of stones and the muffled voices of quarrymen impinged upon the atmosphere, quickened into life for a fleeting moment on a drowsy summer afternoon, or was it my imagination running wild?

It was here that I watched the movements of the little creatures, the shy ones - mice, voles and grey squirrels who dwelt in this secluded and deserted spot. But they were not entirely safe, for a pair of kestrels nested each year on a ledge high up on the quarry face, and pathetic balls of fur scattered on the floor, told of their ravages.

I loved the Valley when it was filled with the rich colours of autumn; when the leaves hung waiting for the first equinoctial gale to blow them to the ground where they would die, permeate the soil and be absorbed by the parent roots of the trees to stimulate new life in next years buds.

I revelled in this kaleidoscope of colour - as yellow, crimson, ochre, brown and orange tinted the withering leaves. I saw the bracken fronds become brown skeletons, cow parsley and alexander heads, now denuded of seeds, stood waiting for the coming gales to crush them down. Before the leaves fell, the fruits of autumn hung heavy on bush and branch, scarlet hips and haws, glossy black sloes, twisted ropes of bryony, and lustrous blackberries.

It was then that Mother, on a fine Sunday afternoon, would cajole Father into a blackberrying expedition to the Valley. Armed with walking sticks for beating down brambles, and wicker shopping baskets which they placed near at hand, they would pick furiously, dropping the berries into enamel milk cans hung from their wrists which, when full, were emptied into the waiting baskets. I enjoyed blackberry picking with my parents and took them to the thickets where the largest berries grew. As I picked, I carried out a ritual of counting each one as I dropped it into my can and eating every fiftieth berry.

As September ended, the sun dipped earlier over the western rim of the Valley, and there was a slight chill in the air. The first winds blew, the leaves sighed as they released their hold. But the mornings were magic, for with the advent of autumn, there came hoar frost, mist and spider's webs.

Four times in my young life I watched this pageantry and was up and dressed before dawn. Father and Mother thought I was mad but did not discourage me from going. I found a vantage point near the humpback bridge and watched and waited for the approaching dawn. My teeth chattered, my hands were numb, and hoar frost on my boots made my feet feel like icicles.

I watched the mediocre landscape gradually transform as through the greyness the first shafts of weak sunshine appeared like pale searchlight beams. During the night the spiders had been active - a fantasy of gossamer was strung on dying stalks and bushes. Mist hovered on the curving stream where delicate rope bridges had been spun across the sedge from bank to bank, as strong in their proportions as any engineering feat devised by man. The Valley glittered with a billion microscopic diamanté jewels as I stood frozen, entranced. As the sun gained strength, the mist lifted, the hoar frost melted, the diamanté disappeared, the foliage and stalks became ordinary dying things again and the miracle was over. Stiffly I turned away and ran through the meadow and up the hill towards home, my body now tingling with the exertion, my mind still overwhelmed by the short pageant of beauty I had witnessed.

For many weeks, as the days grew shorter, I could not visit the Valley, not by my own choice, but because my parents objected, saying it was too wet; I would be bogged down, and the stream would be swollen and dangerous. They did not understand my feelings, but I kept faith with them and volunteered to fetch the weekly cream for Mother from the mill so I could see the Valley in its grey shroud; the sleeping, twisted elms, the battered sedge the angry brown stream gnawing at the corner stones of the bridge, and the rain-sodden cow paths.

Mrs Hawken must have understood my longings when she saw me standing in the mowhay one day.

"You love the old Valley, don't you, Jack? I've watched you playing there many a time. I was brought up here beside it; I know every inch of it and I believe you do too."

"Yes, Mrs Hawken," I said. "I think I do, but not for long."

She looked surprised. "Why? What is happening? Your Mother hasn't said anything."

"Father has got a job up in the village. We only heard yesterday, and we are leaving Lane End at the end of the month."

I hoped she didn't see the tears in my eyes.

Packhorse Bridge, Trescore

Part Two: Trehemborne

10

To Chapel on Sunday

The womenfolk in my family were strict Wesleyan Methodists and regularly attended the granite-built chapel next to the Board School, three quarters of a mile away from Rose Cottage; so it was only natural that I was introduced to Services at an early age. On Sundays I was dressed in my best brown velvet blouse with matching short trousers, white socks and brown shoes. My Aunt, had a good soprano voice, and was a member of the chapel choir. She tried to teach me to sing, but was unsuccessful.

St. Merryn Wesleyan Chapel

Before we set out Aunt made me stand on a chair, and she would say, "Now Jack, Sing! You know all the words." I had learned the words of several pretty hymns from the Sunday School Hymnal, but my voice was thin and reedy, so when I hit a top note Gramfer said I sounded like a crowing bantam. Encouraged by my Aunt my tortured vocal chords poured forth:

Suppose the little cowslip
Should hang its golden cup
And say I'm such a tiny flower
I'd better not grow up.

I followed up with several verses of *'All things Bright and Beautiful'*, and that lovely hymn imprinted on my mind a love for Nature which has remained with me throughout my life. At Christmas I mutilated the tune of *'Away in a*

Manger', and to this day, whenever I hear it sung, for a moment I am a small boy standing on a chair making squawking noises.

When my performance ended, we left home for Sunday School which began at half past ten in a drab building alongside the chapel. Here we sang such hymns as, *"There's a friend for little children above the bright blue sky."* Those who could read mouthed one verse each from a chapter in the New Testament. Some of the younger ladies of the chapel congregation took it in turns to teach us.

When Sunday School ended I went to the chapel porch and joined Gran who had arrived, dressed as always in a sober black costume, surmounted by a toque which sat regally on her head, and was decorated with a large white bird's wing.

"Were you a good boy?"

"Yes Gran."

"Now go and do Number One."

"Yes Gran," and off I scurried to relieve myself against the wall of the small enclosed area behind the Sunday School. Girls were sent to the more civilized earth closets at the Board School a hundred yards away.

The grownups exchanged pleasantries in the porch and when the clock showed eleven o'clock, we all trooped in and sat in our allotted seats for the morning service.

The chapel was built in 1907, and was about thirteen years old when I first attended. The porch screen, tiered choir, and rostrum were made of pitch pine, as also were the hard, straight-backed seats of the wide centre aisle and short side aisles. Oil lamps with white shades hung on long chains from S crooks in the ceiling; in later years they were replaced by hissing pressure lamps before electricity came to the parish. The windows were leaded-lights set in granite surrounds, with obscured glazed panes relieved by formal red and green flower and leaf motifs which reflected long coloured shadows down the sloped reveals and sills when the sun shone through them.

Gran's pew was third from the front in the left hand aisle; this gave me a good view of preacher, choir, and a fair expanse of congregation if I looked sideways. But any attempt to twist my head around to see who was sitting behind us, immediately produced a hard jab in the ribs from Gran's elbow.

It was the custom in those days to rent a sitting, and this gave one a sort of congregation status. Woe betide anyone who sat in a pew which had a brass card holder screwed to the front of the hymnbook shelf with someone else's name written on it. Gran could seat four of our family in her seat, but some of the more prolific elders rented a whole long pew in the centre aisle to accommodate their families.

Blue strip carpeting was laid between each aisle, with matching hassocks in each pew. The tiered choir sloped down on either side of the pulpit, or rostrum

70

as it was grandly called. Directly behind the preacher stood an harmonium which, at the beginning of each hymn, wheezed asthmatically, and the organist's head and shoulders, just visible over the top, swayed pendulum-like from side to side as she manipulated the foot pedals to imbibe the aged instrument with life-giving air.

There was a good all-year-round congregation, and during the Summer season, many fresh faces from Plymouth and Devonport swelled our congregation, some of whom owned holiday homes in the parish.

To the left of the choir was a doorway which led to a small vestry where the preacher for the day relaxed before taking the Service. Preachers were planned, and came from various parishes. Some were literate, others illiterate; some were refined and put their aitches in the correct place, and others, truly rural, spoke in the broad, velvety North Cornish brogue which happily has never been stifled by education or progress.

Morning Service lasted an hour and a quarter sometimes longer. To me it was eternity. I counted the square panes of glass in the windows, the number of green leaves and red flower heads of stained glass, I counted the choir, and those whom I could see in the congregation. The seat got harder and harder, my backside felt numb, so I transferred my weight from one buttock to the other; I picked my nose; I drew finger lines in the light layer of dust on the hymnbook shelf; I moved the hassock with my toes and I counted the faint ticking of the clock. The preacher droned on and on.

My feet did not reach the floor, but by easing myself slightly forward my left toe could just touch the twin hot water pipes which provided an elementary form of central heating. I discovered that if I tapped the top pipe lightly, and then transferred my toe to the lower pipe, a few seconds later, I could feel a vibration in that pipe which had travelled right around the chapel. I did this once too often, for I slipped and my shoe struck the top pipe hard, and a tremendous DONGqqqqq! echoed through the sermon-laden atmosphere, and continued donging around all four walls. The preacher stopped in mid-flow and, obviously seeing me cringe, said in an awe-inspiring voice, "Madam, kindly tell the small boy to desist in order that I may continue my sermon."

Gran, her face like a thunder cloud, pointed a stern finger at me and said, "Shhhhh!" which ended my boredom and silenced me during the remainder of the service.

This public rebuke cut Gran to the quick, and we walked home in silence.

"Gran, what does desist mean?" I asked her later that day, after she had spoken at length to the family of my behaviour and her humiliation.

"I don't know, and I don't care. But if you do it again, I'll break your damned little neck!" she said. That was the only time I ever heard Gran swear.

Harvest Festival Sunday was always a joyful occasion, and every year an abundant collection of fruit, flowers, vegetables, home and farm produce filled the chapel. Each window recess was decorated with rows of glossy apples, little triangular mounds of tomatoes, jam jars filled with chrysanthemums, dahlias, michaelmas daisies, intertwined with plaited ropes of corn and miniature sheaves of corn. The choir, pulpit and altar was always a glowing panorama.

I well remember one such Sunday when I was a lad of ten years, sitting as usual with Gran in the same pew. On the edge of the pulpit stood a row of apples and pears, interspersed with dahlia heads, flanked each side with glass vases holding tall plumes of pampas grass. On the crisp white cloth of the altar table below stood loaves of homemade bread, yellow pats of butter ornamented with ribbed bas-relief swans and thistle heads; dishes of scalded cream and a variety of large and small cakes. An enormous golden pumpkin girdled with wheat heads stood on a dais above them, with plates of brown eggs, scones, saffron cake and pyramids of black grapes. On the floor stood sacks of potatoes and corn, green globes of cabbage, bunches of carrots, leeks and beetroot. On the coming Tuesday evening, this wonderful display would be taken into the Sunday School and a grand auction sale would take place.

On this particular Sunday - I was now quite well-behaved and, having mimed my way through *'The sower went forth sowing'* (my voice had become so flat it could put a Choir out of tune), and having listened to the parable of the Prodigal Son - I resigned myself to the inevitable lengthy sermon.

Our local butcher was the preacher for the day, and I had listened to his exhortations on several occasions. He was always eloquent, and sometimes demonstrative. Today he was both, and regaled the large congregation with his text: *'Whatever a man soweth, that shall he also reap.'*

He had reached the point where he likened those persons who had lived unblemished lives, to ears of wheat when on the Judgement Day they would be separated from the tares those who had lived evil lives. The wheat would be gathered into a Heavenly Granary and the tares would be consumed by the fires of Hell.

With arms outstretched and fists clenched, the preacher suddenly brought them together with a wallop onto the top of the pulpit. Fascinated, I thought I saw a large red apple move slightly. Then, once more - Wallop! and the apple did move. Lurching slightly to the right with arms wide open and fingers extended, the preacher's hand brushed against a delicately poised head of pampas grass which swung, lightly at first; then it gathered momentum, brought the other heads together, and now, top-heavy, the arrangement lost its point of balance and tipped forward. The cut-glass mouth of the vase gaped as water gushed forth, the whole decoration fell slowly, bringing down first a dribble of tomatoes, then a marrow which, like a green rolling pin, swept down pears, eggs and onions. The vibration toppled the moving apple over the edge of the pulpit and it bumped heavily down onto the pumpkin which mercifully was too heavy to be dislodged, and cannoned off and landed in the dish of cream. The chaos of falling offerings was like witnessing an earthquake as they cascaded down and surged towards the petrified congregation. I sniggered, and received the anticipated dig in the ribs. Our preacher was not embarrassed as he surveyed the wreckage in the silence after the last apple had rolled to a standstill.

"Amen! Amen!" he intoned. "And now we will sing the closing hymn: '*All is safely gathered in, 'Ere the Winter storms begin'*'."

The harmonium groaned out the first line; the choir and congregation stood up and sang lustily; many smiles were hidden behind hymn books held in front of faces. Those who had spent loving hours in assembling the display knew that they would be spending the afternoon recreating it.

The Service ended, and some of the older boys rushed down the aisles and began salvage operations which were gratefully appreciated by some of the elderly ladies, who never knew how many apples were pocketed under the guise of public-spirited action.

There were other chapel functions: Prayer Meetings on Tuesday evenings, when those who were more lucid in their religious expression, were individually called upon to pray, and gems, both literate and illiterate poured into the sanctimonious air, spiced with occasional 'Praise the Lord', 'Hosannah!' and moans of fervent approval from the indoctrinated. Gran never prayed, but she was impressed by some of the efforts, particularly if the praying was done by a visitor.

I attended a few of these evenings as company for Gran. We sat in our appointed seat, but those who would be called upon to pray usually sat in the front pews. Unholy thoughts sometimes passed through my mind as I surveyed the rows of nodding bald heads and stuck-out ears. What targets they would make if only I had my catapult! What could blotting paper pellets soaked in ink do to those shining domes? My peashooter-could make those ears ring and waggle!

Magic Lantern lectures were sometimes given by an official from one of the Missionary Societies, who was also involved in the Deep Sea Mission for Fishermen, and were very popular. A huge white sheet was hung in front of the pulpit and choir. The lantern and its stand stood on a trestle table top laid on pews halfway down the centre aisle. When the hissing pressure lamps were ceremoniously doused by the caretaker, the lantern lens became like a white lighthouse beam silhouetting many of those bald prayer meeting heads and sending wicked thoughts through my own head again. The operator lifted the beam above these excrescence and it was a magic moment when the first slide was placed in position showing the title: 'A Missionary's Journey through Africa' or similar evangelistic theme.

As each garish hand-coloured glass slide was projected, an enthralling tale of life among the Kaffirs, Zulus, and Pygmies was unfolded by the operator. We saw beehive huts, war canoes, and the majesty of the Victoria Falls, herds of elephants, giraffes and antelopes. We saw white garbed children singing hymns under the watchful eyes of stolid missionary ladies who wore pith helmets, white blouses, heavy voluminous skirts and elastic sided boots. Stalwart male missionaries looked out of place in frock coats, batwing collars and bowler hats as they stared stonily at dances, performed by stark naked tribesmen, and I longed to ask Gran why all the dancers had their genitalia carefully painted out.

Social Evenings in the Sunday School were very popular and were organised by Miss Lavinia Bragg, affectionately known as Vina. She was a gentle, dear soul who taught the very young at Sunday School, and she had theatrical leanings.

A Social comprised a mixture of monologues, dialogues, short humorous sketches such as *'Aunt Mary's Will'* (for four females and one male), solos, duets, and on rare occasions, and a visiting conjuror.

The entertainment began at seven o'clock when Vina appeared in front of the red curtains which hid the rickety stage and announced the first item. Vina had a peculiar habit of sucking her tongue and loudly drawing in her breath at intervals which sounded as though she was eating hot soup. Boys in the audience loudly imitated her, much to the annoyance of their elders who Shhhhh'd them to be quiet.

Outside, a large black portable furnace bubbled hot water for the tea and refreshments which followed after the final curtain. A trestle table held plates of meat paste sandwiches, splits and cream, together with jaw-stretching wedges of sponge roll laced with strawberry jam, and a variety of buns - faith refreshments, all of which had been willingly donated.

A silver collection followed, and the green baize bottom of the collecting box was always covered with little silver three-penny pieces, sixpences and the odd shilling.

Games such as Passing the Parcel, Railway Stations, and Twos and Threes followed for about three quarters of an hour. By ten o'clock it was all over; a chapel Steward would thank Vina for her excellent entertainment, and Vina, smiling happily, would thank us all for attending and promise us another Social in the near future.

During my childhood years I regularly attended chapel. In addition to the morning's events there was also an afternoon Sunday school, and an evening service. In later years, when we moved up into the village Mother and Father abandoned the Chapel in favour of the Church, but Gran and Aunt Gladys remained faithful to the Wesleyan Methodist faith.

11

Gran's Little Quirks

Gran Carne

Gran had some odd little quirks and superstitions, and would never look at the new moon through a window pane; neither would she point a finger at the moon. One evening I said, "I've seen the new moon Gran," and she opened her purse, took out a silver sixpence, rushed outside and held it up to the moon. "Now I shall have good luck for a month," she said, smiling as she replaced the coin in her purse. Gran hated ravens and their guttural, "Cawkk, cawkk"; if one flew overhead she would shake her head and say, "There's going to be a death in the parish." Sometimes she was right, and she would purse her lips and mutter, "There'll be two more!" and when this did happen Gran would almost appear to be relishing the news as she informed us, "A cawkking raven always means death."

It was an ill omen if any bird tapped upon the window panes; and if one flew into the cottage Gran would instantly proclaim an imminent death within the family. This happened once, but the relative was a distant cousin in America, it was several weeks before the news reached us - but Gran remembered the incident of the sparrow and loudly proclaimed it.

Once I brought some May blossom indoors, and was promptly sent out and admonished, "Don't you ever bring those flowers indoors again, they are unlucky!"

I often sweated uncomfortably during May month because Gran was adamant that, "No one should ever cast a clout 'til May is out." She was right on more than one occasion during that fickle month of varying temperatures, when I tried to conceal a snivelling cold through discarding my vest. If ever I had a sore throat Gran would say, "Come here Jack, I'll soon cure you." She would wrap one of Gramfer's sweaty socks around my neck and, despite the awful smell (Gramfer only washed his feet once a month) a cure often took place.

If things did not go as Gran intended, she would shake her head and say philosophically: "Man proposes - God disposes. I must get on and make the best of it."

I was very fond of sweets, and consequently developed a hollow tooth at the back of my lower jaw which made me howl in agony. Gran had a remedy in the form of brown wrapping paper which she cut into several squares like postage stamps. She then chewed each one vigorously and placed them into a saucer where a few drops of Gramfer's 'medicinal brandy' had been poured. Making sure that each well-chewed little wad was saturated, Gran then ordered me to open my mouth wide and between my sobs would somehow implant a wad into the aching cavity. This operation produced an immediate beneficial effect which lasted about an hour before another was inserted. I was always cured by the time the saucer was empty.

Gramfer was less successful in dealing with my teething troubles. One day I discovered that a bottom front tooth was loose and, after tonguing it back and forth for some time, I showed it to Gramfer.

"We'll soon put that right, Jack boy," he said. "It'll have to come out."

Gramfer went to Gran's workbasket, found a reel of thread, cut off a piece about five feet long, and made a loop at one end.

"Now, Boy, you stand with your back to the table and grip it hard."

I did as instructed. "Now face the back door."

Gramfer placed the loop over my loose tooth, slackening and gently tightening the thread until he was satisfied. Then he opened the door and tied the end of the thread around the brass door knob.

"We're ready now! Hold tight Jack!"

Petrified, my hands gripped the table as I watched Gramfer move towards the door. Suddenly he lifted a leg and kicked the door hard; I felt a shooting pain in my gum and let out a loud wail as something flew out of my mouth as the door slammed shut.

"There, Boy, 'tis all over. I told you I'd soon put it right," laughed Gramfer, approaching me with the tooth swinging on the string. I put my tongue across my lower gum. There should have been a small gap, but my tongue went right across one which was an inch wide. I felt a cavernous hole with blood oozing from it. Horrified I saw not one tooth, but three dangling from the thread.

"Aw! Bugger me - I've scat out three. My eyesight must be failing. I was sure I'd only put the loop around the loose 'un."

Gran arrived, having heard the commotion. I exposed my bloody, gap-toothed grin to her startled gaze.

"You poor child, what has he done to you?" she cried, nestling me in her arms.

"YOU should know better, John - that tooth would have come out on its own, now just look - the boy's got a great gap there and it'll take months for the new teeth to grow!"

I felt rather silly though until the new ones grew, but I could make a shrill whistle through that gap which the other children couldn't copy, and that was some compensation. Gramfer also gave me a shilling on the quiet, and I changed it into pennies which enabled me to buy a plentiful supply of sweets for several weeks to come.

During early schooldays when I stayed with my Grandparents and Aunt at Rose Cottage, I joined the children of the hamlet and explored every ditch, nook and cranny in the hedges; I made hiding places in the green iris flags by the mill pool where sedge warblers nested in the spring. We threw stones at moorhens, and went on concerted bird nesting expeditions in the fields. We were not content in taking one egg from a nest, but each one of us took an egg. I sadly recall the desecrated and deserted nests we left in our wake – 'strubbing' was the Cornish word for that activity

We played rounders, football with sorbo rubber balls, hopscotch and tipcat along the then quiet road between the cottages and the hill.

At sundown Gran would emerge from the front porch and call loudly: "Jaack! Jaack! Time to come in!"

If we were in the middle of a game of Hide and Seek I could not acknowledge her call because I would have given away my hiding place, so I kept quiet. Meanwhile, Gran, losing patience, would again shout loudly: "If you don't come quick. I'll sting your legs, my boy!" and on several occasions she did so, for near at hand was a large tamarisk bush, from which she plucked a long, slender twig. When I finally arrived full of excuses, she would let fly with it, and my bare legs stung from her ministrations

Gran was a disciplinarian, I thank her for being one, but she was always kind and just; she never chastised unless it was necessary. I dearly loved her. Throughout her long life she was greatly respected by everyone in the parish, and when Gramfer died of pneumonia just before Christmas 1935, Gran then aged seventy-five bade farewell to Rose Cottage and went to live with Aunt Gladys who was then happily married. Gramfer's funeral was held on a cheerless, rain-lashed Boxing Day but the parish did not forget him for young and old left their festivities and the church was full as they came to bid him farewell.

During Gran's final years she come to live with my family until she was laid to rest in the double grave above Gramfer one June afternoon in 1960; she had reached the age of ninety-seven years.

Gran loved flowers, and would often say, "Let them bring flowers now, I don't want them when I'm dead." And flowers she had, for she was now confined to bed and everyone who called brought her a posy. The second part of her wish was not granted, for the grave and a large area around it was piled high with tributes.

RULES

OF
ST. MERRYN PIG CLUB,

JULY, 1887.

1. That the club shall consist of an unlimited number of Members, also that the Society shall not be broken up nor the stock divided so long as any ten Members are willing to support the same; and if any member or members shall otherwise propose, he or they shall forfeit the sum of two shillings, and on refusing to pay the same shall be excluded the society.

2. That there be four stewards chosen annually out of the members for the purpose of collecting subscriptions and fines, visiting and deciding in cases of sick pigs, and marking all pigs belonging to the club; and that each member shall be at the risk of his pig until he give notice to the nearest Steward of marking the same, either personally or in writing; and should the said steward neglect to mark the aforesaid pig within five days, he shall be fined the sum of one shilling; and should the said member neglect to enforce the fine on the steward, if proved, he shall also be fined the same as the steward. Should any member have more than two pigs marked in one year, he shall pay two-pence to the steward for marking each of the others, also the fines so collected to be paid over immediately to the Treasurer.

3. That each member shall pay or cause to be paid on the first Tuesday after every quarter day the sum of six-pence, or be fined the sum of three-pence, to be paid to the steward appointed for that purpose, at such time and place as the said steward shall direct, and if such fines and subscriptions be not paid up by the next collecting day, the member so neglecting shall be excluded.

4. That any member lately losing his pig, shall within ten days after the sum being affixed, receive of the treasurer the price to be awarded at one farthing under the butchers' buying price, and to be at the whole weight of his pig; and if in cases of sick pigs any member shall kill his pig before finding any disease, or giving notice to the stewards, and afterwards there should be a failure, except pease shall in no case receive any benefit, and in case of pease the loss to be decided by the stewards, and in case where stewards are called they shall immediately proceed to value the pig, and so on as called on, and if the pig should recover, the four stewards shall decide on the loss, and in default of any steward or stewards neglecting their duty, unless prevented by sickness or extreme necessity, and then to send their key by one of the members to act in their behalf; and not to be later than seven o'clock every quarter night, shall be fined six-pence, and default of payment to be excluded.

5. That any member shall dispose of his interest in the club to any person the majority of the club may approve of, but the party so becoming a member shall not come to the full benefit of the club for the space of three months after, and in case of the death of a member his interest shall descend to the Widow or Children if approved of.

6. That if any new member wishes to join the society may at any quarter meeting by paying two shillings and sixpence entering money, and risk his pig three months, and pay his quarterage regularly so long as until an accident should occur, when all the members will again advance their quarter arrears, and then to be free as the standing members.

7. That any member refusing to serve in the office of a steward after being duly elected, or neglecting his duty shall be fined the sum of one shilling. the fines to be paid the same in this case as in rule the fourth, and no substitute allowed.

8. That in case of the sudden illness of a pig, one of the stewards will be sufficient to decide whether or not the said pig shall be killed, but the whole must attend to decide on the loss.

9. That no member shall in any case have more than one pig in the club at a time, and that must not be a breeding sow, if known.

10. That in any case when the club shall come to a loss of two pounds, each member shall pay the sum of three-pence or extra if required to the collecting stewards and so on for every two pounds the stewards are to give notice of such loss to the members, and the fines to be the same in this case as in rule the third.

11. That any member imposing or attempting to impose on the club shall be immediately excluded.

12. That in case of the sudden death of a pig, the stewards shall give notice for the sale of the carcase, and the said pig to be sold to the best advantage within 24 hours for the benefit of the club.

13. That any new member after joining the club before becoming a free member, shall be entitled to one quarter of the value of the pig, if lost.

14. That no member shall feed and kill more than twenty score weight. in one year, on the risk of the club, unless recommended to do so by the stewards.

15. That all disputes shall be settled by ballot.

16. That the club hours are from 6 o'Clock until 8 p.m.

17. Any member insulting the stewards, or interrupting business in club hours, shall be fined for the first offence six-pence, second offence one shilling, and in default of payment, or third offence, to be excluded, and if disputed, to be settled by ballot, as in rule fifteenth.

18. That these rules shall be strictly attended to, and stand good until the next annual meeting.

E. BENNEY, Printer, ST. COLUMB.

78

12

Pig Killing Day

Gramfer kept a pig, for pork and bacon were essential items in the food-chain of survival in those days after World War I, when a man struggled to maintain a family on wages of fifteen shillings (75p) per week.

The pig, purchased when only a few weeks old, was given VIP treatment: it was fed on the best pig-meal available, supplemented by bread, potato skins and scraps kept in a large bucket outside the back door called the pig's pail. As the pig grew older and larger it became increasingly valuable and an increasing liability. What a calamity if it sickened and died! What hardship and hunger would follow in its wake! And so, everyone who owned a pig joined the local Pig Club which was efficiently administered by a President and Committee with a strict set of rules dating back to 1887. Dues were levied and recorded, and a panel of Stewards could be assembled at any time of day or night to visit a sick pig. At the sty it would be decided if a veterinary surgeon was required, and if so, he was summoned immediately. Stewards would, if necessary, sit up all night with a sick pig. If a pig died, compensation was paid out of the Pig Club funds.

One evening at Rose Cottage I sensed tension in the air when Gramfer came in swinging a hurricane lantern and announced to Gran: "There's something wrong with the pig. He's gone down on his hind legs and I can't move him. You go and keep watch, Beatrice, while I fetch two of the Stewards."

Gran took the lantern, donned a dilapidated old mackintosh, and still older galoshes and kept vigil with the pig as Gramfer set off on his bicycle. I watched him light the little oil cycle-lamp, check the tyres, and pedal off into the rainy darkness, wearing an old oilskin, a large hessian sack over his bowed shoulders for protection.

At this hour I should have been in bed, but I was overlooked in the crisis. I crept up the garden path, through the open pen and peeped through a crack in the wall of the whitewashed, cobwebby interior of the sty. The floor was dung-strewn and oozing urine; the fifteen score pig was sitting on its haunches with front legs sticking out at an angle, its head lolling, ears flapping, and its breathing stentorious. Gran was sitting on a tea chest, her face impassive in the yellow lamplight, one hand gently stroking the pig. My shoes began to take in water and I hurried back to the warmth of the kitchen.

My Aunt was out for the evening. Being alone in the cottage, it seemed like eternity before I heard Gramfer return with the Stewards and walk up to the sty where they remained for some time.

Gran returned first and was amazed to see me sitting in front of the fire, but she was too preoccupied in brewing tea for the men to berate me, so I sat and listened. It transpired that Gramfer had made a mistake; the pig was not sick, but had become so overweight that its legs could not bear its body weight. As pigs were for the sole purpose of fattening up, there was no question of putting the animal on a diet. Johnny Prynn, one of the Stewards in attendance, was also a professional pig-killer. Gramfer and Gran decided that Johnny should kill it on the forthcoming Saturday morning, so he agreed to arrive at half past eight. I heard no more for I was ushered off to bed by Gran, strangely without a telling off.

Among the important tasks that had to be carried out before Saturday was the cleaning of the killing-stock. The stock - a short-legged table about six feet long and two feet wide, with shaped carrying handles at each end, and legs about eighteen inches long, was brought from the straw house and taken down to the pump trough which was filled with water. Gran, armed with scrubbing brush, pumice block and soap, scrubbed away all traces of last year's bloodstains, spiders and woodlice which had gathered on it.

Saturday morning dawned, I was up, washed and dressed by half past seven. The family was already at their tasks. The large copper in the washhouse bubbled hot water as Gran fed the fire beneath it with sticks. My Aunt washed the cutting-up knives, and opened up large brown-paper covered bars of salt. Father arrived from Trevorrick, having taken the day off from work, followed soon after by Mother. Gramfer and Father discussed how they would secure the pig so that it would not run amok in the garden, for during the past two days it had eaten only small amounts of food and could now stand on its legs again. I did not hear their final decision as Mother shouted: "Jack, your breakfast is ready. If you don't hurry you'll get none!" I sat down to two boiled eggs, a thick slice of bread and butter, and a large cup of strong tea which tasted slightly smoky.

"Now mind you keep out of sight when the pig is being killed, and don't get in anyone's way, or you'll be sent upstairs," admonished Mother.

At that moment there was a knock on the door. Johnny Prynn had arrived. Johnny was a pleasant little man with a pink, freckled face, ginger moustache, gimlet eyes and a balding head. He wore an ancient leather jerkin, cord breeches, brown leggings and shapeless boots; a red and white spotted handkerchief was knotted around his neck. He dropped a long sharp knife and a coil of thin rope on the table.

Rubbing his hands together, Johnny said: "It's a lovely day for the job - if it stays fine. Not too hot for hanging the pig, and no blow-flies to bother us."

"The water's boiling, and the killing-stock is under the big apple tree. The men are waiting for you in the garden, Johnny," said Gran.

"Good, then we can start right away," nodded Johnny, picking up knife and rope and walking out.

80

I followed Gran down to the washhouse where she set out a line of battered buckets, and placed a galvanized dipper on top of the copper.

"Now, we're all ready," she said, and continued to issue last minute instructions.

"Milly! Make sure the dog is chained up. Remember she got at the tripe last time."

"Gladys, see that the steps down to the river are clean, and put your waders down there. You'll need them when you wash the tripe."

"And YOU - where do you think you're going?" Gran had spotted me edging towards the door.

"You stay right in the kitchen until the pig is killed. 'Tis no sight for a child."

My imagination was already stirred, for I had never witnessed a killing, and I was determined to do so today. At that moment Joe Brown the Postman arrived, and Gran was preoccupied for a few moments. I slipped away, unnoticed, and squatted down behind a row of gooseberry bushes betwixt garden and orchard.

The pig-pen gate was open, with Johnny Prynn, Gramfer and Father inside the sty. Silence. Shuffling, and a loud agonised squeal rent the air. The pig waddled out into the pen with the rope tied to a foreleg. Johnny Prynn with knife bared, grabbed an ear and pulled the head of the animal upwards whilst Father held on to its tail. I closed my eyes as the knife descended, and when I opened them it was buried in the pig's throat. The squealing changed to gurgling as a fountain of dark red blood cascaded down. Johnny Prynn withdrew the knife, flicked blood from its blade with dripping fingers and shouted: "I've slicked 'im first time! Let 'im run!"

The pig, gurgling and squealing ran from the pen and made for the orchard, its head lolling, eyes clouding and its front legs streaming with blood. Gramfer pulled at the rope; the pig swung around, panted past the violet bed and currant bushes until it was facing the killing-stock, then unexpectedly, it turned and, with a spurt of dying strength, ran twice around a tree trunk until it was being strangled by the rope. After much swearing and pushing, the men detached the rope from the pig's leg. It was now unsteady, and the gurgling was more pronounced. I squatted, terrified, and could feel and smell sweat running down my body. The pig sank down on its knees and keeled over near the killing-stock.

"He's dead, but he wasn't an easy one," said Johnny.

Suddenly the spell was broken. Gran spotted me, crept up, and gave me a sharp slap on the head which sent me reeling. I fell over, and she hoisted me to my feet, her face livid as she hissed: "Why can't you do as you're told? Get into the house - and stay there!"

Trembling, and with a smarting ear, I watched from the kitchen window, but the proceedings were now partly obscured by the gooseberry bushes. The men turned the dead animal onto its back and, holding the legs, lifted it up to the stock and turned it over on its side with blood still dripping from its throat. Mother appeared with a bucket of earth and sprinkled it liberally on the trail of blood until it was all covered up. I discovered later this was to keep flies at bay should the day become hot.

Gran and Aunt Gladys appeared, carrying our galvanized bath which they placed beside the stock and, together with Mother filled it with buckets of water from the washhouse. They then fetched three enamel jugs, dipped them into the bath and in turn poured jug after jug upon the carcase as the men began scraping off the black hair with what looked to me like cut-throat razors. They are shaving the pig I murmured to myself. I was now feeling quite relaxed and was standing on the kitchen table where I could see over the bushes that the pig was changing from black to a creamy-brown colour. After a while the carcass was lifted to expose the un-scraped side, and Gran, Aunt and Mother made several more trips to refill the bath.

I decided it was time to move, jumped off the table and stood by the back door and shouted, "Can I come and see the pig now?"

"Come along then," Mother called back, "but keep your feet clean."

The pig lay in repose on its right hand side, its head, snout and ears clean and cream coloured; its scraped tail stuck out over the end of the stock. The air was heavy with the overpowering smell of hot water, scalded flesh and bristle, I was suddenly overcome with nausea. I ran into the orchard feeling sick; my shoes squelched in the earth and blood trail, and I slumped down under the nearest apple tree. The dreadful feeling soon passed off and I watched them finish the scraping. Sunlight sparkled through the apple blossom buds, and blood spots on the white violets glistened like rubies.

A fresh operation began when the men moved the carcass to the high wooden frame from which my swing normally hung, but had been temporarily removed by Father. Johnny Prynn secured a rope around each of the pig's hind legs; Mother fetched a chair, placed it under the frame and, balancing precariously, Father pushed the rope ends through each of the heavy screw-eyes under the lintel. They all pulled hard on the ropes, and the pig rose vertically, a trifle lop-sided at first because Johnny Prynn wasn't as strong as the others.

"Pull! Pull! Hold on to him!" shouted Gramfer, and he whipped the end of the rope around the left hand jamb, and now the pig hung straight, with legs apart, and its head about eighteen inches from the ground. The stock was pulled away and gathering bath, buckets and jugs Gran, Mother and Aunt Gladys walked back to the cottage. It was eleven o'clock and time for refreshment or crib as we call it in Cornwall.

I was given a slice of saffron cake and a glass of milk and ordered to sit on the well-cover where I could keep an eye on the pig and chase away any marauding animals. I sipped my milk and nibbled at the cake. The sun made me feel drowsy. Suddenly I was wide awake and staring. A large ginger cat was sitting on its haunches with its front paws embracing the head of the pig, and it was about to lean forward and start eating. I noticed a big clod of earth about two feet away from me, and I wriggled towards it, cupped it in my hand, leaned back and threw it. The clod struck the cat cleanly on its neck and with a loud Miaow! it fled across the stream. I ran to the pig and wiped the splodge of earth from its face with the cuff of my jersey so that no one would be the wiser.

Johnny Prynn and my family returned, and Johnny with a flourish, delicately plunged the point of his knife into the belly of the pig, and with a long, downward stroke, made a continuous cut which exposed the entrails. Gramfer then gave Johnny two sticks, each about twelve inches long which he placed horizontally, one at each end of the cut, leaving the body wide open. The intestines started to billow out, and Johnny plunged both hands into them, and with a sucking noise followed by a pungent smell they fell out and were caught in buckets by Mother and my Aunt who were standing by.

"Now we'll let 'im 'ang for a while," said Johnny, and to me: "Something for you Jack. Blow this up," and he picked out a bag-like object from a bucket and squeezed it. A jet of liquid spurted past my face. I took hold of the warm object, it smelt of pig's pee.

"Go on - Blow!" said Johnny. I began to feel sick again.

"Wait! I've got just the thing for you," said Gramfer, and he produced a goose quill from his pocket and stuck it into the neck of the flaccid object. "now you can blow."

I blew, revolted by the strong, warm smell.

"Blow harder," urged Johnny, and the thing assumed the shape of a skin football.

"Now, keep hold of it and don't let any wind out," urged Gramfer, and as I gripped the sticky neck, he knotted a piece of thin cord around it. "Now, put it somewhere in the sun to dry, and you'll soon have a good football to play with." That was the first of several pig's bladders I received during those childhood years.

The stock was now swilled down and placed near the suspended carcass in preparation for cutting up. A hot pasty lunch was served and, remembering the onslaught of the ginger cat, I volunteered to keep watch over the pig again.

Johnny Prynn cut up the carcass during the early afternoon. The shoulders, hams, legs, ribs, and chops were carried to the kitchen table where Gran was in charge of the salting operation.

Gran scraped the white glistening sides of a large block of salt and, gathering the powder in both hands she rubbed it briskly into the pork which was then removed by Mother and placed in layers in the kieve in the larder.

A rich oily smell of boiling fat filled the kitchen. Gran stopped salting for a moment, wiped her hands in her apron, and lifted a large enamelled pan of sizzling fat from the stove. Moving majestically across the kitchen, her strong hands holding the pan by its handles at arms' length, Gran said loudly, "Out of my way or you'll all be scalded!"

Mother produced a brown earthenware jar called a stug, and between them they poured the boiling fat into it then carried it to the back porch where it gradually solidified into pure white lard.

During the afternoon I was given a treat, partly, I think, to keep me out of mischief. Mother clamped a battered old mincing machine to the kitchen table, well out of Gran's way, placed an oval plate in front of it and by its side a bowl full of chunks of pork, liver and fat. Mother fitted a little circular disc which was perforated with several star-shaped holes, and screwed it to the orifice facing the plate. Gathering a handful of the mixture Mother pressed it firmly into the mouth of the mincer and began turning the handle. With a slight squelch the meat was drawn into the internal worm-screw. I watched, fascinated, as two more handfuls disappeared into the hungry mouth of the machine. Suddenly, from the lower opening there emerged six star-shaped skeins of minced meat. As Mother turned the handle and fed in more of the mixture, the mincemeat settled gently on the plate and gradually evolved into a delightful pink pyramid.

"Now Dear, you can have a go," said Mother.

"Take the handle in your right hand; keep turning it, and put some meat into the mincer and press it down."

I did as I was told and felt very important. Mother removed her mincemeat, and my pyramid began to grow as greasy coils of meat spiralled onto the plate. Soon I was reaching out automatically and feeding more pieces into the mincer. Practice made me careless, rather than perfect: my movements became automatic and my eyes focussed on Gran who was rubbing salt into a hind quarter of the pig.

Suddenly I was screaming with pain; I felt the cold bite of steel on my fingers, and I thought I had chopped them off; Mother had not mentioned the danger of pushing them down into the spiral mechanism of the mincer. Gran rushed to my aid, turned the handle slightly forward making me yelp even louder, then backwards a little, and I was released. My index finger was turning black, and the nail was oozing blood. I wanted to cry, but Gran took my wounded hand, kissed it, and gave me a piece of crackling which was cooking on the stove.

"You've done very well," said Gran, and I realised that I had pushed the whole of the bowl of meat through the mincer, and the only thing left to mince was my hand. Mother put a piece of adhesive plaster on my injuries and the pain eased when we went into the front-kitchen for tea.

My Aunt produced a list of people to whom we should give pork. "There are eight up at the farm so they'll need a large piece. Thea and Arthur next door aren't big eaters; the Brays were very good to us when they killed their last pig, and remember the lovely chops that Rachael at Trescore sent us." And so the discussion and allocation went on, until everyone was included. Johnny Prynn made his selection, and after Gramfer had paid him for his day's work, he packed up his knives and rope and went home, saying he looked forward to his next visit.

The gift pork was carefully wrapped in greaseproof paper and put into a basket for Father to deliver later in the evening. The salting was finished, and the kieve in the larder was filled to the brim. Father reaffixed my swing and the killing-stock was returned to the straw shed. I wandered into the orchard, idly kicking my newly acquired bladder ball. The ruby spots on the violets were now black splashes, and the sun was low behind the apple trees.

Mother and Aunt put on Wellington boots and went down to the stream with the buckets of entrails. They both bent down and faced the swift flow of shallow water and, taking skeins of tripe from the buckets, they held them so that the water flushed out the excreta; then they turned the tripe inside out, placed it in an empty bucket on the bank and repeated the operation.

Suddenly Nellie, an old brown and white mongrel appeared and made straight for the bucket, and withdrew a skein of tripe.

"Hey! Look!" I shouted, and Mother yelled to Father who was in the washhouse, "Quickly Herbert, a dog's eating the tripe."

Father sprinted after Nellie who zigzagged through the currant bushes holding on tightly to her prize; behind her trailed a long ribbon of tripe which stretched like elastic as it became entangled in the bushes. Father hurled a clod of earth at Nellie, hitting her on the hindquarters, and with a yelp she dropped the tripe and disappeared. With arms outstretched Father unravelled the tripe and looked as though he was winding wool.

But soon there was more excitement when my Aunt shouted, "I've lost the maw, 'tis going down under the bridge!" (The maw was the pig's large intestine, and was considered a delicacy in those days).

Now is my chance to help, I thought, and forgetting to take off my shoes and stockings I rushed down the steps into the stream. As I neared the culvert the water deepened and reached my knees. The maw grazed a rock, and I hoped it would be caught up on it; but it slithered past and entered the left culvert. Aunt shouted: "Come back, you'll be drowned. Never mind the old maw!"

I could see daylight at the far end of the culvert, some twenty feet away as I stumbled into the half-light of its dank interior. My feet sank into soft mud, the water was now above my knees. The maw was floating like a jellyfish towards the exit where I could see the dim outlines of ferns growing from the sides. I was now almost bent double, when the maw caught against a small dead branch. I stumbled towards it, grasped its slippery exterior and holding it against my chest I paddled towards the exit.

I heard excited voices from the road above me as Father was briefed on this latest calamity. A water rat plopped from a crevice and slid down over my shoulders; my knees buckled with fright. I emerged into the daylight and found myself in a small pool at the end of the bridge.

"I've got it! I've got it!" I yelled, and held the dripping maw above my head. No sooner had I said this than I sank up to my middle in the muddy water. Father peered down at me, clambered down to the edge of the pool and pulled me to the bank.

"I've saved it. Dad," I cried, as he took the maw from me and tried to look stern, but I knew he wanted to laugh.

"You'll catch it from your Mother when she sees the state of your clothes. I ought to kick your arse for this," but Father did nothing of the sort, and I scrambled up the bank, crossed the road and ran through the bicycle shed hoping to escape, but Mother was waiting, and she caught me.

"Just look at you! Look at your shoes! Look at your trousers! Oh, you bad boy, you're always getting into mischief."

Mother dragged me to the pump trough; stripped off my clothes and scrubbed me all over in the cold water. I was shivering when she brought a large towel, wrapped me in it and sent me up to the bedroom. It was a repeat performance of my washing day mishap, but without spectators. I hurried through the warm, fat-smelling kitchen, down the front passage and up the stairs. Safe in the sanctuary of the bedroom I towelled my cold body vigorously, put on my slippers and my nightshirt, because I couldn't find any spare clothing; then I sat in the window seat, alone with my thoughts.

Darkness crept down over the meadow, and the window panes of the distant farmhouse quivered yellow as the lamps were lit. I watched Father depart on his bicycle with a large basket of pork strapped to the carrier which he would soon distribute to friends and neighbours. A sparrow twittered for a moment in the ivy outside the window; then all was silent.

I began to feel hungry, and crept down the stairs and along the passage; my nostrils twitched at the smell of frying. The paraffin lamp cast mellow light on the flowered kitchen wallpaper, and white table cloth which was laid for a meal. Gran was holding a frying pan over the stove; Mother, Aunt Gladys and Gramfer were sitting on the hard kitchen chairs watching her. I braved the anticipated telling off, sidled over to Mother and put my hand in hers.

"I'm hungry. Mum," I whispered, and I lied, "I couldn't go to sleep because my stomach's rumbling."

Mother lifted me onto her lap. "My finger nail has gone black," I said, and held it up for inspection (I had forgotten about it until this moment).

Gran mumbled something between the frying pan and the fire, then turned to me and said: "Now that you're here, you'd better have some hogs' pudding, because you did help to make it."

Gramfer, sitting in his corner by the stove, beckoned to me. "Come over here Jack, it's warmer." His face crinkled into a contented smile and I slipped away from Mother and was caught up in a pair of brown, hairy hands with broken finger nails and set down on his rough, corduroy covered knees.

Pleasant chatter and cooking smells enveloped me, and Gramfer's chest was warm against my back. He whispered in my ear, "Have a drop of this," and pushed my hand against a big white cup. I raised it to my lips with difficulty and took a deep gulp of the brownish liquid, having never before experienced such a taste. It was bitter, fizzy, and I thought I would be sick. Gramfer felt me shudder and jogged my arm to lift the cup again. I felt certain it was going to kill me, but I couldn't let Gramfer down, so I took another swig, and another. It began to taste better; the lamplight seemed more golden, and the wallpaper pattern danced up and down. I felt delightfully drowsy.

Will Buckingham pig killing.

Gran brought the frying pan to the table and dished out sizzling slices of hogs' pudding and tender bits of pork. Gramfer turned our chair around to face the table and, using my fingers, I ate from his plate. Soon we were all eating, and there was no sound but the rattling of the cutlery. Replete, I reached for the white cup again, and was about to take another swig but was halted in mid gulp by Gran who dropped her knife and fork and, pointing at me said: "Look John, the boy is drinking your beer! You have been encouraging him. You ought to know better."

Gramfer smiled. "I hear the boy has had a busy day, and a little sip won't hurt him." Whereupon I felt very tired and dizzy and, leaving Gramfer, I stood up, went to all of them for a goodnight kiss and wobbled my way down the passage where I met Father. My last recollection as I dragged myself up the stairs was Father saying loudly,

"What on earth has happened to Jack? He's smelling like a brewery. What has he had to drink?"

I heard Gramfer laugh, and say, "About half a pint - but he's got to learn sometime."

Gran said, "You ought to be ashamed of yourself." That was all I heard, for I fell asleep on my bed and my pig-killing day was over.

This is a steamroller that use to work the Mawgan St Merryn area and would have been used to repair the holes using the broken stones 'cracked' and prepared by Granfer Carne.

13

Stone Cracker

Granfer Carne

When Gramfer was not trapping rabbits and farm labouring, he earned extra money as a stone cracker. In those days there was no stone crushing plant in the local quarry, so stone for road making and repairs had to be reduced in size and graded by hand. Sometimes Gramfer worked at an hourly rate, sometimes on a piecework basis, neither of which were very profitable, but nevertheless sup- plemented the weekly cost of living. The roads throughout the parish were not tarmacadamed as they are today, but heavily potholed, holding deep pools of water when it rained, and in dry weather they sent up clouds of choking dust when traversed by vehicles. Cartloads of chunky Cataclew stone were dropped at various points along the parish roads for the stone crackers who had been notified previously of their forthcoming arrival by the local road surveyor.

Gramfer was always willing for me to accompany him if the stone was not too far from home, and Gran did not object to this outing - I think there were times when she was glad to have me out of the way. I always dressed in my oldest clothes, and carried a toy hammer when I set off with Gramfer who carried his hammers in a hessian sack which he slung across the handlebars of his rusty old bicycle; he did not ride it on these occasions, but used it merely as a means of transporting his tools. Gramfer also carried our food for the day in a leather satchel which he slung over one shoulder. Our mid-morning crib was usually a meat sandwich and a slice of saffron cake; for our mid-day meal there was a large pasty for Gramfer and one of proportionate size for me, and squares of half-inch thick heavy cake for both of us. For drink we were provided with bottles of tea - still warm at crib time, stone cold at mid-day, but there was usually some left over for an afternoon drink for me. Gramfer always produced a bottle of ale at this time. I enjoyed my cold tea - we could not afford the luxury of vacuum flasks.

Gramfer wore an old grey tweed cap, a ragged coat with pockets bulging with red and white spotted handkerchiefs, a tin which held coils of chewing tobacco, a pouch for his smoking tobacco, and always two boxes of matches. "Never get caught out Jack boy," he would say, "you can strike half a box in a wind and still not get your pipe to draw." Gramfer chewed and smoked alternatively, and spat intermittently onto the stone heap. A pair of goggles with blue anti-glare lenses, each with a fine wire mesh fixed in front of them to prevent them being broken by flying chippings, was perched above the peak of his cap, and pulled down when he was working. His shirt was of coarse striped twill, collarless, with a front stud; he wore brown corduroy trousers, and boots of heavy leather which had never seen brush or polish, but which he rubbed frequently with oil to increase their waterproofing. Around his calves were strapped leather leggings, and when these were not on, his trousers were tied with binder twine below the knees. When he cracked stones or trapped rabbits, there was much kneeling involved, so he wore thick leather knee pads.

I remember one of those outings on a hot day in June. We left home at half past seven, with Floss, Gramfer's wire-haired terrier padding on behind us. Our destination was Hillhead, some three hundred yards beyond the village crossroads where we were confronted by a huge heap of rough, bluish stone. Gramfer chuckled, spat on his hands and said: "We'd better get tucked into these, boy. They'll take several days to get through." I did not realise at that time how grateful Gramfer was at this sight, for he was going through a period when work was scarce. Gramfer parked his bicycle against the hedge, removed an array of hammers from the sack which he folded and placed beside the heap of stone; the satchel containing our food and drink was carefully placed under a bush.

"Come on boy, let's start," said Gramfer, and we knelt down beside the stone. At first he used the heavy sledge hammer, and split several of the large rocks into small pieces. I hammered on one of these but only bruised the surface, so Gramfer said, "You'd better use this small hammer of mine, the head of yours is going to fall off any minute." Kneeling wasn't at all comfortable, but Gramfer had foreseen this and produced a small square of coconut matting from his sack for me to kneel upon.

Gramfer took off his coat draped it over the back of the stone heap, and rolled up his sleeves; the hair on his mahogany tanned arms glinted in the sunshine as he gripped the hammer with stubby fingers whose nails were ragged and short through scratching earth at rabbit holes when he set his gins.

Using his various hammers Gramfer now made two piles of broken stone, the larger stones would be used as ballast, and the small stones for binding. My little pile also grew and I found it tiring work.

As the sun rose higher, Gramfer tilted back his cap, and sweat formed in little runnels on his balding forehead now covered with a thin layer of dust. His dark glasses reminded me of Blind Charlie. Floss lay asleep in the ditch;

Postman Brown at Treyarnon Point.

languidly I continued to break up small stones and began to feel bored, but not for long, as it was now crib time. Gramfer opened up the satchel and handed me a piece of saffron cake and my bottle of warm tea which went down well.

We heard approaching footsteps, and Joe Brown the postman came over the brow of the hill pushing a wicker contraption which looked like a basket with a lift-up lid, supported on two bicycle wheels. It contained an assortment of letters and parcels which he would deliver throughout the parish after reporting at the Post Office on the crossroads. Joe, a quaint little man, not more than five feet tall, wore the blue-black uniform of the period with red braid around the edges of the jacket, and a red stripe down one trouser leg; on his head was a flat-crowned peaked cap. Joe had just walked two and a half miles from the main Post Office, had trundled his load down a hill with a one in four gradient, and up another hill of equal steepness. His beady little eyes twinkled, and his walrus moustache twitched as he chatted to Gramfer. Soon he was on his way, his feet pitter-pattering as he accelerated along the level stretch to the crossroads.

From my ground level position I gazed at several passers-by travelling in both directions, all of whom were on foot, and spoke to Gramfer. Then up the hill came Maria - Aunt Rye, to her intimates. Tall, thin and wizened, she wore a black silk blouse heavily encrusted with small, bugle-like beads which glittered in the sunlight. Her full skirt was rusty black, and her elastic sided boots had seen better days. On her head was a black boater-style hat to which was attached a black fishnet veil. She was the wife of Gran's brother Jim, and they lived in one of the small cottages in the shadow of the church. Maria paid frequent visits to the public house, a stone's throw from her cottage, usually carrying a white jug which Gramfer told me later was for refills of ale.

"Are you going to give Aunt Rye a kiss, Jack?"

I could have killed Gramfer for saying that, but there was no escape. Aunt Rye bent over me, lifted her veil and pursed her thin lips for my offering. I kneeled up, lifted my face and suddenly recoiled at the strange aroma which she breathed over me. She put her arms around me and delivered a slobbery wet kiss on my mouth which I thought would never end.

"What a fine boy he is, John," said Aunt Rye. "He's got his Father's looks and his Mother's eyes."

I managed to break free from her grasp, picked up my hammer and banged away at a stone, for fear that she might want to kiss me again. Gramfer and Aunt Rye chatted for a while, and I noticed how unsteady she was on her feet when she left us.

"What was that smell that was coming from her, Gramfer?" I asked.

"Maria has been on the beer this morning, and she's had a swig or two of rum, that was what you could smell Jack. Rum's good for you when the weather's cold. You shall try some, one day."

"I don't like the smell, and it has made her wobble," I said.

Gramfer laughed. "She's only a bit tipsy, it'll soon wear off. She's probably drunk it on an empty stomach."

Soon after Maria was out of sight a large man in a bowler hat, corduroy jacket and whipcord breeches appeared in a pony and trap. The elderly beast snorted and wheezed with the effort of pulling its heavyweight passenger up the long slope.

"Hullo Mr Hawken, nice day for travelling!" said Gramfer

"Can't stay to talk John, I'm on my way to Porthcothan. Got to have a word or two with my brother."

He gave the pony a flick with the whip and was gone. Gramfer said, "That was John Gray; he's all set for a row; they're always falling out over something."

The morning wore on; I dropped my hammer and decided to explore the field behind us. Gramfer did not object.

"Be very careful of the ditches, they're deep and I might not hear you shouting if you fell in."

"I won't go near them Gramfer," I promised, and crawled through the five bar gate followed by Floss who had just awakened.

The field was full of uncut hay, which came up past my middle as I weaved my way slowly towards the farthest hedge, enjoying the tickle of the grass stalks on my bare legs. I stopped to examine their feathery heads and sat down in the clover hoping to find one with four leaves. Mother had told me that it was lucky to own one, as clover plants normally had only three leaves. But my luck was out, I couldn't find any, so I lay back in the grass and listened to the trilling, bubbling song a skylark overhead. I cupped my hands to my eyes and scanned the blue sky until I found the tiny up soaring bird. I watched it hover, motionless; the song ceased and the bird plummeted to earth not far from where I lay. I hastened to the spot, but there was no nest and no bird. Little did I know that a skylark always lands some distance from its nest as a decoy to intruders.

Brown butterflies clung to grasses and wavered into flight as I brushed them aside, and when I reached the far hedge, small blue butterflies fluttered over patches of yellow coltsfoot. I tried many times to catch them when they had settled, but just as my fingers were about to close together on the wings, away they would fly.

Floss foraged in the ditches, and I remembered Gramfer's warning. Those that I saw were deep, with great trails of brambles growing from them, all sprouting evil looking thorns. I whistled to Floss and she emerged with head cocked to one side, evidently wondering why I had cut short her activities.

As we made our way back to the roadside Floss suddenly yelped and jumped excitedly into the air, and I almost jumped out of my skin, as a whirring and flapping of wings arose from all sides. A covey of young partridges took flight, but they were out of sight before Floss could extricate herself from the hay.

Gramfer's pile of cracked stones was now much larger, and he said, "I'm glad you're here Jack, we'll have our dinner now." Floss, tired from her exercise, curled up and went to sleep in the shade.

Gramfer's pasty was about nine inches long, mine was about half that size. Today, whenever I eat a genuine Cornish pasty, be it is hot or cold, from the moment I bite off the crinkled end and feel the succulence of chopped meat and the flavour of potatoes, wedded with traces of gravy, and the feel of my teeth entering the crisp crust, I am transported back in time to a roadside with a heap of stones; I am washing that pasty down with cold or luke-warm tea under the smiling gaze of my long departed Grandfather.

After our meal, out of courtesy to Gramfer, I cracked a few more stones then asked him if I could go for a walk to the village.

"Of course you can Boy, but keep well into the side of the road, or you might get run over. And keep out of mischief - your Gran'll be sure to find out if you do, and you won't be allowed to come with me again."

A few people were chatting outside Mrs Old's shop when I went in and bought four gobstoppers with my pocket-money penny. I popped a red one into my mouth; it would last most of the afternoon if I sucked it slowly. I crossed the road, and around the corner I saw the open door of the Smithy.

Octavius (everyone called him 'Tavis), the Smith, was shoeing a horse. The beast was inside, with its hindquarters in the doorway. 'Tavis, facing the road, was straddling one of its legs and fitting a hot, iron shoe to the hoof, which sizzled and threw off a cloud of acrid smoke.

In the dim interior of the Smithy, farmer Bennett pipe in mouth, cap pushed back from his forehead, was patiently holding the horse's head.

"Hello, young Jack, what are you doing up here?" asked 'Tavis.

"I'm helping Gramfer crack stones at Hillhead, and I've just come up to buy some sweets." I replied, pushing the gobstopper into my cheek so that I could speak properly.

"Well now, you can give him this message - say that 'Tavis has finished repairing his gins and will put them outside the door for him to pick up when you two go home today."

I promised to do this, and 'Tavis said, "You can go inside if you wish", his pink face smiling through rivulets of dust and sweat which trickled down his brow as he moved the brown, knobbly legged horse. I sidled past into the forge with its open, slated roof across whose principal beams were laid a number of lengths of long, rusty iron bars. The floor was thick was hoof parings, iron filings and dried dung, and a spider spun busily in one corner of the small cracked window pane. The fire glowed red on its raised hearth in the gaping chimney recess; the ancient leather bellows connected to it, crouched nearby like a wrinkled water butt. Behind the bellows was a deep, dank pit housing the steam coal which fed the fire. The pit always exuded a pungent smell, and years later I learned that 'Tavis damped down the coal when he wanted to relieve himself, as also did waiting farmers if nature called.

I was about to say Good afternoon to Mr Bennett when the horse decided to move a hind leg on the ground, and also the one that 'Tavis was holding. 'Tavis let go, and the horse let fly with both feet, neighing loudly, and pushed him through the doorway. Mr Bennett jerked the horse's reins tightly and shouted, "Get up! You great bugger, I'll break yer bleddy neck if you don't keep quiet!" and his thick arms closed around the animal's neck like a vice. I knew they were swear words because Gramfer used them, and if Gran heard him she would give him a good telling off.

'Tavis moved smartly forward to grasp the horses hoof again, and the beast retaliated by letting off a loud fart and cascading a load of dung over 'Tavis's shoulders. 'Tavis didn't swear at this indignity, because I knew he went to Chapel, and Chapel people never swore. Mr Bennett, having quieted the horse, threw back his huge Henry-the-eighth head and roared, "Annie won't be able to get near you when you get home tonight." (Annie was 'Tavis' wife).

It was time to go, for the heat and the smells made me feel uncomfortable. When 'Tavis finished the shoeing I ran out into the sunshine and away down the road to Gramfer. He laughed at the tale I had to tell, especially at what Mr Bennett had said.

"Don't you mention any of those swear words at home, mind, otherwise you won't be allowed to come with me again, but I'd like to have seen Tavis's face when the horse messed over him," laughed Gramfer.

Four o'clock came; we finished off the cold tea and the remaining heavy cake, then at five o'clock Gramfer said, "There, Jack boy, that'll do for today" and he stood back and eyed his efforts (and mine) with satisfaction. Soon the hammers were put back in their sack, and with the empty food satchel, were slung over the handlebars. Gramfer kicked a few loose stones back onto the heap, whistled for Floss who was hunting in the field. We waited until she appeared, bobbing up and down in the hay to maintain her direction.

I told Gramfer his gin traps were ready. 'Tavis, Mr Bennett and his horse were gone; four traps stood against the closed door. The crossroads was empty.

94

We went happily along the road and down the hill to Rose Cottage, and during teatime I gave a full - almost full, report of my stone cracking day with no mention of Mr Bennett's swear words, but a graphic description of Aunt Rye's breath instead.

Mr and Mrs Hawken of Porthcothan farmhouse in their trap.

Treyarnon House

Waterbeach Hotel at Treyarnon

View of Treyarnon

14

Bird Beaters

Sometimes during the long winter evenings the men folk indulged in the sport of bird beating. Today such an activity is outlawed, and anyone caught would have the wrath and full weight of every organization connected with bird life and Natural History thrown at them.

As I grew up I began to love birds, the pleasure of observing their beauty, flight and habits increased steadily over the years. Today I rejoice as I watch birds of many species feeding happily on my lawn and pecking at nut-filled containers hanging on the apple trees; and my thoughts go back to the 1920s when things were very different.

On a dark, windy night, usually one when there were intermittent showers, when my family were gathered around the kitchen fire at Rose Cottage, Gramfer would say, "Tis a good night for bird beating, how about going out for an hour?" Father, and Harry who was courting Aunt Gladys, would nod in agreement, push back their chairs and head for the back door.

"Please, may I come with you?" I would ask

Mother would look at Father for his decision, and if he nodded, I could go. But sometimes Gran had the last word.

"The boy can't go out in this weather, he won't be able to stand against the wind, and he's been a bit chesty this week."

"Don't mollycoddle him, he'll be alright, we'll see that he's dressed up properly," Gramfer would say.

"No John! He is not going out tonight. You shouldn't encourage him!"

Even Father kept quiet; for he got on well with Gran, and never attempted to argue with her.

I remember one November evening when I was allowed to join them. We went down to the washhouse where the ritual of preparation began. I put on a pair of stout old boots and mud stained gaiters; a jacket gleaned from a long-forgotten jumble sale, and over it a black oilskin from whose pockets I took a pair of woollen gloves with holes in the fingertips. Thus attired, my ensemble was completed with a scarf draped over my head knotted at the chin, and the ends tucked into the recesses of the oilskin.

The grownups put on their workaday boots and leggings, ragged coats, oilskins and mackintoshes. Father wore a decrepit trilby hat, kept in position by elastic sewn under the brim and secured under his chin. Harry had a cap which he put on back to front, and Gramfer sported a battered, mud-caked bowler hat which had seen many funerals.

A hurricane lantern hung from a ceiling crook and swayed as gusts of wind blew through the open door, making us look grotesque in its wavering light. Father and Harry took down two Powell & Hanmer acetylene gas lamps from a shelf, unscrewed their bases and tipped out spent carbide from a previous expedition. From a rusty tin they took a blue paper bag which contained lumps of evil-smelling carbide, and packed it into the empty lamp bases. A jug of water was poured into the reservoirs of the lamps, and when the regulators were unscrewed, we heard the water gurgling down onto the carbide which began to hiss, and a strong smell of gas then poured from the burners. Both jets popped when Father put a match to them, and the washhouse was flooded with dazzling pale yellow light. Father and Harry adjusted the flame of each lamp, timed back the water regulators, and closed the hinged metal and glass fronts. Gramfer prodded Floss with his boot; she arose unwillingly from her bed of old sacks and stood with ears cocked in the doorway. Against one wall amid a collection of brooms and brushes stood three bird beating sticks, each about three feet long, and similar in appearance to American baseball clubs.

"Ready, then?" said Father "Get your sticks." He unhooked the hurricane lantern and handed it to me to light my way. The washhouse door slammed shut as I followed them up the path, through the vegetable garden and past the orchard where the trees screamed in the wind, their branches clanking like hollow bones. My eyes watered as we clambered over the wooden stile into Trehemborne Meadow.

A half moon shone spasmodically through the rushing rain clouds, and a few stars flickered and vanished as we stumbled through the sodden grass. My lantern bobbed as the wind tore at it; the flame guttered and wallowed but kept burning. I looked behind me and could see the pale shape if our lighted kitchen window, and for a moment I wondered why I had been so foolish to come out on a night like this.

The gas lamps cast their glare on the cowering bushes as we re-traversed the windward side of the hedge. Sometimes Father would shout, "Mind the brambles!" and we detoured sharply away from the wicked prickles of arching stems growing out past the hedge into the meadow. Then the hedge turned at right angles, and for a moment we were sheltered from the blast. We clambered through a slippery-sided gap in the hedge and over a stream whose muddy verge sucked at my boots which started to take in water through the lace holes.

We headed up the valley; Father and Harry turned on the water in their lamps and the fermenting carbide produced much more light as the beams shone into the flaying branches of bushes, bare except for the silvery green leaves of the ivy, whose berries bobbed aimlessly in the blast.

"Look! There's a bird!" said Harry, directing his lamp beam high into an ivy bush. A blackbird, hypnotized by the sudden glare, perched with staring unblinking eyes; its yellow beak opening and closing noiselessly. Father lifted his stick, took aim, and brought it crashing down on the bird, which, with a futile flapping of wings, teetered down into the stream. Gramfer picked it up as the lamps focused down on it. The bird's eyes were closed, flecks of blood stained the once yellow beak. Floss jumped up and down excitedly and sniffed the victim as Gramfer transferred it to his sack.

We stopped frequently as the lamps pinpointed bird after bird huddled against the storm. Few birds escaped the sticks, and by the time we had searched three hedges, a collection of thrushes, blackbirds, starlings and two wood pigeons filled out Gramfer's sack. A thrush which had not received a lethal blow tried to flutter away, but was caught by Floss who shook it until its feathers flew skywards in a tiny cloud. Gramfer grabbed it, and its little claws scratched frantically against his mackintosh as he twisted its neck.

The rain eased off and pale swathes of moonlight swept across the fields; more stars appeared, but the wind seemed to grow stronger. We reached a clump of elms whose branches scraped and ground together in agony, and saw nestled close against one of the trunks the creamy-brown form of a barn owl, which sat with a haughty, unblinking stare in the beams of the lamps.

"Mustn't hit that bird, 'tis the farmer's best friend," said Harry, "but we'll make him fly," and he rattled the trunk with his stick. The owl took flight in a low swoop with its talons down, and in passing over us, caught a claw in Father's hat as he gazed upwards. The elastic tightened under his chin and nearly choked him, and there was blood on one of his eyebrows. We laughed at Father, who wasn't too pleased, and he said, "That darned bird may be the farmer's friend, but he isn't one of mine," and, wiping his eye, he growled, "your turn'll come! Just you wait and see!"

We left the elms to climb the high hedge into the adjacent field. Gramfer went first, pushing his way through a wilderness of furze and brambles. Father hoisted Gramfer up and he stood swaying in the teeth of the gale amidst the thorn bushes on the top. Gramfer leaned down and pulled Father upwards, whilst Harry pushed him up with his shoulder. I stood fearfully awaiting my turn as Harry was pulled up, and the three gas lamps described erratic beams in the sky as the men strove to stand upright. Father, now held by Gramfer and Harry, crouched forward to pluck me up. I never knew what happened next as I was in mid air, and rising. Father straightened up and, with furze scratching my legs, I reached the top, my hurricane lamp dangling close to my chest and feeling very hot.

At that moment a tremendous gust of wind blew out Gramfer's lamp as he was manoeuvring to face the drop into the field. He lurched forward and, as Father's and Harry's lamps were pointing in my direction, Gramfer fell into the blackness below.

A scream and a shout pierced the gale, followed by a terrible snorting;

then a sound like thunder as something white and shapeless passed below us. I thought I had seen a ghost. Gramfer was shouting words I had never heard before when we shone our lights down upon him. He was lying on his back in a furrow, with his bowler hat jammed down over his ears; his sack lay open, and dead birds were strewn around him. Somewhere in the distance there came neighing, snorting, and the thump of hooves. In the lamplight I saw my ghost, an old grey and white mare which had been sleeping beside the hedge.

We climbed down, and Father hoisted Gramfer to his feet.

"For Christ's sake, get this bleddy hat off! It's squeezing my ears, and I can't see a thing!" yelled Gramfer.

"Here, Harry - hold my lamp," said Father and, putting one hand each side of the bowler, he jerked it upwards taking Gramfer with it shouting, "You've cut my ears!"

Father handed Gramfer his hat, and I picked up the birds and returned them to the sack. Gramfer, still shaken, said, "I thought I'd landed on the Devil himself, and could feel his hot breath."

"If you'd landed astride the old mare you'd still be over there riding her," said Harry, lighting Gramfer's lamp, and we could still hear her snorting somewhere in the darkness.

"I think we'd better start making tracks for home," said Father, and we were, once more in the teeth of the wind. Traversing the Marsh Park field was difficult and meant walking in, or straddling, the sodden ploughed furrows, and my wet feet, forgotten during the excitement, were now feeling cold. My nose dribbled; I couldn't find my handkerchief, so I had to put a finger to each nostril and blow away the snot.

We reached the stile which led to the Meadows, and were once again on the leeward side of the hedge. Father saw a bird and, halting, said to me, "You have a go at this one Jack," and, taking my lantern, handed me his stick. This was to be my first attempt at bird beating so, holding the stick with both hands, I brought it down through the thicket onto the light-blinded bird. I heard a little squeak, and saw a flurry of feathers, I had killed a fat hedge sparrow. It was warm when I picked it up, its little dead eyes stared at me accusingly as I popped it into Gramfer's sack. I felt pleased at what I had done as Father handed me back my lantern.

As we reached the last meadow, the rain started again; borne on the north wind its drops were horizontal stinging needles of icy water. I stumbled on, my eyes screwed up, my head bent, my scarf sodden. Father and Harry were urging Gramfer to move faster. Suddenly he became annoyed, wheeled around, shone his lamp on them and shouted, "I can't go any faster - you carry the bleddy bag!" and thrusting it into Harry's arms stomped forward with surprising agility for an elderly man. His anger was only momentary, for as we climbed over the stile into our garden he was chuckling that the women would have their work cut out picking the birds, if we were to have birdie-pie tomorrow.

Back in the washhouse we stripped off our sodden outer clothing, changed our footwear, put out the lamps and went back to the warmth of the kitchen and the inquisitive demands of Gran, Mother and Aunt to see the catch which was quickly emptied onto a sheet of newspaper on the floor. The final result was: six thrushes, eight blackbirds, five starlings, two wood pigeons and one hedge sparrow. Up to the age of eleven I went out many times on these bird beating expeditions and killed my quota of birds, the largest being a wood pigeon. Father once killed a hen pheasant which was squatting in the bottom of a ditch. What feasts those birds made, and what pleasure Mother had from sorting through the speckled feathers to make ornaments for her hats.

Today I shudder at those nights of slaughter, but they formed part of a different way of life, when wild birds formed an essential part of the human food-chain by providing sustenance when money was short. I must admit though, my little hedge sparrow's minute legs and breast were the tastiest morsels I ate for many a day, and after seventy years, I can still savour those luscious moments when my teeth bit into my very own bird.

Cottages at Trevoyan Lane End

Treyarnon bathing pool where Jack spent many a happy hour. (Jack is centre picture with back to camera standing on the rocks)

On Constantine Beach

15

Family Picnic

**Jack sitting on the trough at
Treyarnon pump.**

Each year, during the long, hot summer holidays I was delighted whenever I heard Gran making arrangements for family picnics. These outings depended upon the men folk obtaining time off from work, so to achieve this Father worked overtime during the preceding week and Gramfer arranged his stone cracking, labouring and trapping schedule accordingly. Aunt's boy friend Harry appeared to have little difficulty in fitting in with any arrangement.

To me the preparations seemed vast as the results of their labours were deposited on the kitchen table. A kettle of majestic proportions which held a gallon of water and usually resided on the stove, was carefully cleaned of soot, together with a bucket into which was placed a few lumps of coal, each piece carefully wrapped in newspaper, a box of matches, a small bottle of paraffin and two empty thermos flasks joined them, and they were with the exception of the coal bucket, placed in a sack.

A large brown teapot, cups, saucers, spoons, tea plates, a bottle of milk and a packet of Lipton's tea were then packed into two straw carrier bags.

Then the forthcoming feast was laid out: an assortment of pasties; beef and potato, turnip and beef, egg and leek; sometimes there were other variations, but only once was there a jam pasty for 'afters' because it somehow got squashed en route and ruined the white tablecloth in which the pasties were wrapped. An egg and bacon pie, thin slices of bread and butter, seed buns, current buns, saffron buns and squares of heavy cake were all carefully wrapped in greaseproof paper and, with the pasties layered into a wicker market basket; finally, a jelly, later to be topped with scalded cream, shivered in a two pound screw-top jam jar.

Each member of the family helped to transport the consignment. The men took charge of sack, bucket and straw bags. The women took turns in carrying the food basket, plus a blanket to sit upon, reading matter and two hand towels.

We usually set off at eleven o'clock for Constantine Bay. If the picnic was held on a Sunday, chapel was missed and Gran would say, "The Plymouth people will fill it up, and I'm not very keen on the preacher who is planned today."

We walked up the hill and took the winding lane to Trevear where dog roses, red campions, honeysuckle, fireweed, meadowsweet and great beds of sinister looking hemlock filled hedge and ditch. From Trevear we followed a footpath to Constantine which joined a rugged cart track and the main road down to the beach. The men followed by a different route on their bicycles with their share of the transportation festooned from the handlebars.

Our favourite picnic spot was on the cliff top near Lacey's Cottage where I spent many happy hours with Mother when she did the cleaning.

Gran immediately took charge and delegated a task to each one of us. The food basket was set down and the tablecloth spread out. I was sent down to the beach to find four large stones to anchor the cloth against a sudden breeze. Father gathered dead tamarisk twigs from the nearby hedge, broke them into small pieces and placed them with the screwed-up newspapers under the lumps of coal which he then doused with the bottle of paraffin. It was essential that the kettle should sit squarely on the pile and not topple over when the wood burned away Having found the point of balance, he handed the kettle to Gramfer who hastened across the Common where, some two hundred yards away stood an old pump in splendid isolation. When the filled kettle was securely balanced

Tremain Andrews and family of Trevethan Farm, Porthcothan having a family picnic.

Father threw down a lighted match; with a whoosh and a burst of yellow flame the paraffin ignited, momentarily enveloping the kettle and soon sticks and coal were well alight.

Gran emptied the contents of the food basket. What a mouth-watering sight it was: the pasties, each about nine inches long were laid one on each plate around the four sides of the table cloth; the pie, cut into segments was placed in the centre, and around it; the jelly on dessert plates shimmered under its topping of golden scalded cream.

When Gran was satisfied with the layout, we sat down, Gramfer and Harry sprawled sideways, their elbows resting on the turf, their heads supported by their hands. They discarded their heavy jackets and displayed wide braces, striped collarless twill shirts with the front studs and buttons unfastened to allow them more freedom; the hobnails in the soles of their boots glinted like little silver stars. Gran, Mother and Aunt knelt on the partly unfolded blanket, taking care that their skirts were well tucked in under their feet, and Father and I sat cross-legged.

The kettle sang; the lid popped up and down; larks trilled over head, and the receding tide mumbled against the rocks. Mother poured milk into the cups and Aunt held out the teapot a few inches from the spout of the kettle as Father leaned over and tilted it forward until the teapot was full. Once during an earlier picnic Mother forgot to remove the lid from the teapot and the tablecloth and food was spattered with boiling water. On another occasion a sudden breeze blew smoke across us and we were forced to pull the cloth and its contents away from the fire. But today conditions were perfect and Gran's pasties were delicious.

Those who eat pasties on plates with knives and forks defeat the purpose of this delicacy which originally was to provide a self contained meal which could withstand battering and bumping underground before being eaten by a miner. There is only one way to eat a Cornish pasty, that is to hold it in one hand and nibble away from the top until the whole of the crust and juicy contents are consumed. We ate our pasties in this manner washing them down with hot smoke flavoured tea, we then demolished the egg and bacon pie, how I loved the taste of the tiny flecks of chopped parsley which permeated the egg, and the jelly, now melting under the strong sunshine and heat from the fire was quickly eaten.

Gramfer made a further trip to refill the kettle and more tea was made and poured into the thermos flasks for consumption on the beach.

Replete to bursting point I stretched out and idly viewed the scene as my family cleared away the remnants of the picnic. Gold and ochre sand rippled from the base of the cliffs as the tide receded. A few children paddled in the rock pools and two men wearing ill-fitting bathing costumes which sagged down below their knees shouted and splashed each other on the tide line. Gran eyed the men with distaste. "The old visitors are here again, there won't be any more peace for weeks to come," she said grimly. As the afternoon ticked away, more people entered the sea, and at one stage I counted fifteen.

It was time to go down to the beach and we made our way down the crooked path and soon found a suitable nook in the shade of the rocks. Mother said, "Let's all go paddling," and everyone took off their shoes and stockings. The men rolled up the bottoms of their trousers and long Johns until they were bunched around their knees; then off came their jackets which they folded and placed with the baskets. Mother, Aunt and Gran now pulled up their long skirts, tucking the hems into the elasticated waists, and to my amusement each exposed an expanse of white bloomers and fading red rings on their thighs where a few minutes earlier their garter elastic had reposed.

Wearing her wide-brim black straw hat Gran headed our procession to the tide line. Gramfer pushed the peak of his cap away from his forehead, and rolled his shirt sleeves up above his elbows; his brown arms exposed daily to the elements contrasted sharply with his white, hairless legs.

"Hey, John! It's about time you washed your feet. There's enough dirt between your toes to grow cabbages!" said Father jokingly.

"That's why I'm going into the sea now. And what about your own? I bet you haven't washed yours since we came here last month!" Gramfer replied.

We all stood at the rippling tide line waiting for a wave to wet our feet, and when it came, the 'Oohs' and 'Ahhs', and loud intakes of breath indicated the rareness of this exercise. Today I wore shorts and could wade further into the sea where I jumped up and down as each wave passed, heedless that my clothes were getting wet during those joyful moments. How interesting it was to view my family as I paddled behind them. Harry stood between Mother and Aunt his girl friend, holding hands and, as the waves flowed past, they all bobbed up and down laughing happily. Father attended Gran who was fully occupied in pulling her knickers higher with one hand and trying to secure her hat which was slipping off with the other. Gramfer had brought pipe and tobacco in his waistcoat pocket and stood with his back to the ocean as he proceeded to light up. I watched

Harry Brewer, Jack's Aunt Gladys's boyfriend, later to be her husband and live at Belmont St Merryn.

several spent matches float away, until at last he was successful. The water was now no longer cold, I flipped a few handfuls at Mother and Aunt who were highly indignant.

"Give him a clout on the head. Harry," shouted Mother.

I flipped a few drops into Aunt's face.

"You little devil! Harry, give him a hard one!" cried Aunt, wiping her eyes. Harry made a gesture, but no contact with my head, he winked at me for unbeknown to them, he was enjoying my horseplay.

There is such a phenomenon as a large seventh wave. Such waves do not come in sequence, but may be the twenty-first, or say, the thirty-fifth, but always as a factor of seven. Today the waves were all about the same size - little slow-moving ridges which broke quietly into gentle cascades of froth as they petered out and died on the sand. Suddenly, several yards away I saw a swiftly rising swell. I turned and ran towards the shore shouting: "Look out! Look out! The wave! Run! Quickly!" They all saw it, turned and followed me but were too late.

Gran's hat fell off, she pulled her bloomers higher but they were now fully immersed in water. Mother and Aunt suffered the same fate but, being shorter were soaked almost breast high. Gramfer stuffed his pipe into his waistcoat pocket and attempted to roll his trousers higher but the water flowed past his middle and a moment later he was shouting swear words I had never heard before as the hot bowl of his pipe cascaded glowing tobacco onto his stomach.

"John! Your language! Shut up!" shouted Gran.

"Bleddy pipe's burned my guts," he answered. "You'd shout loud 'nough if 'twas you!"

Father and Harry were both soaked but took little notice as they waded to rescue Gran's hat which was sailing away with the now receding wave. Father grabbed it and as he held it up it leaked like a colander. That was the end of our paddling and we all went back to our pitch.

The women took off their bloomers, laid them on the rocks and decorously knelt down and spread their skirts and petticoats around them like bell tents to dry in the sun. Soon Mother and Aunt were happily reading the *'Family Journal'* and *'Peg's Paper'* while Gran dozed with her mouth open.

The tide was now well out, I joined the men on the far side of the rocks where

Jack's Aunt Gladys Carne, later to become Gladys Brewer

they had stripped off their trousers and hung out their long Johns to dry. They had replaced their soaked trousers and did not appear to mind their wetness.

"We're going musseling now. You can come if you wish," said Father, and we went back to our pitch where he collected the bucket which had held the coal, and Gramfer foraged for the sack in which the kettle was carried.

We clambered over the wide expanse of rocks which embraced the southern arm of the bay. Here at low water hung thousands of mussels, their blue-black shells glistening in the sun. For more than half an hour we plucked them from the rocks until sack and bucket were full. Father said, "I'll take the sack," and without effort heaved it over a shoulder. Harry took the bucket, and Gramfer having cleaned out his pipe re-lit it with better luck this time.

"I've got a mark as big as a half crown on my belly, but the salt water has stopped the burning," he said.

"Let's have a look," said Harry. Gramfer pulled up his shirt, and sure enough there was an angry looking red weal.

"When you get home, rub some goose fat on it," said Harry, "It's fine for burns. I've used it several times."

"Dad! May I stay here a while? I want to look in the pools," I asked.

Father hesitated for a moment, then he nodded. "Yes, but be sure you to watch for the turn of the tide, and if I call, mind you come back quick." Then he turned and with the others walked towards the shore.

There were many pools, some shallow, some deep and mysterious, and I waded among them to my heart's content. I watched darting prawns and blenny fish (known locally as molygranites); brown beaded anemones hung in clusters and I squeezed several and made them squirt water. I moved flat stones and watched small crabs scuttle away. Out on the furthest rocks a flock of oystercatchers kept up a continuous 'kleep-kleep' rising frequently, circling low over the water then settling again. I became completely engrossed in the wonders of the pools until my reverie was broken by Father's voice.

"Jaaack! Jaaack! Time to come back! Hurry up now! Tide's on the turn!"

I waved acknowledgment and reluctantly clambered back over the rocks.

The tablecloth was laid on the sand and tea was ready. Everyone seemed to be quite dry now after their ducking. We ate cake and buns and drank the thermos tea which had a peculiar flavour and wasn't as nice as our earlier smoky tea.

Three large gulls suddenly swooped down from the cliff top and hopped close to us. We recognised them from previous visits for they lived in semi-captivity at a large stone and slate house which nestled behind the dunes near the beach head. They took food from our fingers, hopping closer and closer after each offering, their beaks snapping and their alert yellow-ringed black eyes glaring stonily. Gramfer tossed small pieces of cake high into the air and, with a flurry of wings and harsh cries the birds soared and dived for these aerial titbits.

Our favourite gull was an old lesser black-back with one leg, so tame that we could stroke his head. He wore a red marking ring on his good leg and remained with the others for several years in the area. When the owners of the house departed at the end of the season, these gulls also left their open aviary and returned the following year.

Father was a very good athlete, and standing up and sending off the gulls in a flurry said: "Come on Boy, I'll race you across to the Island. Go on. You've got one minute's start!"

Away I went with the last bun I'd eaten lying heavily in my stomach. I too enjoyed running, so I knew Father would soon overtake me, but I was more than half way to the rocky outcrop before I heard his approaching footsteps. As we jogged along comfortably he taught me how to regulate my breathing as I ran and what to do if I developed a stitch in my side. I wondered how he could run so easily for today he was wearing, like the others, heavy hobnailed boots. I was wearing brown sandshoes with rubber soles. Father was pleased with my efforts and when we returned to the family I did my best to conceal my gasping and panting.

The sun was losing power now, but there was still the long delicious evening to come. Visitors departed to their lodgings for their evening meal, we too gathered up our belongings; the rocks were bare, bloomers and long Johns had long been removed. We carried our gear to the cliff top, the men loaded their bicycles and mounted. As they set off Gran's admonition rang in their ears, "Don't you stay too long in the old Pub, there's work to do when you get home!" but she was smiling for she had enjoyed her day.

We trailed across the Common to Treyarnon Bay and stopped to chat with Ben Pinch and his wife who were sitting outside their cliff top cottage enjoying the evening sunshine. Today no trace of that building remains.

Leaning tamarisk bushes blocked out the sunlight in the short lane which led from the beach past a grey stone farmhouse, and the drop in temperature made me shiver. We reached a gateway which led to several fields and a well defined footpath. Cows quietly chewing their cud ignored us as we passed by. We hoisted our picnic gear over the high stone stiles between grass fields, and into the last one at Trevear where corn, flecked with scarlet poppies, was beginning to ripen. Here I found the domed nest of a field mouse hanging between stalks, as I shook them slightly the occupant stared at me beady-eyed from the opening before scurrying down the stalks and vanishing into the weed forest below.

Near the end of the footpath at Trevear stood an old house sited on a stony outcrop above the narrow lane, and there on the garden wall I saw for the first time, Mrs Dora Bray's gramophone whose voice I had heard wafting across the meadows to Trehemborne. This magnificent instrument had an enormous pink horn attached by a connector to a wooden box from whose polished sides protruded a cranked handle for winding up the mechanism within. Surmounting the box was a green baize covered turntable and swan-neck sound box.

As we approached, Mrs Bray appeared and wound up the instrument. When this was done she thumbed through a pile of records, selected one and placed it on the turntable. Mrs Bray loved her gramophone and when the weather was fine she brought it from her parlour and played it outside on the wall for her own, and her neighbours' enjoyment. It was the only gramophone for miles around, I wondered later whether these recitals were broadcast through an element of snobbery. Then Mrs Bray saw us approaching.

"Hello Beatrice, Millie, Gladys! I haven't seen you for weeks."

My relations dropped their burdens and soon were engaged in rapid conversation with Mrs Bray. I was ignored and longing to hear that instrument speak. Suddenly Mrs Bray's grown up daughters popped up like three Jacks-in-the-box from behind the wall where they had been sitting reading.

"Come on Mother, Mrs Carne would like a tune," said Annie the middle sister, "and Millie's boy there is looking some glum." (I was at that moment bored to tears with their conversation.).

The chattering stopped and Mrs Bray dropped the sound box lightly onto the record and released the spring which controlled the turntable. With a loud hisss the record started and I nearly jumped out of my skin as the full-throated volume of a choir belted out *'God be with you 'til we meet again.'* I stood transfixed, enthralled through several verses, and was word perfect with:

> *'Til we me-ee-eet*
> *'Til we me-ee-eet*
> *'Til we meet on that beautiful shore...*

I dug Mother in the ribs and whispered, "Ask her to play *'The Laughing Policeman'.*" Before Mother could speak Mrs Bray who had heard my request, found the record and put it on. At close range the policeman's voice was terrific and the three girls began to laugh, louder, and louder still, and soon we were all laughing. And I laughed louder still when I noticed their titties bouncing up and down and Mrs Bray's bun wobbling on top of her head. It was so much better than hearing it from across the meadow.

Reluctantly we left the Brays and walked down to the lane. I looked back, the gramophone was silhouetted against the evening sky. In the lane sloes were forming on the blackthorn bushes and the scent of meadowsweet and honey-suckle was almost overpowering. We reached the main road junction and were quickly down the hill to home. The men had already arrived and put away their bicycles. The sun had sunk behind the grey mass of Trehemborne Farm. A moorhen called her mate from the mill pond; sparrows shuffled to roost in the ivy-covered front wall of Rose Cottage.

We went indoors and dropped our gear. Gramfer had fed the pig and lit the lamp in the 'front kitchen'. The mussels were cooking in a large black boiler

110

on the kitchen stove. From across the meadows came the strains of *'The Sheik of Araby'*. Gran drew the curtains, Aunt and Harry were canoodling somewhere outside, Father and Mother were ready to cycle back to Trevorrick Lane End.

It had been a wonderful day. I settled down in the window seat to read my Children's Newspaper. It was the year that Howard Carter opened the tomb of Tutankhamen, and my mind was agog with the descriptions of its wonders. I read, and read until Gran took away my paper, saying, "If you aren't careful you'll strain your eyes." Reluctantly I went upstairs to bed.

**The cottage in Trevear where Mrs Bray lived and played her
gramophone on the garden wall.**

Two photographs of Trehemborne Farmyard. The lower featuring the farmer's two daughters, the Miss Campions, milking.

16

Schooldays

At half past eight on the morning of 31st January 1921 I left Rose Cottage for my first day at the Council School. Gran and Aunt Glad stood in the front porch and watched Mother and I hurry up the hill to the school where I would be a pupil for the next six years.

The Headmaster stood on a little raised dais behind a spindly legged desk in the main classroom. He eyed me ferociously behind gold pince-nez spectacles as we entered.

"This is Jack," said Mother.

"Is that his full name?"

"Well, he's really called Herbert John, but.."

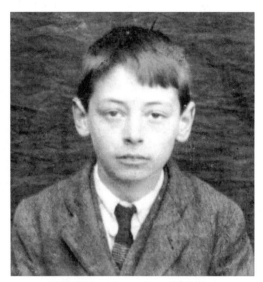

Jack as a ten year old boy

"Herbert John Ingrey," intoned the Headmaster. "Where was he born?"

"Rose Cottage, Trehemborne," said Mother. "He was due to start school last September but his whooping cough lasted a long time."

The Headmaster continued writing, and chatting with Mother, while my eyes roved around the classroom over the rows of long desks; past the black Tortoise stove with iron fireguard around it, to the coloured map of the World hanging on the wall.

"Take the boy in there," said the Headmaster, pointing to a door, "and speak to Mrs Williams."

We went into the Infant's classroom where Mother left me in the care of a plump, comfortable-looking lady.

"I shall be waiting outside the gate at twelve o'clock to take you home to dinner," said Mother and, squeezing my hand, she went out of the room.

As Mother left, the Headmaster, who had watched my handing-over from the doorway, took up a large hand bell and rang it. Immediately there was a thunderous sound of running feet; both rooms filled with children. I was caught up in a melee as they pushed their way into one half of the room which held five rows of desks with tip-up seats set in sloping tiers. Mrs Williams sat me in the second row with four other boys.

On the right hand side of the room were larger desks for the Standard One children. Mrs Williams spoke to them for a while, then they started up a monotonous non-stop sing-song which I learned later was the method used for teaching the multiplication tables. I was given a slate and a piece of chalk and told to copy letters of the alphabet from the blackboard, which I enjoyed, because I knew my ABC having been taught this by my Aunt during the weeks of my whooping cough.

A bell rang in the Big Room, and we all went out into the small Infant's playground. Two or three children asked me my name, and I told them; they told me their names and allowed me to join them in a game called Tag. The bell rang again and we dashed back to the classroom for another lesson. We were shown a large coloured picture of a baby lying in a cradle near a river, with a beautiful lady bending over it; Mrs Williams related the story of the finding of Moses in the bulrushes.

Mother was waiting at the lobby door at twelve o'clock and was anxious to know how I had fared. We hurried home for my mid-day meal which I gobbled down, it was soon time to hurry back for the afternoon session.

We made things from plasticine while Mrs Williams talked to the older children, I made a cat and a mouse, plasticine was no novelty to me for I had made many animals with my own clay.

At half past four Mother again awaited me. She did the three treks up and down the road during those long winter months until I became accustomed to the routine and joined other children who were going my way.

Mrs Williams was middle aged, with a round face, rosy cheeks, and hair parted in the centre which ended in a bun at the nape of her neck. She always wore thin woollen jumpers, cut low at the neck which revealed an abundance of large, rolling breasts when she moved. Her skirts were drab, and her black stockings did not match her brown shoes with flapping leather tongues. Sometimes mischievous children broke up pieces of chalk and placed them on her chair. When she stood up, the back of her skirt was white, but I did not find this trick at all amusing.

Mrs Williams taught me many more bible stories from the coloured illustrations and I processed through the Garden of Eden to the death of Abel; the building of the Ark and Noah's zoological collection; the Flood and its aftermath. I was taught how to count, add and subtract on an abacus frame with rows of wire partly filled with coloured, moveable beads. I was shown how to hold chalks and draw simple coloured pictures on my slate of flowers and leaves gathered by the older children on their way to school. This was my introduction to Nature Study and my love of the countryside which grew stronger as I grew older.

School began at nine o'clock, we all stood to attention behind our desks with hands clasped, as we joined Mrs Williams in The Lord's Prayer which I knew perfectly through my Sunday excursions to Chapel. Some children were not so lucid as they mouthed in parrot fashion: *'Our favver chart in 'eaven, allo be thy name...Kingdum cum...done on Earf-f'give us trespuss...power and glory...ebber and ebber...Hamen!'* At the end of the morning session we sang Grace before breaking off for dinner:

> *'Be present at our table. Lord,*
> *Be here and everywhere adored.*
> *These creatures bless, and grant that we,*
> *May feast in Paradise with Thee.'*

Children who lived in outlying farms and hamlets brought their dinners with them; pasties of which there were many varieties ranging from 'beef and teddy' (beef and potato), 'teddy and turmit' (potato and turnip), leeky (leek), 'cheese and teddy' (cheese and potato); beef and onion, jam, rabbit and parsley, and fowl. Others brought sandwiches made of beef, ham, eggs or jam. Children from poor families had to be content with slices of bread and dripping, or bread sprinkled with sugar, damped down with cold tea. There was also 'teddy caake' (potato cake), and ''eavy caake' (heavy cake), both about half an inch thick and cut into irregular rectangular shapes. These meals were washed down with luke-warm tea brought in bottles wrapped in newspapers to retain heat; in Winter the tea was poured into enamel mugs and warmed on top of the Tortoise stove. An enormous lady with a stethoscope dangling from her neck, and carrying a black Gladstone bag, billowed through the classroom door like a ship under full sail, once every year. She was the School Doctor, she examined every child, starting with the infants and ending with the teenagers. Her examinations lasted a whole day.

A clotheshorse was brought from the Headmaster's house, and set up near the stationery cupboard, its frame opened at right angles and draped with a blanket. Mrs Williams' chair was placed behind it, the privacy of the infants was thus assured. A bowl of water and a towel were placed on a side table, when all was ready, the Doctor vanished behind the temporary screen.

The Standard One children were sent out to play and the individual examination of the infants began. The Doctor's voice was low and kindly as she extracted information from each of us. Some children remained behind the screen longer than others, and occasionally I heard the Doctor tut-tutting and sighing.

Then my name was called, I stood before the lady who was sitting squarely on the chair, her enveloping thighs overflowing the seat.

"Your name. Boy?"

"Herbert John Ingrey, Ma'am." (We had been briefed to be polite.)

"Clothes off. Boy."

I took off my jersey and vest, slipped down my braces and stood between her vast, shrouded legs. She tapped my chest with a plump finger, examined my eyes and teeth, looked into both ears, ran a hand down my spine and examined my hair through a magnifying glass.

"Your Mother keeps you nice and clean. Boy. How often do you wash?"

"Three times a day, Ma'am."

"Good. And when do you bath?"

"Friday night, Ma'am, before my Aunt has hers."

"Remember, cleanliness is next to Godliness. You may dress."

I put on my vest and shirt, and was about to tuck them in, when the Doctor said, "Not yet, Boy. Trousers down."

I undid my fly buttons and pulled my trousers down.

"And your underpants. Boy."

She prodded my ribs, lifted my penis with a pencil, held it for a moment, pulled back my foreskin and said: "Cough! Once more, cough!"

My penis jumped off the pencil.

"Have you ever had whooping cough. Boy?"

"Yes, Ma'am, last year."

The doctor leaned over the side table, made some notes, and released me from her imprisoning legs.

"Pull up your trousers."

I thought my examination was over, but there was more to come.

"Now, shoes and stockings off. Boy, and feet up here." She indicated her lap and, wobbling, I put up one foot at a time. She smiled and seemed to be quite interested in something.

"Did you know you have webbed toes?"

"No Ma'am." I thought it was normal that the second and third toes of everyone's feet were joined half way up, and Mother hadn't said anything about it.

"You should be able to swim like a duck," she laughed. "That's all Boy. Put on your shoes and stockings." As I made my exit, she called loudly, "Next child please!"

I stood before this pleasant lady Doctor once each year until I was twelve and, like other adolescent boys, became more embarrassed each year when I had to strip. We were now examined in the Girls Rear Lobby, and scrupulously shielded from female intrusion. Much banter was exchanged during these later examinations, "I bet she thought you had a big one!" or, "Weren't you ashamed to show that little thing?" and once a boy came out with a red face, looking very embarrassed, but refused to tell us why. Weeks later, when he was leaving school, he told us, "She kept poking my cock and I got a bit hard, and she told me to go out and put it under a tap."

Puberty was a mystery that was never mentioned by our parents. Those best informed were the sons and daughters of farmers who lived closer to the

116

land, and from them, we, the ignorant, gained a smattering of biology and, more often than not, many distorted versions of the facts of life.

Some children were not as clean as others, reports of personal hygiene were made by the Doctor, and a note containing a sharp reprimand sent to delinquent parents.

In the Infants' Room I progressed to Standard One; slate and coloured chalks were discarded, I was given a copy-book printed with guiding lines, specimen letters of the alphabet and simple words like cat, dog and hat, to copy. As I filled the pagers, the words became longer - riv-er, walk-ing, shop-ping, mead-ow, and so forth. I copied each word laboriously with a broad nibbed pen, often wiping the nib with a small piece of cloth, for at this stage I was messy. When I arrived home my ink stained fingers were painfully cleaned with pumice stone.

Within two years I moved to the Big Room and was sorry to leave kind Mrs Williams. Here was a world of bigger boys and girls under the supervision of the Headmaster. Geography, history, arithmetic and English literature dominated my curriculum, together with elocution and singing; later there would be practical work in the school garden which was the Headmaster's pride and joy

The severe, stone-built Victorian school building followed the pattern of many others in the County, with high sliding sash windows, and still higher ones with pointed heads in the gable walls. Two lobbies were attached, one for Boys, the other for Girls. The main block comprised the Big Room which faced the Boys' playground and the smaller Infants' Room which overlooked the main road. Stone boundary walls enclosed the school building and embraced the playgrounds. Two ranges of stone earth closets set back to back within the dividing walls of the playgrounds provided our toilet accommodation. Both closets stank horribly in hot weather, the Boys' urinal was often choked and fly infested. From time to time workmen whitewashed the closet walls and tarred the back channel of the urinal.

The grit-surfaced playgrounds held water when it rained and were not surfaced until many years later. A small bell tower and spire graced the apex of the steep, slated school roof, but it was not in use when I attended school; in latter years it was dismantled, and today a chimney stands in its place.

Leading off the south side of the Boy's playground was the school garden, meticulously laid out into rectangular plots, intersected by ashes paths, by-products of the Tortoise stoves. An immaculate green painted galvanized tool shed contained a regimented range of garden tools - almost a complete set for each boy, together with wheelbarrows, edging boards and bags of manure. I did not gain access to the garden until I reached Standard Five, unfortunately, I was not a very good gardener. Each plot was shared by two boys, and on it was grown a succession of vegetables and flowers. We went through the process of Spring digging, dunging and bed preparation; every stone and foreign body was removed and the plots were scrupulously raked. A full range of vegetable seeds were planted along lines of tightened string. We watched with interest the sprouting of the young plants, recording their growth in a Gardener's Diary. Potatoes also occupied a large portion of each plot, one year there was great consternation when a Colorado beetle was discovered. Flower cultivation ranged from daffodils in Spring, to hollyhocks, asters and lupins in Summer and chrysanthemums in the Autumn.

The garden was visited during each summer holiday by a panel of experts and judged against other schools in the area. Sometimes our garden topped the list, much to the delight of the Headmaster.

Mr Nancecarrow and the young gardeners.
Back Row: **Arthur Geach, unknown, Dennis Kestle.** *Front Row:* **John Duffy, Ted Rossiter, Mr Nancarrow, Raymond Bray, Clifford Newcombe.**

Each year, an epidemic unfailingly hit the school: measles, mumps, chicken-pox, scarlet fever, whooping cough, all took their toll; there were also isolated cases of diphtheria. I contracted chicken-pox and mumps; scarlet fever passed me by, but I did not contract measles until I was almost twelve years of age and it came at an awkward time with later repercussions.

For weeks I had been studying for the Minor Scholarship Examination which, if I passed it, would ensure me a place at County School. Very few pupils had graduated from our school, but the Headmaster evidently thought that I had the necessary intelligence to pass the entrance examination. I swatted at home during late spring and early summer evenings, and read *'Westward Ho!'*, the book upon which the literature paper was to be set. I disliked arithmetic, and was not very good at it, but geography and history, upon which there was a general knowledge paper, held no qualms for me.

Two days before the examination I suddenly felt uncomfortable. Mother thought it was examination nerves, but during the afternoon of the day before the exam, my face became flushed and I felt very dizzy. Mother hurriedly contacted the Headmaster who decreed that I must go, if at all possible. That night I went to bed with aching limbs, a glass of hot lemon and a tot of Gramfer's brandy.

Next morning I could hardly bear to dress or swallow my breakfast. But I had to go, and Father drove Mother and me to the Station which was seething with a crowd of boys and girls with their parents, all of them lively and chattering like magpies. We stood alone, I felt terrible. The train arrived and we entered a carriage with four boys and their mothers. During the journey Mother chatted with the parents whilst I sat subdued and embarrassed thinking that everyone was looking at me. We walked the half mile from the Station to the County School and, with dozens of other children gathered in the Assembly Hall for a roll call. Each one of us was allocated to a teacher who led us to the allotted examination rooms. I worked through the papers as though I was in a trance, and when we broke off for lunch, I could hardly swallow my sandwiches. The examination lasted until mid-afternoon, and my skin began to itch. I felt myself going in and out of focus, the feeling got worse in the train where I felt sure that all eyes were now upon me, and Mother in an unguarded moment voiced the opinion that I might be sickening for something - and how right she was! Next morning I was covered in a rash; the District Nurse arrived and diagnosed measles.

A few days later, Father brought news that I had given several children measles, furthermore, it was spreading like wildfire to others who were in the classroom where I had taken the examination. Some three weeks later I recovered, and the incident faded from my mind. July and the summer holiday came, and with it the examination results. I had passed, despite measles and my mediocre performance. The Headmaster was delighted. I left the Council School and a new world opened up to me in September when I transferred to County School.

As I stood on the Station platform a cry went up: "That's him! That's the boy who gave our kids the measles!" A ginger-haired, blowsy, common looking woman bore down and pointed an accusing finger at Mother who had come to see me off.

"You should never have brought him! But from where you come from, I don't suppose you knew any better!"

All eyes were upon us; I piped up in a thin voice, "But measles didn't stop me from getting a scholarship."

The woman glared, and another voice butted in: "What does it matter? The kids would have caught measles from someone else. And who are you to talk? You haven't been living here five minutes and you think you own the place. You're only a foreigner, so shut your mouth!"

Someone else butted in: "Your boy didn't pass, did he? And you're jealous because you've got to pay for his schooling." Everyone seemed to be on our side and my heart warmed to Mother's rescuers.

From that morning onwards for five years, I made the long journey from my home to the Station and the County School, but back now to continue my reminiscences of those early days. Each season brought its particular game or pastime, and during Winter and Spring hoop trundling was especially attractive on frosty mornings. I acquired my first hoop shortly after I was allowed to go to school on my own. It was a wooden hoop purchased from the village shop where they stocked them in various sizes.

From Rose Cottage the going was hard; the hill was short but steep, and thereafter, although it was easier, the road was still rising almost to the school gates. Several children from the hamlets used this road, we ran non-stop races which ended in exhaustion when we parked our hoops inside the playground walls. Going home was all down hill, we whacked our hoops with various propellants (mine was a piece of bamboo cane) and sent them hurtling ahead of us. There were mishaps, many unfortunate pedestrians suffered the full impact of wood or iron hoops upon their bodies. I have seen wooden hoops broken into pieces, and iron ones flung over hedges by angry victims.

My favourite hoop was an iron one made by 'Tavis the blacksmith. Father placed the order a week before my birthday, he told me it would be ready on that day. I ran straight to the smithy after school. There was 'Tavis juggling with a red-hot glowing circle of iron on the forge with a long pair of tongs. I watched him dip it into the water pit by the bellows; an acrid cloud of white steam arose and the hoop cooled with a sizzling, sucking sound. 'Tavis turned and saw me.

"You're right on time, my boy, but I've been very busy, and your hoop had to wait. Many happy returns of the day. How old are you, then?"

"I'm eight, Mr Brenton."

"What a lovely age, I can't remember when I was eight!"

'Tavis hung up the hoop and smiled.

"Seeing it's your birthday, I'm going to make a truckler for that hoop as a present. But you'll have to wait while I heat up the iron."

A truckler is an iron rod about eighteen inches long, with one end bent into a crook for steering the hoop; the other end is shaped into a small circle through which the forefinger and thumb are placed.

'Tavis pumped the bellows, and with his tongs, heated the iron in the forge; then with one hand he placed the glowing iron on the anvil and, with the other he hammered it, making red and orange sparks fly in all directions as the truckler took shape. After dipping it in the water pit, 'Tavis took down the hoop, and handed it to me with the still warm truckler.

120

"Now Jack, have a go, and tell me what you think of it."

I trundled my present down the road towards Hillhead, listening to the swish of hoop against the truckler as I steered and weaved in and out of the uneven, potholed road. The hoop was perfect, I had complete control over it. 'Tavis was leaning over the half-door of the smithy when I returned. I told him how good the hoop was, thanked him for the truckler, and from the smile on his dust-streaked face, I could see that he was satisfied with his handiwork.,

The Marble season followed hoops, almost every boy carried a small cloth bag containing an assortment of glass alleys, glazed clays, and large alleys called 'taws'. In the playground we squatted on our haunches and flicked marbles with thumbs whose joints were often calloused and ingrained with dirt through being in frequent contact with the ground. We played several variations of the game; the most popular one was to shoot a large glass taw at marbles lying within the perimeter of a circle scratched in the dust, or inside a chalk line, to hit a marble hard enough to knock it outside, when it was claimed by the shooter.

Leapfrog, or 'jump backs' as we called it, was played continuously during Winter and Spring. The easy way was straight forward jumping over the bent bodies of players standing a few feet apart. The benders were called 'pillars'. When the last pillar had been jumped over, he began jumping over those who had already jumped and taken up new positions. Pillars started from a kneeling position with the head bent forward, and chin tucked in; then gradually moving higher and straightening up. This was an exhilarating but somewhat dangerous game, for if after taking off, and with hands upon the pillar's shoulders, one leaned a little too far forward, it was inevitable that one would crash-land and end up with cuts and bruises. If the pillar decided to bend lower just as one leaped, the leaper fell backwards and stood a good chance of bruising the base of his spine.

Another form of leapfrog consisted of two teams. One team selected a hefty boy who stood with his back against a wall; a second boy placed his head firmly into the first boy's stomach and gripped him firmly around the waist. The remainder of the team followed, bending over and tucking their heads into the buttocks of the boy in front. The opponents lined up in single file a few yards away, then at a given signal, the first contestant jumped and attempted to land as near as possible onto the boy who was furthest away. The remainder of the team followed in quick succession until all were suspended in a heaving, wriggling mass, holding on until someone below caved in, or they themselves were thrown off by stronger boys below. If you were small and were landed on by two heavily built boys, the pain was excruciating, for you could not move your head, for it was a disgrace to bend the knees.

Summer brought a short spate of Top spinning, and many tops of vintage years, handed down from father to son, appeared in the playground. Some tops were home-made for boys whose fathers were carpenters. These were sometimes carved out of hardwood with a nail at the spinning end. Tops were made to spin by winding cord around their bodies then, with a flick of the wrist it was thrown to the ground and the cord jerked; a skilful operation in which I was never very successful. Softwood tops were sometimes split apart by boys who owned tops with nails or spikes in their spinning ends, I have seen many a fight and bloody nose as a result of such destruction.

The Conker season was short, possibly because there were only a few chestnut trees in the parish, but somehow we always managed to acquire a few. We immersed our chestnuts in vinegar to harden them, then baked them in the ovens of our Cornish stoves, and rubbed them with Kiwi boot polish until they gleamed. During these operations the conkers were pierced with a nail or metal skewer and threaded onto a tough piece of cord or leather bootlace.

My conkers never seemed to last very long despite my attempts at hardening them, and it was usually the school bully whose nut was 'King over all'. The game was simple to play: Your opponent dangled his conker at arm's length; you approached, and with one hand twisted the end of your conker string firmly around a finger, and with the other hand drew your conker out horizontally until it touched your opponent's conker. This determined the distance you should stand away from him. You then brought your hand back to your shoulder and your conker swung behind it. Taking aim, you then jerked your arm forward and if your aim was good, your conker hit your opponent's with a resounding smack, hopefully splitting it apart. Each player had three consecutive strikes, continuing alternatively until one conker was smashed. Sometimes a draw was agreed upon, then a replay took place on another day. There were vicious undertones in this simple sport: If you had a grudge against an opponent you could always misfire and bring your conker down with devastating results upon his knuckles. Wearing gloves was, of course, banned, in any case no one would dare do it and be labelled a sissy.

When we played football, our goalposts were marked by chalk on the playground walls. Windows were often broken when the ball sailed out over the road and hit passing vehicles and pedestrians, the outcome was often altercations and canings. On one occasion, a ball sailed over the goalkeeper and landed in the back of a passing horse and trap. The driver, who was the local trapped rabbit collector, gave the pony a sharp thwack and sent it galloping, and the ball was never recovered. Those football games were all rough and tumble, with few rules, and the tremendous pushings, shovings and buttings by the older boys resulted in bleeding knees from flying falls, and violent bruises from steel-tipped toecaps. The ball often landed in the front garden of the house on the opposite side of the road, but the owner never complained for she kept a shop and knew there would be a drop in the sale of sweets if she did so. Sometimes the ball sailed into the school garden and landed among the winter greens; the

122

retriever's deep footmarks would invariably be noticed by the Headmaster and an inquest held; if nobody owned up, we were all given one stroke of the cane. We played cricket with sorbo rubber balls, chalked-up stumps, and created similar repercussions as when we played football. A wildly swung bat sometimes caught a young, often unwilling wicket-keeper full in the mouth with the loss of some teeth, and on one occasion I was bowled out for a duck, plus a bleeding nose.

Catapults were all year round favourites. We made them from short, 'Y' shaped branches cut from apple or hawthorn trees which we stripped of bark, dried, and trimmed into traditional catapult shape. Each arm of the 'Y' was incised deeply with cuts which formed a bedding for waxed cord which bound the square-shaped elastic to them. When the two equal lengths of elastic were in position, a piece of soft square-shaped leather was pierced and secured at each end, thus forming a sort of sling. Anything that could be fired was used for ammunition: marbles, stones, hazel nuts, oak apples, rubbers and even hard sweets. We set up empty tins on top of hedges for target practice, and rattled them with small beach pebbles. We shot at wild birds without much success, but scored heavily on the ducks in Trehemborne millpond. During school hours we used a modified form of catapult made from elastic bands twisted around thumb and forefinger. Wads of blotting paper, soaked in ink were surreptitiously placed in the pencil-groove of the desk, and when the Headmaster's back was turned, careful aim was taken at someone's head or neck, in the front row. The unexpected agony of a direct hit on the ear; the ruining of a clean white shirt, the camouflaging of many a tear was well known to me when I first moved out into the Big Room but, as I grew older, I too enjoyed scoring direct hits from the back row.

We made pea-shooters from dried hollow stalks of cow parsley and allied plants during the autumn and winter months, when ivy bushes, laden with hard, green berries provided ideal ammunition. A playtime pastime was to lie in wait for passers-by behind the playground walls, or the garden hedge, and pepper them with concerted broadsides On one occasion this activity did not pass unnoticed. Several of us were hiding, in tight formation, behind the garden hedge, and already we had scored several direct hits on unsuspecting ladies who were walking past. Unbeknown to us, one lady had gone straight to the Headmaster and vented her indignation. As a result every boy received one stroke of the cane because nobody owned up to the incident.

We always posted a look-out and on another occasion, Fatty Foster, whose father was a Coastguard, signalled that Holy Joe was coming. Joe, pink faced, bald headed, and so nicknamed because of his enthusiastic religious fervour, came peddling around the bend, his bicycle laden with builder's tools and materials. As Joe drew level, all lips were pursed for a concerted bombardment. It never matured, for there came a swishing sound, and across everyone's backside the stinging pain of several quickly administered strokes from the Headmaster's cane. He had watched our activities from the window, crept quietly down the garden path and at the crucial moment, administered in seconds, a simultaneous caning.

Once I collected twelve strokes of the cane for deliberate cheating at arithmetic. One afternoon the Headmaster left his textbook which contained all the answers in the end pages, on his desk, whilst he was instructing boys in the school garden. I copied two pages of the numbered references and answers and, for several days I entered them at the foot of my sums, assuming that it was unlikely for him to check the body of each sum. Alas, my deceit was my undoing, for one morning he found an obvious and blatant error. I had entered the answers to four consecutive sums one answer ahead of what it should have been. I was hauled out in front of the entire Big Room classes. The Headmaster was livid, his usually pale face was scarlet, his eyes bored into me like twin gimlets. He took the supple cane from his desk and flexed it almost double.

"Left hand out!" he almost screamed. I received six vicious strokes.

"Now, your right hand!" and six more followed. I could have cried with agony from the stinging pain, but I bit my lips and held my breath.

"Ask him what he has done, and don't any one of you, boy or girl, ever attempt to do the same thing, or you'll receive the same punishment!"

Of course, everyone knew by the end of the day, and I became a momentary hero when I displayed the white welts on my palms which lasted for two days. I did not tell them at home, but someone else did. I was less than popular with Father and Mother who were embarrassed to have a son who was a cheat.

Wet days in Winter meant no games in the playground. The entire complement of Big Room boys congregated in the Boy's Lobby which became a writhing, seething mass during playtime break, when another game was played.

Everyone stood in lines with their backs against the two long walls of the lobby. At each of the end doorways stood three of the biggest boys. Suddenly, a boy would be squeezed out of his position against the wall and he would be set upon and pushed towards one of the end doorway. As the victim stumbled from side to side, he was pushed back into the centre again, and when he reached the end, the big boys sent him hurtling back. This went on until the unfortunate boy howled in agony. If he was made of sterner stuff, he retaliated and hit out at his assailants with no holds barred.

I remember well the first buffeting I received; the surprise of being hurled down the middle; feeling my jersey being torn, my stockings falling down; seeing the delight in the eyes of someone you thought was a friend; smelling the sweat of bodies through warm, half-wet clothing; losing my cherished cap and trying to retrieve it as it ballooned high overhead from the kick of a mud-caked boot, and trampled on when it fell to the floor. When I bent down to retrieve it, there was the feeling of numbness caused by a well-aimed kick on my backside.

There were times when some of the youngest boys were hung upside down by their bootlaces to the hat and coat hooks, then when the bell went for resumption of lessons, the older boys forced the younger ones to do the untying, whilst they went innocently back to the Big Room. These bullies did not always escape for sometimes the Headmaster sensed what was going on and stood ready with his cane as they passed through the classroom door. Yes, those were rough and tumble days, and I experienced all those indignities - but I had my own back as I grew older.

School Holidays were long: two whole weeks at Easter; six weeks during August and September; and two weeks at Christmas.

We 'scrambled for nuts' in the playgrounds on breaking-up day for the Christmas holiday, or if the weather was wet, in the Big Room, where all the desks were stacked back against the walls. The Headmaster appeared with a large sack filled with assorted nuts, which he threw into the air by the handful, and everyone - boys and girls scrambled for them. There was always enough for all, the infants held their scramble separately. Empire Day followed the same pattern each year. The Vicar arrived in his clerical garb and delivered a lecture on the glories of the great British Empire; the Raj, Australia, New Zealand, Canada, South Africa, and the far flung islands. On these occasions, the large map hanging on the wall over the Tortoise stove came into use as he pointed out each Dependency which was coloured red. After a closing prayer we all stood and fairly raised the roof with *'Rule Britannia'*, which had been well rehearsed during earlier singing lessons.

Today the whole face of schooling has changed; education has taken an entirely new form; but in my early schooldays each child learned the basics of the few subjects taught and could certainly produce better handwriting than the mediocre scripts of children today. We had no radios, television programmes, video machines, DVDs or computers; but from the simple, dog-eared text books, lined exercise books, steel pens, practical gardening, needlework, and dedicated teachers who were not afraid to use the cane, there was ingrained in me and my contemporaries a stability and outlook which, though it may seem old-fashioned and outdated to today's generation, we would not wish to change for all today's technology.

Mill pond Trehemborne, Porthcothan or Mawgan.

**'Holy' Joe Brenton and family at Primrose
Cottage, Trethias.**

126

17

By Pony Trap to Newquay

"I'm going to Newquay with your Uncle Jim tomorrow. Would you like to come with us?" asked Gran.

It was a Friday evening in late July and school had closed that day for the summer holiday. Tomorrow night I would be sleeping at Trevorrick Lane End for five weeks before returning to Rose Cottage where I would stay from Monday to Friday during the coming winter term.

"Oh, yes please Gran," I said.

"Off you go to bed then, because you have to be up early and we mustn't keep your Uncle waiting."

Reluctantly I retired for it was still daylight, and my eight year old mind was churning with anticipation of the journey as I sipped my Ovaltine nightcap.

Early next morning I was smartly dressed in my new sailor suit and black patent shoes with sparkling brass buckles. Around my neck hung a lanyard from which dangled a small whistle that Gramfer had brought me last year from Summercourt Fair.

Gran looked elegant in a white blouse with puffed sleeves trimmed with lace, and a white and grey striped skirt. On her head was a white straw hat with turned-up brim, garnished with a small bunch of artificial cherries. She looked so much younger and not nearly so severe as she did in her Sunday chapel-going clothes.

We waited outside the front porch for Uncle Jim's arrival. At Gran's feet rested a square wicker basket covered with a white cloth, beneath which lay a large piece of salted pork wrapped in butter muslin. She had also packed three cups, some saffron buns and a bottle of hot tea.

As the clock was striking nine Uncle Jim with his pony and trap came clip-clopping down the hill, and drawing up in front of us he dismounted. Although it was high Summer, Uncle was dressed in his thick Sunday-best grey suit, heavy black boots, grey trilby hat and an unbuttoned brown overcoat which disclosed a heavy silver watch chain festooned across his waistcoat. He was a few years older than Gran, but the resemblance between brother and sister was unmistakable; his high cheekbones were ruddy; he wore a neatly clipped moustache and his grey eyes twinkled.

"You're ready then Beat, I see young Jack's coming with us. He'll be able to help the pony up hills, wont you, my boy?" I began to have doubts. Wasn't I going to ride all the way?

Gran handed Uncle the basket which he stowed under the seat where I glimpsed a brace of rabbits, and a bag which twitched violently and from whose interior came an angry cackling sound. A contented looking shaggy brown pony stood between the shafts. The large iron-shod wheels had painted spokes and polished hubs. The dual seat was high, with a narrow padded backrest.

"Now, Beat, up you get," and as Gran put a foot on the step Uncle put both hands under her bottom and hoisted her up.

"Oh! You're as rough as you were when we went to school. I can manage. Let me go!" Gran seemed annoyed and tossing her head made the cherries on her hat bob up and down, but she was secretly enjoying her brother's attention as she wriggled and sat bolt upright on the seat. Aunt Glad who was seeing us off said, "Mother, you look like a Duchess sitting up there."

Uncle Jim then unfastened the backboard and let it down to its slightly off-horizontal position.

"Come on Jack boy. Up you get!" he called, and he lifted me off ground. The next moment I was sitting on the floor of the trap with my legs dangling over the backboard.

"There's a cushion for you, and put your back against that bag, the old cockerel inside won't hurt you."

I squirmed around until I felt comfortable. Uncle Jim looked under the trap where the pony's nosebag was fastened to make sure it was secure, then he hoisted himself up beside Gran and took the slender whip from its holder.

"Right then. We're ready!"

Uncle Jim jerked the reins and off we trotted to visit relatives whom I had yet to meet.

I counted the clip-clop of the pony's hooves as we headed for Lane End where Gran asked Uncle Jim to stop.

"Milly doesn't know the boy's going to Newquay."

Gran shouted, "Milly, are you in?" Mother appeared in the doorway and was surprised to see me dressed in my sailor suit. Gran explained why, and Mother said: "He'll be out of mischief if he's with you, and I've got several bundles of washing to get through today, so he wont hinder me. And Jack, be on your best behaviour and mind your manners."

"Yes Mum," I nodded. "I promise, and I'll tell you all about it tonight." We drove on past Porthcothan Farm where I had lived before we moved to Lane End and down the hill over the stone bridge where the stream meandered like a silver snake across the beach to the tide which was half way out and where several children were already paddling. As we climbed Trevethan Hill the pony's harness tightened against its flanks as it strained forward. We slowed down. Uncle Jim dismounted and walked beside us with one hand on the wooden shaft and began pushing to assist the pony. Dogs barked in the yard beside the farmhouse whose tall arch-shaped windows peered out from weathered stone walls.

Trevethan Farmhouse, Porthcothan in the snow.

On the opposite side of the road was a shallow well and Uncle taking a small bowl from under his seat, dipped it in the water and gave the pony a drink.

We passed Efflins farm and approached the straight, high road which led through six fields, passing Bedruthan Steps on our right. Behind us the hump of Trevose Head protruded into the Atlantic with the tower of the lighthouse standing like a stick of white chalk behind the brown curve of Constantine Bay. Sea pinks hung in faded clumps on the windswept hedges, mingling with blue scabious and starry white stonecrop.

Each field had a gate at either end manned by two or more children like me on holiday, who laboriously pushed their gate open when a vehicle approached. The road was a public highway, but it was inconvenient to dismount from ones conveyance, prop the gate open, drive through and close it again, because of the enclosed flocks of grazing cattle. Six fields meant seven gates, and the children were, no doubt the offspring of local farmers or their friends. I envied their enterprise as Gran threw down a penny to the grimy, upturned faces. They scrambled wildly for each coin. At the end of the day many vehicles would have passed through and their takings would be considerable. They closed each gate immediately we had passed through and their eyes were alert for the next arrival. During our passage I noticed that there was much pushing, punching and hair pulling among the participants. One big boy tried to dislodge me by pulling at my dangling feet as we passed through the last gate at Trenance. I shook myself free and had the satisfaction of kicking him in the face and sending him sprawling in the road. I think it was because Gran had run out of pennies that he retaliated on me shouting, "Mingy! Mingy!"

We cantered down the hill into Mawgan Porth where marram grass covered the sand dunes reaching up from the beach to the higher ground. Beyond the bridge the road rose steeply to a right angle bend with a green cliff hanging menacingly behind it. Tucked away on a ledge stood a Coastguard's cottage, and beyond the bend a steep and seemingly endless hill.

"We'll let the pony have a breather," said Uncle, and drew up near the entrance to the cottage where the verge was flat and grassy. He dismounted, helped Gran down; and lifted me from my not too comfortable seat. Gran produced the cups, poured out the tea and we sat and ate the saffron buns. An open-top char-a-banc filled with visitors came slowly down the hill, and the occupants shrieked with excitement as the driver misjudging the sharpness of the bend and nearly drove into us. With a grating of gears he went back and forth several times until the cumbersome vehicle negotiated the bend and climbed slowly up the other hill back firing as it went, pouring a cloud of smoke from its exhaust pipe.

We were ready to continue our journey and I stood waiting to take my seat.

"Not yet. Jack boy, your Gran is the only one who's going to ride up the hill. You push from behind, and we'll soon be at the top."

"Now Beat, up you get," Uncle Jim hoisted Gran and her bag into the trap, this time she made no comment.

Uncle walked beside the pony, patting its matted brown coat from which arose a small cloud of flies. I placed both arms under the tailboard and with head down, pushed hard with my legs.

The hill seemed endless. We passed two cottages on the left; I began to sweat; I put my head between my arms, closed my eyes and plodded. The pony jogged slowly and the trap swayed slightly from side to side. An age passed, I opened my eyes and looked about me. Uncle's trilby hat was pushed back from his forehead and his overcoat flapped with each step he took. Gran sat erect and solitary, her head nodding back and forth like a pendulum, her straw hat glinting sunbeams. Uncle chewed tobacco and occasionally spat into the hedge. A crow perched on the single sagging telephone wire whose poles I had counted and counted and now lost track of.

The pony suddenly broke the monotony by simultaneously relieving itself in both directions. I clung to the tailboard and lifted my feet off ground in an attempt to avoid the yellow cascade which hissed between the shafts and flowed rapidly down hill; wind breaking followed and a series of plops. Gran now less dignified, pinched her nostrils together and said, "Pooh!"

I began to laugh but not for long, for I was treading in dung, soft like under baked buns and my shoes were caked and sticky with the stuff. I shouted out in alarm; Uncle Jim came back, patted me on the shoulders and said: "Tis all right Jack boy, a bit of hoss shit never hurt anybody. You just walk along the ditch and it'll soon wear off." This I did, and Uncle Jim was right.

At last we skirted the hilltop and reached Trevarrian village where Uncle said, "Take the reins Beat – I'm going into 'The Travellers Rest' for a pint of ale."

Gran was not very pleased to hear this. "You've only just drunk your tea."

"I can't help it, 'tis the weather. I'm boiling over."

"Well, take your coat off."

"I can't, I might catch cold," and he went into the public house, only to reappear a few seconds later with a disappointed look on his face.

"It don't open for half an hour." "Good, let's get on our way then," said Gran triumphantly as Uncle remounted.

We trotted through Trevarrian's sister village Tregurrian whose cottages seemed to lean forward to prevent us intruding on their privacy, and down through the fern filled valley to Watergate Bay. Uncle said we could have taken a shorter route, but it would have been difficult for the pony to go down the steep hill without slipping.

Watergate Bay, now famous for surfing, seemed to me on that faraway morning to be merely a long stretch of uninteresting sand with a hotel tucked under the cliff face. Bathing towels hung from windows, but there were only two bathers in the sea.

Again I was required to dismount and help push the trap around another steep hairpin bend and up a much shorter hill. Then the going was easy as we jogged the narrow road between low stone hedges. Suddenly, Gran said, "There's Newquay!" I peered excitedly around the side of the trap for my first view of the town. It looked so large and sprawling, and a great hotel crowned a headland, with houses clinging below it and a curving sandy beach was thickly dotted with holiday makers.

Gran had been calling out the names of places as we passed through, now it was Porth, leading up to the junction with the main road into Newquay where the traffic immediately increased. Several cyclists and a procession of cars sped past, one of which honked its horn loudly making the pony jib and Gran almost fell forward off her seat. I had never before seen so much traffic. Then a brightly painted contraption like a jingle with a roof on top supported by four twisted brass posts drawn by a pony trotted past. In it sat a man with a walrus moustache, wearing a white coat, ringing a large hand bell. It was the first time I had seen an Italian ice cream cart and its owner, Senor Staffeiri.

Uncle stopped at a large house named Whitegate.

"We're going to call on Willie," said Gran.

Willie was the eldest of Gran's brothers and he held an important position in the Newquay Electric Works.

"We've made good time, it's just half past eleven," said Uncle consulting his watch and tethering the pony to a gatepost. A bevy of relatives, none of whom I could remember having seen before, immediately surrounded us and I became the focal point of many hot kisses and exclamations of, "How he's grown!" and, "He's just like his Mother!"

Soon we were all drinking tea and I was introduced to my new Uncle Willie who promised to take me on a tour of the electric works when I visited Newquay again. From the front garden he pointed out the large ugly building with its tall chimney stack looming over the streets. On a later visit he kept his promise and I stood in awe before the generators with their rows of clock face dials on which needles flickered.

"When I pull down this switch I can put out all the lights in Newquay," he told me, and was not very enthusiastic when I asked him if I could have a try.

We left our relatives and turned into the road leading down to Trenance valley. As we were driving under the high arches of the viaduct a train passed over whistling and billowing clouds of steam as I stared upwards with mouth open in amazement.

"Look, Trenance Lake!" called Gran, and my attention was drawn to a glittering sheet of water edged with reeds and alive with ducks and gulls. We passed beside adjacent gardens and up a short, steep hill where on the left was our destination, a pretty slate-roofed cottage with whitewashed stone walls. An open porch covered the front door and several small windows peeped out through a profusion of pink roses and honeysuckle. In front of the cottage was a flower filled garden, where Tom and Emily Crews stood, peering down and waving to us. Soon the pony was unharnessed, tethered in an open-ended shed by the roadside and fed from its nosebag.

"I don't think you've met your Aunt Emily and Uncle Tom Crews before," said Gran, introducing me, and I wondered how many more aunts and uncles I was going to meet. Aunt Emily viewed me through rimless pince-nez spectacles, kissed my forehead and made me very welcome. She was rosy cheeked and unwrinkled, with grey hair piled up in a bun on top of her head; she wore a black and white striped blouse and a purple skirt over which was hung a white apron tied at the back with a large bow; she was the essence of neatness, birdlike in her movements, outwardly prim, but entirely warm and friendly despite the severe expression which her pince-nez gave her.

Uncle Tom was short and plump with blue eyes; leg-of- mutton sideburns partly hid his red cheeks, and a bowler hat was pushed far back on his head. He wore drainpipe trousers and his shirt sleeves were rolled back to his elbows for he had been gardening.

We were ushered into the parlour where a large pitcher of mixed gladioli filled the fireplace; above it on a high mantelshelf sat two ferocious china dogs, a chiming clock and several brass candlesticks. Black leather chairs and a sofa were draped with antimacassars. A circular table was covered with a pink velvet cloth from which dangled scores of tiny velvet balls and in the centre stood a vase of white carnations. The ceiling was painted white between brown varnished beams, the crooked walls were papered with a pattern of gold stripes and pink rosebuds.

In the front kitchen (we would call it dining room today) Aunt Emily had set out her best cutlery on a white tablecloth, and soon we were tucking into roast chicken, with broccoli, new potatoes, broad beans and thick gravy. Gran helped me cut up my leg of chicken, but Uncle Tom said, "Go on, let the boy use his fingers, they were made before forks," and he demonstrated. We ended our repast with junket and cream liberally sprinkled with nutmeg.

After the meal Gran helped Aunt Emily wash the dishes in the tiny scullery. When this was done we walked down to the public gardens and along the lakeside, returning to inspect the greenhouses and potting sheds where Uncle Tom was employed by the Town Council.

Another train went hissing and clattering over the viaduct and several people waved from the carriage windows as it slowed down for entry into Newquay Station.

The afternoon sun beat down on us as we were conducted through Uncle Tom's own cottage garden. Straight rows of peas and kidney beans staked with bamboo canes were full of buzzing bees, rows of banked potatoes, feathery leaved carrots, parsnips, turnips, leeks and lettuce. There wasn't a weed to be seen. Rows of jam pots filled with flowers for sale to passers-by adorned the road hedge, but the front garden was for pleasure only.

We all sat on an old white painted seat and Aunt Emily pointed out to me the moss roses, dahlias, carnations, marigolds, delphiniums and a host of other flowers, the names of which I could not remember then, but which became familiar to me in later years. Bee hives stood half hidden in a corner behind mallow and rosemary bushes; and boys love which gave off a lovely scent when I picked the leaves and rolled them between the palms of my hands. Apple and plum trees with half grown fruit were trained against the back wall of the shed where the pony was asleep standing up.

Aunt Emily told me that she often entertained young people, and for this reason she kept a store of children's books. For me she produced a large one called Chatterbox, and I whiled away the remainder of the afternoon on the seat, ploughing through the hundreds of pages and pictures, attempting to read some of the text. From within the cottage came a steady buzz of conversation between Gran and Aunt Emily, while Uncle Jim now stripped to his shirt sleeves pottered in the vegetable garden with Uncle Tom.

Tea time - and a glorious repast met my eager eyes: Cucumber sandwiches, egg and bacon tart, splits and cream, lemon cake, honeycomb, and raspberries.

Aunt Emily poured the tea into wide-mouthed cups with awkward fancy handles, so heavy and difficult to hold that I was fearful of spilling the contents over the white lace tablecloth; but somehow I managed even though she kept up a barrage of questions all the while - how was I doing at school? - could I get my sums right? - did I know my tables...?

Seven o'clock struck and Gran said it was time to go home. Uncle Jim harnessed the pony and put aboard two sacks of vegetables; Gran clutched a bunch of rose buds; Uncle Tom gave me a shilling, and Aunt Emily, beaming behind her pince-nez gave me a bundle of 'Comic Cuts', a smacking kiss and helped me up into the trap. Uncle Jim now garbed in his overcoat sat up beside Gran, and I waved and waved until Trenance Cottage was out of sight.

The road leading out from Newquay was still busy with holiday makers and cars.

"Tis the old visitors here again, I can't abide them," muttered Gran. Little did we realise we were witnessing a foretaste of the future when Newquay would be the main North Coast resort, and the coastal road and our beaches would be overrun during the summer months of the years ahead.

I did not have to dismount until we reached Watergate Bay, but this time we bypassed Tregurrian, taking instead the steep hill past the hotel which seemed to be longer than the Mawgan Porth hill. I had eaten too much tea and was out of breath and panting when we reached the summit. What a relief to enjoy the canter down to Mawgan Porth! Alas! I had to dismount once more, this time to pull back and dig my heels in to assist the pony negotiate the steep drop at the hairpin bend, but I was allowed to stay on board during the climb up to Trenance.

At Trenance and Bedruthan the first and last gates were closed, but those between the fields were wide open and unattended; the children had left with their takings and cattle were beginning to lie down for the night.

The sun was low on the horizon as we passed Porthcothan Bay; the tide was full and shimmering; swallows darted and gyrated overhead; ten minutes later we arrived at Lane End and the end of my journey.

My parents came out to meet us and helped unload our share of the gifts. Uncle Jim tethered the pony and Father invited him in for a glass of beer. Gran, Mother and I drank tea. Suddenly my legs ached and I felt very tired. I heard them say, "He's been a very good boy and got on well with Tom and Emily..." But that was all, for I fell asleep; my tea went cold, and when I awoke I was upstairs in my bed.

It was morning and I had five weeks of summer holiday before me.

18

Village Concerts

Most of the cultural activities of the parish took place in the Big Room of the Council School and although they were rare events, their content was quite diverse.

Once a year the 'Flutterbyes Concert Party' arrived from Truro with a repertoire of monologues, solos, duets and dances which they performed with professional aplomb. Their star artist was Mr Clifford Gay, a sort of Ken Dodd of the era. His sparkling, locally slanted repartee had us rolling in our seats, and, his jokes were scrupulously clean.

From Delabole, that straggling village of slate built around the famous quarry, came the Delabole Optimists. Their star comedian was 'Boxer' Rowe, a short, chubby, balding, India-rubber-faced little man whose humour was simple and homespun. But when Boxer removed his dentures, his facial contortions endeared him to the audience for he was the very image of Popeye the Sailor, and even more resembled the late Les Dawson of the 90s.

One of Boxer's specialities was a comic song with the following chorus:
When Father papered the parlour you couldn't see him for paste!
Dabbing it here, dabbing it there - paste and paper everywhere.
Mother was stuck to the ceiling, the children stuck to the floor,
I never knew a blooming family so 'stuck up' before.

Boxer interpolated the words with exaggerated miming of pasting, hanging the paper, falling over the bucket, and with the paper finally coming unstuck and enveloping him.

In another favourite sketch Boxer played the part of a backstage effects man. At a given moment when the heroine, complete with baby, alone and abandoned by her seducer, would cry, "The night grows cold. We have no place to sleep. What shall we do for snow is beginning to fall?"

Boxer, standing on a pair of steps behind the backcloth, his head visible to the audience, and holding up a bucket filled with confetti, from which one hand had plucked a fistful, would wait in anticipation. As the despairing girl cried once more,

"The night grows cold..." Boxer would say loudly to an invisible prompter:
"Shall I snow now?" Again no answer. Then, in a louder voice,
"Shall I snow NOW?"

Silence. Then, lifting the bucket he emptied the contents over the poor girl's head, roaring, "Here dear, have a bloody blizzard on me!"

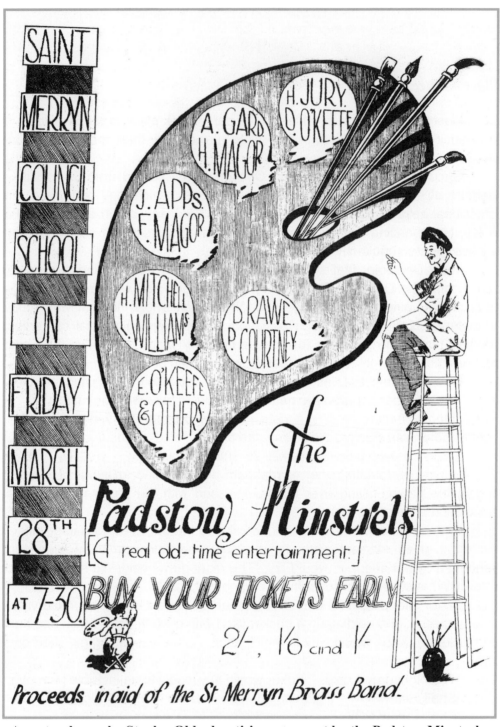

A poster drawn by Stanley Old advertising a concert by the Padstow Minstrels at St Merryn School in aid of St Merryn Brass Band, this shows the quality of art work produced by Stanley Old.

Concerts were usually held during school holidays, but occasionally they occurred during term time which meant that certain advance preparations had to be carried out on the Friday afternoon before the stage was erected for the Saturday evening performance.

The long desks which filled the Big Room were re-orientated to face the western end of the room. The adjustable tops were unscrewed and turned vertically to form a back support to the attached seat. Each desktop held three recessed inkwells which were stuffed with wads of blotting paper to prevent leakage, but invariably some unfortunate person suffered a ruined dress or suit, for the older boys always managed to remove one or two of the wads after the inkwells had been checked and pronounced safe.

The stage components comprising a number of trestles arrived and were lined up in three rows. On the trestles were placed a covering of scaffold boards and table tops borrowed from the Methodist Sunday School. The front of the stage was then draped with blankets secured by drawing pins to hide the trestles, but although the structure appeared to be Jerry-built, it never once collapsed during a concert.

The curtains and the framework upon which they operated arrived from a local builder's shed where they had been carefully stored since the last concert. The intricate system of cords and runners was then unravelled and tested, for sometimes there was a failure during a concert. The mishap, however, provided good entertainment, for the audience thoroughly enjoyed the struggles of the unfortunate operator, and loudly applauded his success when, with a swish the curtains moved once more.

Stage props were stored in the rear Girls' lobby, and the artistes congregated there and also in the Girls' main entrance porch. The only public entry to the Big Room was therefore, via the Boys' entrance at the other end, this was also the only public exit.

Fire precautions were almost non-existent - one bucket of water on the floor at each end of the stage and, compared with today's regulations would be a fire officer's nightmare.

The headmaster's upright piano faced the stage at the left hand end in order that the accompanist could see the artistes and prompt them, adjust the timing should they race ahead, go slow or wander off-key.

If the concert was by a non-local party, their manager usually sent stock posters to the concert organizer some two weeks in advance. Dates and times were inserted and the posters distributed and fixed at strategic points throughout the parish.

Admission prices rarely varied. Tickets were sold in advance from selected outlets; reserved seats in the two front rows cost three shillings and sixpence; behind them were several rows at two shillings, and the back three rows were priced at one shilling and sixpence. Surplus tickets were sold at the door on the night of the concert.

Posters for concerts in which parishioners and visitors were involved, were usually hand drawn by Stanley Old who had returned to the parish after a career in London, bringing with him his talents of commercial artistry and entertaining. His posters, drawn on thick card were works of art and a joy to behold. Cartoon figures, clowns, balloons and streamers complimented the extravagant wording which described the format of the show.

Concerts began at 7.30 pm; doors opening at 7.00 pm. Ticket holders were the first to be admitted, and usually arrived early for in the Boys' lobby a milling stampede began as non-ticket holders surged forward and were held at bay by a perspiring door-keeper who, for the first twenty minutes, allowed entry of ticket holders only. Thereafter, like Solomon at the judgement seat, a ticket seller sat at a card table inside the door and dispensed tickets for unreserved seats, and when they were gone he sold standing room only places at a shilling per person.

Seats filled rapidly and the buzzing of conversation filled the air. Sometimes there was altercation if double booking had occurred and someone tried to squeeze into an already filled line of seats.

I attended many concerts, and cull at random, sights and sounds from those happy evenings which flash up from the depths of memory:

Oil lamps hang down on long wires from the high ceiling and cast a yellow radiance on the audience; a faint whiff of paraffin flavours the unventilated air as the windows steam up. Two or three youths who cannot afford the admission money are outside looking in and tapping on the window panes in the hope that someone will wipe off the condensation to enable them to see the show.

The homemade row of footlights comprising twelve electric light bulbs burst into bloom when an unseen hand connects them to an accumulator battery beneath the stage. The candles on the piano are lit by the accompanist who then opens the lid, sets music on the stand and adjusts the height of the revolving stool. Thumps and bangs begin to emanate from the stage as performers stumble up improvised steps from the rear and side and wait in the wings; a momentary billowing of curtains as someone leaves a door open. Now the oil lamps are drawn down with a map pole by the school caretaker, who turns down their wicks to a glimmer of light, then pushes the lamps up again.

Zero hour, a head peeps from the left side of the curtains and nods at the accompanist who sits for a moment with hands poised over the keys. With a flourish he bangs a tremendous multi-note cord as the heavy curtains draw back and the Flutterbyes brisk signature tune, *"Here we are again, happy as can be..."* is belted out by all eight performers, setting the seal of success on the evening as act after act flashes by. Solos, duets, tap dancing by leggy girls in frilly skirts;

138

a conjuror in top hat and tails, and an hilarious sketch brings the first half of the programme to an end.

During the ten minute interval the lights go up, then down again, with much shuffling those men who left their seats to go outside to relieve themselves against the playground walls, squeeze back into them again to the annoyance and discomfort of those who remained seated. The second half of the programme follows a similar sequence as the first half, and the two and a half hour show ends with a dazzling finale of favourite tunes and many curtain calls.

Locally produced concerts varied in quality and were slower in tempo than the Flutterbyes and Optimists; nevertheless they were very satisfying, and the August Visitors Concerts always produced packed houses with a nightly change of programme.

Stanley Old, who lived at Constantine Bay, excelled himself for through his contacts, he knew if any theatrical persons were staying in the area, and if so, they were gently coerced to take part.

In appearance Stanley Old was a cross between George Robey the comedian and Prime Minister Stanley Baldwin, and his favourite act was a one man marionette show. A Punch and Judy style booth was placed between the centre of the drawn stage curtains, and when the curtains of the booth parted, Stanley's head with a tiny marionette's body attached below it was revealed. As Stanley's head moved, so moved the little arms and legs, and he drew gales of laughter with his stream of comic songs and jokes. A supply of headgear, whiskers, spectacles etc, handed to him each time he drew the curtains produced a new character; in turn he was yokel, curate, fisherman, butcher, schoolmaster and anyone else for whom there was a hat.

Among the male singers were Archie Gard from Padstow, and Jack Collins a young fisherman from Port Isaac. Archie was tall, heavily built, and created a presence as he stood poker straight and impassive for the pianist to strike the opening chords. Suddenly the room would reverberate with: *'Trumpeter, what are you sounding now? Is it the call I'm seeking?'* and his voice would make my hair stand on end. As an encore Archie sang *'Asleep in the Deep'*, and his great bass voice seemed to have the power of rolling thunder as it travelled down the scale to subterranean depths.

Jack Collins who had a fine tenor voice was lean, with ginger hair and a ruddy complexion, smaller in stature than Archie, and on stage was immaculately dressed in black suit and bow tie. Jack was very popular and sang in numerous village concerts in Cornwall where his repertoire included *'The fishermen of England'* and *'When the Ebb Tide Flows.'*

Visitors brought a mixture of talent. One soprano whose renditions of *'Cherry Ripe'* and *'Come into the Garden Maude'* were like the trillings of a skylark. This lady evidently enjoyed entertaining, for with hands clasped on her bosom, and eyes closed, she trilled long and loud oblivious to a high-pitched squealing 'Miaowwwwwwwwww' from some uncouth youth sitting in the back row, as she strained to reach high C. Neither did she appear to notice the suppressed sniggers which rippled through the audience, nor the indignant hiss and icy glare of one of the organizers standing beside the piano.

Perhaps the most famous artiste to appear at these Visitors concerts was a young, fair haired boy in shorts who stayed at Harlyn Bay. He played the piano, a second one placed on the stage for the occasion. The boy's style and expression brought encore upon encore, for there was something of genius in his performance. Today, Joseph Cooper concert pianist, broadcaster, and TV quizmaster, is a household word.

We were held spellbound by a gentleman who recited with magical intonations and gestures 'The Green Eye of the Little Yellow God', and Kipling's 'If' as an encore. He transported us to the mountains beyond Kathmandu, and the exploits of Mad Carew for one moment, and the next moment we were walking with Kings and not losing the common touch. The aftermath was that our headmaster made us learn the complete poem by heart because of its uplifting qualities. That same gentleman had other uplifting items in his repertoire, for many years later, on an all male coach trip, I heard him recite 'Eskimo Nell' to thunderous applause.

Boys from the school performed at some of the concerts, and one favourite item which recurred was the Stick Drill performed by some fifteen boys aged from eight to fourteen years. Precision was the keynote and the headmaster obtained it after many rehearsals, classing the exercise as physical culture.

The sticks, each about three feet long, were as thick as broom handles, and each one was divided into equal painted divisions of red, white and blue.

The basic movements started from the attention position with the stick pressed vertically against the side of the body, one hand above the other. From this position a number of gyrations were performed: Stick against chest - out - in - up above head – down - bend to the left – up - bend to the right - up - bend forward - up above head again - then stick behind and down - up and rest on shoulders, and so forth.

The exercise was performed to the staccato tune of the 'Keel Row' on the piano by the headmaster who did not look down at the keys, but straight ahead and enveloped each boy in a wide angle glare. Woe betide anyone who let slip his stick or moved the wrong way.

During rehearsals we hummed in time to the piano, but those in the back row mouthed these words:

> *The monkey cocked his tail up, his tail up*
> *The monkey cocked his tail up*
> *And showed his dirty Bum.*

The big boys, those in Standards Five and Six, stood in the rear rank, in front of them the smaller boys from Standard Four and in the front row the young boys from Standards Two and Three.

PT kit was unknown in those days, but almost everyone had at least one white shirt and a pair of Sunday-best trousers or shorts, and these were worn with black boots or shoes specially polished for the occasion.

Stick drill always produced one or more victims. A boy with long arms would, when his stick was horizontal, push it hard into the neck of a smaller boy in front of him. As the drill progressed, the unhappy boy was pushed fractionally nearer to the edge of the stage and footlights. On one occasion the curtains swished together leaving one boy outside, amid loud cheers from the audience. The eagle eye of the headmaster rarely missed this activity, and three strokes on each hand with his thin black cane was the painful reminder when administered during the next day at school.

On one occasion a joker rubbed lard on a number of sticks before a rehearsal, and they flew through the air like javelins. No one owned up, so the whole contingent received a caning.

The village brass band performed on occasions under the direction of our Vicar, the Reverend A L T Mugford, who was also its founder. At that time we lived at Lane End, and when asked what instrument he would like to play, Father selected the soprano cornet. Prior to a concert the band held many rehearsals, and in addition to these Father held his own sessions in our sitting room. Hour after hour he blew, and the piercing brass voice of his instrument went up and down the scales, sometimes falling flat when half way up, from whence he started again from middle C. Father also practiced triple tonguing and the resulting discords rebounded from the open-beamed ceiling and made the oil lamp flicker.

I suffered with Mother hours of undiluted agony, as night after night the awful outpourings rent the air, and if we dared criticise the performance, we were told, "Bloody well go for a walk!" Father knew he was making a hash of things but, to give him credit, he gradually improved and sometimes sweet notes filled the air. The vicar's party piece was a simple melody entitled 'Humpty Dumpty', which was played on every possible occasion, it was practiced in our home until we grew to loathe it. Other gems, simplified for village bands were 'Over the Waves', 'Poet and Peasant' (Rossini's version), 'Star Spangled Banner' and the hymn 'Abide with Me'.

The stage was too small to hold the complete band so it performed from the floor, and the instrumentalists created a tremendous upheaval when they moved into position during the interval. Trombones clashed with music stands, triangle and tenor horn became entwined, the big drum blocked the walkway, music sheets fluttered to the floor. Added to the melee was the arrival of chairs for the bandsmen and angry exchanges sometimes took place between occupants of front row seats and bandsmen who inadvertently trod on their toes. Finally the band settled down and, with instruments poised, they waited in anticipation for the lifting of the vicar's baton.

The Reverend Mugford was not an example of sartorial elegance; in fact, his suit was shiny and green with age, but it mattered little to him as he stood facing his 'Boys', with baton raised during the hush before the resounding volume of *'Humpty Dumpty'* swamped the room. Those sitting near him would hear him singing 'ta-ta-t-ta, ta-ta-t-taa', as baton gyrated and the volume of sounding brass reached crescendo.

All those bandsmen have long since gone, but I still see them through the mists of memory: Bill Walters who played the euphonium, his leathery cheeks expanding like twin balloons as he oompahed with the 'big end' as he called it. Once someone pushed an old sock into the throat of the instrument and Bill's cheeks reached near bursting point as he blew harder and produced only a muted rumble; 'Bucky' Welsford, forehead wrinkled like a ploughed field, with trombone fully extended, lifting a small valve from which an excess of saliva dripped onto the floor during a moment of rest; Percy Tummon, impassive behind his big drum, seeming to know exactly when to give it a single or a double thump; Edwin Rossiter, standing beside him, giving an occasional rattle on his kettledrum, or bending over to hit one delicate blow on his triangle; Father playing solo trills on his cornet - the culmination of the torture he put us through at home, Mother and I now sitting on tenterhooks for fear his triple tonguing would go off key.

The Reverend Mugford died soon after his tuition had borne fruit, but the band carried on under a new conductor for some years until he left the parish. Then there was a steady decline in interest and the band finally broke up. During dramatic items there were sometimes moments of acute embarrassment both for audience and players when a locally produced, often under-rehearsed sketch was under way, and an unfortunate girl dried up in mid line, from the wings would issue a monotone low-voice prompt, with no reaction on stage except a rising flush on the poor girl's cheeks; then the whole sentence would be repeated loud enough for the back row to hear, and hopefully the connection was re-made and the show proceeded, when performers did not speak loud enough, reaction came promptly from the audience, "Speak up! We can't hear ya!"

I never reached stardom and apart from performing in the inevitable stick drills my only memorable moment was to sing, with actions, the long drawn out song *'All in a wood there grew a tree, the finest tree you ever did see....'* As each new line was added, so the whole of the words were repeated again and again, culminating in a bird's nest and the hatching of the eggs, etc. And all the while *'The green grass grew all around'*. I was, and still am, incapable of singing a single line in tune and could ruin any choir. When my turn came to sing *'And in that nest there was an egg, the finest egg you ever did see.'* I sang in my tuneless dirge like voice *'And in that egg there was a nest, the finest nest you ever did see'* and the roar from the audience was like enveloping surf in my scarlet embarrassed ears. However, the song continued and the boy next to me sang *'And in that egg there was a bird...'* and there was applause at the end, but my parents were not pleased, for my humiliation was theirs also.

The proposed Parish Hall was eventually built, and concerts continued in the new improved environment with a permanent stage and electric lighting.
Alas, village concerts are no more. Bingo and Discos have long since taken over. I sit before my TV set now watching rubbishy Game Shows and listening to the dubious patter of comedians, how I hanker for those crowded paraffin-lit perspiration filled evenings when entertainment was homemade, clean, and not generated by the flip of a switch.

Lady Astor opening the St Merryn Parish Hall

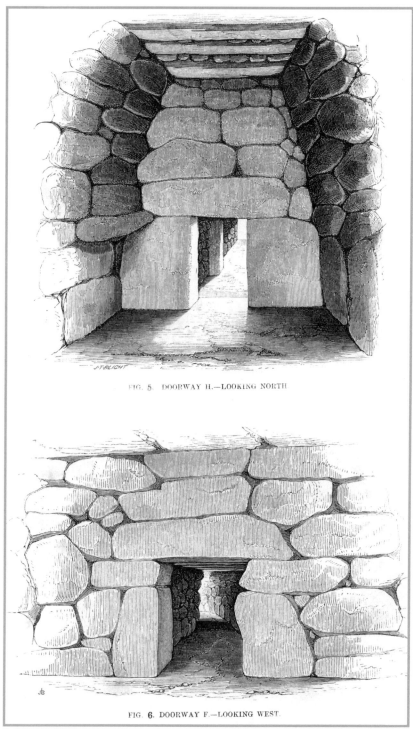

FIG. 5. DOORWAY H.—LOOKING NORTH

FIG. 6. DOORWAY F.—LOOKING WEST.

The above illustrations are a pair of line drawings of the fogue at
Halligye drawn by J. Blight, taken from a late nineteenth century
publication.

144

19

Away to the West

Father acquired an ancient belt-driven Douglas motorcycle together with a dilapidated sidecar chassis with wheel attached, he spent many hours tinkering and coaxing a new lease of life into the sputtering engine. A friend came and welded the chassis to the machine and Father spent even more hours thereafter making a sidecar from plywood salvaged from orange boxes, and a sheet of tin which he bought from the blacksmith. Mother was not impressed and said, "That thing you're making looks like a coffin, and I'm not riding in it!"

"It won't look like that when I put on the hood and windscreen," Father replied, "and it'll be quite comfortable."

In due course, the hood, salvaged from a long defunct perambulator was fitted; a narrow curved piece of plywood formed the windscreen and Father then painted the whole of the bodywork and wheel with dark green paint.

Mother called the motorcycle combination 'His new toy' and it resided under a tarpaulin in our back garden during the late winter and spring months of its rejuvenation. On Saturday afternoons and Sunday mornings if weather permitted. Father took to the road and with a barrage of bangs and clouds of smoke he embarked on trial runs. Once he was missing for three hours and

13 year old Jack with Simeon Norris on one of his summer holidays

Mother, becoming worried set off on her bicycle to find him, taking me on the carrier.

We were fortunate in knowing that he had set off in the direction of Treyarnon and there we found him pushing the cumbersome vehicle, sweating, swearing, out of breathe and all because he had run out of petrol!

Mother was told where the petrol can was stored in our garden shed; how to funnel it into a bottle, without spilling it, and above all to cork the bottle properly.

Mother rode away and I helped Father push the machine along the lane, and we were surprised when she returned quickly having found the can without difficulty.

Father put the petrol in the tank and dropped the empty bottle in the sidecar.

"Jack can ride back with me," he informed Mother and, pointing to the sidecar said, "In you get Boy, we shan't be long now."

Simeon Norris in his
chauffeur's uniform at
Trelewarren.

It was a very uncomfortable ride, and when we reached Lane End Father noticed the grim look on my face and said, "When I put the cushions and backrest in it'll be all right."

Mother regularly corresponded with her elder sister Mary who was married to Simeon Norris and lived in West Cornwall. Uncle Sim, as I called him, was chauffeur to Sir Courtenay Vyvyan of Trelowarren, a beautiful, ancient mansion set in parkland and woods in the parish of St Mawgan-in-Meneage near Helston.

One Wednesday in mid-August a letter arrived inviting us to spend the coming Sunday with them. Mother had mentioned that we now possessed a motorbike and sidecar and Uncle Sim had written to say there was no excuse for us now not to make the journey.

"How far is it?" I asked.

"About fifty miles each way," replied Father.

"A hundred miles!" I could hardly believe my ears. It was like going to the moon and back.

Mother fussed, flapped and worried whether we would get there safely, and Father spent every available minute in tuning the engine to perfection and ensuring that Mother would be comfortable.

Sunday morning arrived, full of sunshine, and we were up and finished our breakfast by eight o'clock. I was reluctantly dressed for the occasion in my winter overcoat, scarf and peaked cap, I was already perspiring when we set out at half past eight. Father opened the little door of the sidecar, and Mother clambered aboard carrying a shopping bag which held a flask of tea and sandwiches for consumption en route. Father had fitted the sidecar with two cushions one as a seat and the other as a back rest. Mother wore her best clothes with matching hat, which looked somewhat incongruous when kept in place by a white silk scarf draped over the crown and knotted under her chin. Father wore his blue serge Sunday suit with the trousers rolled tightly around his ankles and secured with rusty bicycle clips above his shiny black boots. Over this outfit he wore his khaki ex army greatcoat. Royal Garrison Artillery cap, and a pair of goggles.

The machine leaped into life at the first kick and stood juddering at our gate as Mother wriggled and ensconced herself within the cramped interior of the sidecar. Father bolted the door, adjusted Mother's back rest and asked, "Are you comfortable, Milly?"

"I said it looks like a coffin, and it feels like being in one, and we haven't started yet," replied Mother grimly.

"You'll get used to it and we shall stop sometimes to stretch our legs," replied Father as he pulled down the two pillion footrests.

Father mounted and turned to me. "Up you get Jack, and make sure your feet are firm."

I followed, shuffling my bottom on the springy leather pillion upon which he had tied a cushion for extra comfort. I put my arms around his waist, my face close against his back and, turning slightly I smiled at Mother who was sitting upright and tense.

With a crack like machine gun fire we pulled away as Father opened the throttle, in seconds we had negotiated the lane leading from Lane End to Trevoyan Farm. The cool Summer air whipped past my ears; the speed was exhilarating - a wonderful sensation, quite different from my first ride.

We halted outside Rose Cottage and Father squeezed the black bulb of the horn vigorously, bringing Gran and Aunt Glad running to the front door.

"We aren't stopping, Sim is meeting us at half past eleven," said Father. They had a quick chat with Mother and Gran gave me sixpence to spend. I wondered why - it was Sunday and all the shops would be closed.

Off we went again, and at Shop crossroads Mother shrieked loudly as the wheel of the sidecar left the road and tilted her up at a steep angle. Above the roar of the engine Father shouted: "Lean, lean towards the hedge Milly when I'm cornering! And Jack, you keep sitting up straight!"

I soon found that by keeping my back straight I could move my head and see each side of the road and not just Father's backside. Hedges were green blurs, broken by gateways where I saw flashes of cows and sheep in the fields. As we passed through St Columb Major the church clock showed a quarter past nine and the streets were deserted.

The chattering of the engine, the swish, swish, as we passed gateways and the occasional whoosh of passing traffic on the main road had an hypnotic effect, and I closed my eyes as the minutes ticked away.

Suddenly there was a change in the rhythm. The engine coughed and stopped and I was wide awake as we drew to a standstill on a bridge.

"Don't worry, the engine's hot and the plug has oiled up," Father said. "Get down Jack, and help your Mother out. It'll be a quarter of an hour or more until it cools down and I clean the plug. Take a walk and stretch your legs."

I opened the door of the sidecar and helped Mother out. She hadn't spoken much during the journey and now she had to lean against the bridge for support because her legs were very stiff.

We were at Tresillian, and before us was the river at full tide. Mother took off her scarf and adjusted her hat as we strolled along the verge beside the long, straight road flanked by sheds and houses until we reached the Wheel Inn with its thatched roof shimmering in the sunlight.

I was so hot now that I had to take off my cap and coat. I asked Mother if she was enjoying her ride.

"The scenery is nice," she said, "and I'm getting used to the noise, but 'tis still like travelling in a coffin. Maybe we can save up and have a real sidecar one day."

We arrived back to the bridge and, to Mother's annoyance Father was wiping oil from his hands with his best white pocket handkerchief, but he said it was better to do that than wipe them on his trousers.

Father changed the subject saying it was time to have our refreshment, so Mother poured out the tea and we ate our fish paste sandwiches.

"Old bike's going very well," said Father, "We're doing twenty-five to thirty miles an hour, but perhaps I should slow down a bit to stop the plug oiling up again."

I reluctantly put on my cap and coat again, helped Mother into her 'coffin' and remounted. Soon we were chugging up the winding tree lined road leading into Truro. As we coasted down into the city I saw for the first time the cathedral with its three spires soaring high over the streets.

There was more traffic now, and Mother and I had some irritating moments as we bumped up and down over the cobbles in the main street. Father overcame this by standing upright on the footrests oblivious of the amused looks of people on the pavements.

We turned up into the long, wide street which led out of the city, and I noticed that we were slowing down until we were moving at snail's pace.

"Get off and walk Jack. I'll wait for you at the top," said Father. "The driving belt is slipping."

We were still moving as I climbed down, then suddenly, without my extra weight, the machine spurted forward and was soon out of sight. When I reached the monument at the top of the street Father was waiting. I was out of breath and bathed in sweat, as I clambered gratefully onto the pillion. Mother was concerned that I might catch cold when she saw my condition. Then away we went and the rush of air soon cooled me down. I had two more short walks when Father felt that the going was too steep for the driving belt, and after we had passed the road junction near Penryn, I lost all count of time until we reached Helston.

Father stopped to enquire the whereabouts of Clodgy Lane for Uncle had advised him that by taking it he could by-pass the town. Now there were signposts to St Mawgan-in-Meneage and St Keverne, and as we drove through the village of Garras, Father said: "We're on the last lap! Now we must watch out for The Double Lodge. Sim says it is on our left."

Two small octagonal shaped buildings with a pair of high iron gates between them came into view, and standing there was my Uncle Sim talking to the lodge keeper who rushed to open them.

Uncle Sim always my favourite uncle, was short and portly, with a round face and smiling eyes beneath a massive brow and bald head fringed with greying brown hair. He was slightly bow legged from excessive horse riding when, during the War he was a groom in the Veterinary Corps.

Uncle greeted us warmly and waved us through the gateway where a car was standing by the left hand Lodge.

"I've had permission to use the car today, and I'll take you for a ride later. Now, follow me!" said Uncle.

We drove through a winding drive lined with shrubs; on past a farm, then through open gateways across green fields into the tiny hamlet of Halligye where Uncle drew up beside his house.

Aunt Mary rushed out and embraced us; a large liver-and-white spaniel waddled from the lawn, sniffed each of us in turn and, apparently satisfied that we were friends, waddled off again. Aunt Mary extricated Mother from the confines of the sidecar and laughingly said: "My backside's too big to get in there Milly. You're the small one of the family."

The remainder of the day passed in a whirl of fleeting kaleidoscopic scenes: The grandness of their sitting-room with its velvet curtains and chintz covered furniture; the huge lunch and cream tea; the green, close-cut lawn where I played with Flo the dog whilst the grown-ups lazed in deckchairs; Uncle's huge vegetable garden with row upon row of runner beans and peas; the black portable gramophone which they allowed me to wind up, choose records and play. Then we were taken to meet the four resident families of the hamlet, all of whom invited us into their homes and made us very welcome.

After tea Uncle turned back the canvas hood of the Overland car, making it into an open tourer and we drove grandly away to see the sights of St Mawgan, St Martin, St Keverne and Manaccan, returning to Trelowarren where he gave us a conducted tour. I was amazed at the size of the empty stables, and the coach house which had been converted into a garage where Uncle now parked the car.

After we had visited the courtyard and buildings where the estate masons, carpenters, woodmen and gardeners worked, Uncle said, "We'll walk back to Halligye and I'll show you some of the estate."

We passed through huge walled gardens; avenues of oak trees which skirted the drives and a gateway built like the turret of a small castle. We walked over lawns which receded into banks of rhododendrons; and then, suddenly before us was the lovely yellow-brown facade of the west wing of the mansion, and a chapel with pinnacles on its beautiful gable end.

"One day you shall see the inside that chapel Jack, and maybe some of the rooms in the house," said Aunt Mary.

"But that wont be for a very long time," I replied.

"Don't you be so sure," she laughed, and winked at Mother.

In a field between Trelowarren and Halligye was a manmade tree-clad mound called The Mount. We walked up the narrow footpath which spiralled around the circumference and from the summit Uncle pointed in various directions to the Lizard, Porthleven, Penzance, Falmouth, Helford - all names which meant little to me and, as we descended Uncle said, "You'll be able to visit all of them with me." Of course, he was joking.

It was early evening when we returned to the house, and time for us to leave for home. Father and Uncle tightened up the driving belt of the motorbike; checked the water and carbide in the headlight; tested the little rear lamp which was connected to it by a long thin rubber tube, and finally, topped up the petrol tank from a can which Uncle brought from his tool shed.

Suddenly Uncle turned to me and said, "Jack, would you like to stay with us?"

"Yes," I said, "I'd like to, one day."

"Would you stay now?"

I was dumbfounded. What was going on?

"Yes - but I've only got my best clothes."

"That's where you're wrong." Mother started laughing as leaned into the sidecar and produced a large parcel from front end. "There's clothes enough for a fortnight, and a spare pair of shoes."

I knew then why she was so cramped on our downward journey; and the odd remarks made earlier that afternoon about visiting places became clear.

"We weren't sure whether you would want to stay, so we haven't mentioned it before. Now, what's it to be? Yes or no?" asked Father.

I was so surprised at the speed of events that I didn't know what to do. Then I said with uncertainty, "I'll stay with Aunt and Uncle."

Aunt Mary immediately reassured me, "If you find you don't like it here dear, we can soon take you home again." That settled it. Mother was shiny eyed as she handed me over; Father mumbling something about me being a good boy as he donned his greatcoat and cap and helped Mother into the sidecar. A small boy, one of several who had gathered to watch the departure, ran and opened the swing gate.

"You're sure you know the way, Herbert?" called Uncle.

"I hope so," replied Father, and with a sputtering and backfiring he started the motorbike. I stood in the road waving to my departing parents until they vanished over the crest of the field.

I was alone in strange surroundings, with an Aunt who had spent most of her life away from Rose Cottage in service, and an uncle whom I had met only twice. Would they be as kind as Gran and Aunt Glad? At that moment I felt terribly lonely and homesick. "I mustn't cry," I told myself, and blinked several times. I felt a wet nose touching my hand and a head nuzzled against my leg. I looked down, and the dog Flo looked up at me. Then I knew everything would be all right.

Thereafter, until I was fifteen years of age, I spent part of the Easter and Summer holidays with my Aunt and Uncle at Halligye, arriving there on the old Douglas motorcycle which was later superseded by a BSA with a proper sidecar.

When Father went to work at the village garage, he drove a small lorry and this enabled him to transport me to Bodmin Road (Now Bodmin Parkway) railway station from whence I boarded a train for Helston. How thrilling and sometimes alarming were those early journeys; the smell of hissing steam and oil; the scramble for a seat; the sudden fear of being alone in a carriage and unable to open the door when the train arrived at Gwinear Road - supposing the handle wouldn't turn and I went on to Penzance! But such fears were groundless. How I loved the lilt of those sing-song words shouted by the Guard as when the train halted at Gwinear Road Station, "Gwinear Roaaad! All change for Praaaaze, Nanceeegollan and Hellllston."

At twelve I was the proud possessor of a Raleigh sports model bicycle equipped with three speed gear. The following summer I pedalled safely away to the West without puncture or accident. My luggage was sent in advance by rail to Helston station where it was duly collected by my Uncle. Aunt Mary and Uncle Sim were prime favourites with the Halligye children. Among them was little Leslie, youngest of them all. He lived in a thatched cottage around the corner, and he had an elder brother named Monty. It was impossible for Leslie to keep clean, for wherever there was mud or muck Leslie would be in it and we often heard his mother's voice rising in despair, "Oh, my tender dear! What shall I do with you? Just look at yourself!" And she would strip him, wash him and soon his clothes would be hanging on the line to dry.

One afternoon Aunt Mary was entertaining Mr Wilkerson, an elderly bald headed gentleman with a huge white walrus moustache, who was at that time engaged in the restoration of paintings at Trelowarren. With him was Miss Consby, Lady Vyvyan's personal Maid. Uncle and I came in from the garden followed by Leslie, who was about five years of age at the time.

Leslie stood in the doorway eyeing with amazement the huge moustache, shining head and piercing eyes of the old gentleman who was confronting him from the sofa and the stern looking lady sitting beside him. Leslie stood there, a dirt stained cherub with grey eyes-staring from beneath a straight-cut fringe of mousy hair. Two red elbows peeped from holes in the arms of his shapeless jersey whose hemline hung down over his shorts and chubby earth stained legs. He pulled up one red sock, and it fell down again as he clutched my Uncle's hand.

Leslie could sometimes be heard singing tuneless little ditties, more often than not the words were incoherent except to his immediate relatives. Uncle Sim possessed a mischievous streak and after introducing Leslie, he said, "Oh, Miss Consby, would you like to hear Leslie sing?"

Miss Consby, dignified and superior as befitted her station, was magnificently attired in a black costume; a fur stole of doubtful origin was draped over her shoulders; upon her head was a toque from which a black veil trimmed with minute bobbles danced before her lined forehead as she nodded her approval. She turned to her friend and said: "I once conducted a children's choir when I lived at Shepherd's Bush. The little darlings were magnificent. But that was such a long time ago. Have you ever sung in public Mr Wilkerson?"

A voice from beneath the moustache rumbled, "Only on Derby Days, m'dear if I had a winner, and then it was *'Nellie Dean'* and *'Money is the Root of all Evil'* all the way home."

Uncle whispered something in Leslie's ear. The boy looked up at him and grinned as he was gently propelled to the hearthrug. He preened himself, clasped his hands together, and stood with feet apart. Miss Consby cocked an ear in anticipation Aunt Mary gave Uncle a strange look as he winked back at her. Leslie drew an adenoidal breath and then exhaled. From one nostril trembled a small dangle of snot. In an off-key treble he sang a tune which had some resemblance to *'The Ash Grove'*, but the words were different and came loud and clear:

I've seen it I've seen it!
I've been right up between it
She's got hairs on her Dicky-di-do
Right down to her knees.

There followed a moment of frozen silence, broken by Mr Wilkerson's vigorous clapping. Leslie wiped his nose on the cuff of his jersey.

"You never heard anything like that in Shepherd's Bush Miss Consby," he bellowed. "Does he know any more like that one?"

"Yes, but he's not singing them in this house," snapped Aunt Mary

Mr Wilkerson gave Leslie a sixpenny piece for his efforts and the boy departed happily. Miss Consby appeared to be oblivious of Leslie's vocal oratory, but Uncle heard later that she related a modified version to the staff in the servant's hall.

At the top end of Uncle's vegetable garden where the stone hedge abutted onto a field, there was a subterranean cave known in archaeological circles as the Halligye Fogou. The entry at that time was near the foot of the hedge and was composed of large stones set around an opening about a square yard in area. Inside was a chamber some six feet high, five feet wide and about fifty feet in length. At right angles to this chamber, at the western end, was another chamber, and extending from it towards the east via a short tunnel through which one had to crawl, was a third chamber somewhat higher, with a pile of fallen rocks to roof level which prevented further progress.

My introduction to this Iron Age fogou was during a game of hide and seek with the Halligye boys. We slithered down through the entrance onto a soft bed of damp, odorous leaf mould, the product of countless generations of wind blown leaves from the hedge.

Arthur, the eldest of our group always carried a box of matches, and although only twelve years of age, he was an accomplished smoker who collected dog-ends of cigarettes. With an end speared on a pin, Arthur would light up and take a few luxurious puffs before the glowing tobacco burned his lips.

Having clambered inside the fogou, Arthur held aloft a flickering match which revealed for a few seconds the dry-stone walled sides and roof slabs, smelling of earth and glistening with condensation. Roots white and snakelike writhed through the stone courses, and others dangled through cracks in the roof joints like witches' hair.

After several matches and dark stumbling intervals, we started to crawl through the tunnel to the furthest chamber, and in doing so I was suddenly filled with horrifying thoughts. Supposing I got stuck; supposing there was a rock fall; would anyone hear my shouts? Claustrophobia enveloped me. I felt sick with fright, and even more so when Arthur struck a match and said: "Bugger! There's only dead ones left. Now we've got to go backwards to get out."

The inky blackness and smell of decay was nauseating; the slow, backward crawling on hands and knees and the frequent contact with pieces of rock cutting into my knees made me tremble with terror, my cup of woe overflowed when I received a hearty kick in the face from one of Arthur's hob nailed boots. However, we reached the end of the tunnel (it seemed like an age but was only about a minute), could now stand upright and, after groping along the walls could see a faint glimmer of light. As we emerged, Raymond the 'seeker' guessed where we had hidden and was waiting for us to emerge from the fogou.

My top lip was swollen and my knees were scarred; there was earth in my hair and leaves clinging to my clothing. When I went indoors neither Aunt nor Uncle were annoyed by my dishevelled appearance. Uncle merely said, "You've been down in the cave, I can smell it."

"Yes, I've been playing Hide and Seek with Arthur, Cyril, Monty and Raymond."

"Arthur had matches, I suppose?"

"Yes, and he struck them all. I didn't like it in the dark."

Aunt said: "I bet that boy was smoking. Don't you start getting bad habits from him. "

I shook my head. I couldn't let Arthur down, he had, after all, given me a draw from a whole Woodbine one previous afternoon.

"No, Aunt Mary, he wasn't."

Uncle said, "Tomorrow I'll take you down there myself, and you shall see the cave properly." And I did, for when we went Uncle carried a large torch and yesterday's fears vanished as we progressed. I learned that the fogou was not far below ground, and the tunnel leading to the furthest chamber seemed much shorter when we crawled through it; but it was still claustrophobic. Uncle told me that many people visited the cave, and in future, when I was on holiday I could act as their guide with torch and candle.

So, during several Easter and Summer holidays I escorted parties of interested ladies and gentlemen through the fogou. Sometimes the ladies twittered nervously if I switched off the torch, and more than one emerged with laddered stockings and dishevelled hair. One occasion I shall always cherish, for it had an unexpected aftermath.

One afternoon in early September, two soberly clad gentlemen, accompanied by two equally elderly, leathery faced ladies arrived by car and knocked at the front door. One of the men who appeared to be their leader, wore an odd kind of trilby hat, a short cape and black knee breeches with gaiters. The other man was dressed in a dark grey suit. Both ladies wore severely tailored tweeds, the whole party seemed to exude an air of cloistered reverence.

'Gaiters' announced to my Aunt that they had come to inspect the fogou, having been informed by Sir Courtenay Vyvyan that illumination and a guide would be provided.

"Yes Sir. Of course. Sir," said Aunt in a most refined accent which she reserved for occasions such as this. She hurried away to collect candle, matches and torch.

I stood a little apart and eyed this awesome assembly with some apprehension. Aunt returned with the lights and handed them to me.

"My nephew will be pleased to show you the cave Sir. It is up at the top of the garden." She turned to me, "Jack, show the ladies and gentlemen the way."

I led the quartette in single file up the narrow cinder path past Uncle's vegetables and under the two rambler rose covered pergolas, past the earth closet with its ever-open door to the grassy area in front of the fogou.

"Isn't he rather young for this sort of thing?" whispered one lady to the other, "I would have thought he'd be afraid in the dark."

"Here is the entrance, ladies and gentlemen. It is easier to go in this way," I called, as I turned and crawled backwards through the opening." Inside I lit the candle and held it high as 'Gaiters' spindly legs shuffled down onto the leaf mould, followed by black stockinged legs as the first lady entered; then a flash of suspenders and white bloomers as the second lady descended with much grunting, gasping and assistance from the 'grey' man bringing up the rear.

The party stood in anticipation as I switched on the torch and pointed it towards the southern end of the first chamber, and began to walk in that direction.

"Hold it high Boy!" said 'Gaiters', and the party went into discussion about stones and things which were quite unintelligible to me. Following their instructions I flashed the light up, down and sideways. We returned past the entrance and entered the western chamber where they spent so much time examining the walls that I fully expected the torch battery would die on them; but this did not worry me as there was plenty of candle and a full box of matches. "Now we come to the most interesting part," said 'Gaiters' to his friends, and to me, "Give me the torch Boy; I shall go first. You follow, with the candle. If someone behind you calls out, try to turn around and give them some more light."

"Yes Sir," I replied as I handed over the torch.

'Gaiters' got down on his knees and entered the tunnel which was once so frightening to me. In the guttering candlelight he reminded me of a black praying mantis as he eased himself through the narrow confines, his legs moving mechanically across the uneven floor. Once or twice he said, "Ughhh! This is painful. Oooghh!" as he came into contact with pieces of rock.

Behind me the ladies were getting down on their knees. "This kind of exercise is no help for my arthritis," said the eldest, "I hope I can get through," as she eased forward.

I turned and shone the candle right under her nose. She blinked like a startled owl, and behind her came an anguished, "Oooch!" as she involuntarily reversed and stepped on someone's fingers.

"We are nearly through," called 'Gaiters' loudly. "We must relax for a moment." He switched off the torch.

My candle flame made wobbly shadows on the tomblike walls. Sighs percolated the confined space; then silence, broken by 'Gaiters' saying, "I have put down the torch and I can't find it." He grunted and made scratching noises.

"Put the candle on the floor in front of you, Boy," he commanded.

I did this, and from my contorted position I visualised him now as a huge black beetle with thin back legs, and arms that waved like antennae. I was bursting with laughter and put one hand over my mouth to suppress it.

Then it happened. 'Gaiters' moved slightly forward, and in doing so grunted and let off a fart a full bodied rumble which ended on a high pitched note which reminded me of a creaking gate; a noise which in no way matched his rather frail bodily proportions. I burst into uncontrollable laughter, and in doing so blew out the candle. Behind me in the darkness came sounds of stifled merriment, camouflaged by deep throated, "Ahems."

"Light the candle, at once!" yelled the arthritic lady in an unladylike voice and, as I fumbled with the matches 'Gaiters' found the torch, emerged into the high chamber and straightened up. I followed and helped the two ladies to their feet, avoiding their eyes as I did so, but the 'grey' man who was grinning broadly, straightened his face as he followed them and winked at me. I felt utterly embarrassed and wondered what would be said, but the group ignored me and continued their examination of the chamber as though the incident had not occurred.

'Gaiters' handed me the torch when they had finished and said, "Now Boy, you can lead the way back." So, with both hands grasping torch and candlestick I squirmed my way through the tunnel and like a cinema usherette escorted them to the fogou entrance. Their faces were impassive, their clothing somewhat stained and dishevelled as they emerged into the autumn sunshine. I led them back through the garden to the front gate where their chauffeur-driven car was waiting. The driver emerged from the kitchen where he had been drinking tea with my Aunt and opened the doors of the car. 'Gaiters' thanked me for being so helpful; both ladies said they had enjoyed the visit; the grey-clad gentleman gave me a half-crown coin for my trouble and, out of ear shot of the others, winked and said, "Don't ever hide your light under a bushel, young man, otherwise someone may blow it out."

Aunt and Uncle verged on hysterics when I told them what had happened, but they did not bother to find out who the visitors were, or from whence they came.

Some years later, I was with a number of boys and girls in our parish church where a Confirmation Service was in progress. We were kneeling in line at the communion rail with heads bowed. An awe-inspiring figure clad in magnificent vestments slowly moved down the line, laying hands on our heads and saying, "Defend O Lord this thy child with thy Heavenly grace..."

The hands were on my head; the words spoken over me; the man moved on. I looked from the corner of one eye. No it couldn't be?...and yet?..,

After the service we went to the vicarage for refreshments, and each new communicant was introduced by our vicar to His Grace who, from a distance, and without his trappings looked quite ordinary.

My name was called. I walked across the room and shook the extended hand. As he held it, the man looked me straight in the eyes, smiled and said: "Well... the fogou boy! You were a very good guide. I enjoyed my visit," and turning to his colleague he said, "He has grown a lot since we saw him."

Then he moved on, and the other man said, "Is your light still shining?"

"No Sir, I haven't been down to Halligye for eighteen months."

After they had gone, the vicar in inquisitive mood, approached me and said: "Jack, tell me, how long have you known the Bishop of Truro and the Rural Dean. They both told me what a good chap you are?"

"Since the day I blew out the candle, Vicar," I replied, and left it at that.

Each Tuesday my Uncle drove the Overland car to Helston where he did the Trelowarren shopping. Armed with lists from the Cook, he left them in various shops and about an hour later he went back to collect each consignment.

Sometimes I joined him on these excursions. At exactly ten o'clock the car came down the drive, and from where I was hidden behind a huge oak tree I listened for two toots on the horn; then I knew I was going, but if there was only one toot then Sir Courtenay Vyvyan or some other person was in the car and my outing was aborted. However, these disappointments were infrequent and I made many pleasant journeys.

At Helston we first called at Pascoe's fish shop; followed by visits to Wakeham the chemist, and Willey the newsagent-cum-toyshop where I spent many pleasant minutes browsing through books, buying small additions of lead animals for my model farmyard, and looking at packets of foreign stamps. Treasons' grocery store was my favourite rendezvous, for there was always a bag of sweets placed on top of the goods for me. The lady cashier sat in a kiosk from whose roof emanated long overhead wires with small containers attached which shuttled to and from the various counters. She detached them as they arrived, removed their contents and, at the pull of a lever she sent them back with a receipt and change like homing pigeons to their lofts. During one of my early stays at Halligye, Uncle announced that Sir Courtenay wished to meet me, and that he had arranged the meeting for half past ten on the following morning.

I was thrown into turmoil. What would I wear? What would I talk about? Aunt Mary quelled my fears.

"You can wear your best suit," she said.

"And your cap," said Uncle. "When you meet Sir Courtenay in the garden you must salute him by touching your cap with your right hand, and say 'Good morning. Sir Courtenay'."

I rarely wore a cap because caps made my face look pinched and small. However, Aunt Mary took it from my suitcase and Uncle said, "Now we'll have a rehearsal."

I walked to and from the sitting room and Uncle pretended he was the great man.

"Good morning. Sir Courtenay," and up went my right hand to slightly lift the peak of my cap.

"No, that's not right, you're covering your face."

I tried again.

"No, put your elbow up straight when you salute."

I managed to get it right and did it several more times, but by the time Uncle was satisfied I was a nervous wreck.

Next morning, immaculately dressed, I set forth, my feet dragging unwillingly past the Mount and along the pathway which bounded the wood. My heart beat fast and my throat was dry as I continually mouthed the magic words of greeting and my right hand made involuntary salutes. I crossed the main drive and entered the estate grounds passing beside a high wall with fruit trees trained against it, and from whose parapet clusters of long stemmed daisies sprouted. I crossed the lawn by the chapel and entered a smaller garden on the left.

A thin, white haired, elderly gentleman was standing beside a sundial with his back towards me, one hand grasped a walking stick, and a second stick was propped against the sundial. A housemaid approached with a brown paper bag which she placed on the sundial. As I drew near he turned slowly, leaning heavily on his stick, and eyed me keenly.

"Good morning Sir Courtenay," I said through dry lips, and at the same moment lifted my hand and touched my cap. To my horror I realised I had saluted him with my left hand, but he appeared not to notice my confusion.

"Good morning Jack," he replied, "Your Uncle Norris has told me a lot about you," and he immediately began asking me how I liked staying with my Aunt and Uncle. Had I walked around St Mawgan, St Martin, and the Helford river? My fears of meeting the Master of this great mansion and estate proved groundless as we chatted.

I told Sir Courtenay I had visited much of the area with my Uncle who carried me on the crossbar of his bicycle.

As we conversed he took a handful of scraps of bread and cake from the bag and strewed the crumbs around us. Immediately there was a loud fluttering of wings and scores of birds descended and proceeded to eat up his offering.

"Keep very quiet, and don't move," he said in a low voice, and held out his free hand which was filled with crumbs. A chaffinch flew up from the ground, perched on his outstretched hand and was joined by a sparrow. Together the birds pecked away for about a minute until Sir Courtenay dropped his hand and picked up the other walking stick. To my young eyes the happening was wonderful, and on the face of this distinguished looking gentleman was a look of pure bliss.

"Always remember Jack, the birds are our friends. They know those who are kind to them. I have been feeding them for many years and they know me. Your Uncle tells me that you too are fond of birds."

"Yes Sir," I replied, "I go out into the fields at home, and my Father takes me to the cliffs to watch the gulls."

Sir Courtenay seemed pleased.

"Thank you for coming," he said. The interview was over. I saluted again, this time correctly, as he turned, supported by his sticks and walked slowly towards the house with a host of attendant birds fluttering around him.

On the last day of that holiday I received a surprise gift from Sir Courtenay Vyvyan, a beautifully illustrated book entitled 'A Bird Book for the Pocket', and I used it for many years thereafter. I even took it with me when I was called up into the Army, but one day it was stolen from my kitbag. It was as though I had lost a close friend.

Those west country days ended three years after I had won a scholarship to Bodmin County School. My parents said it was necessary for me to earn some money during the holidays to offset the ever rising costs of my schooling and clothing.

I caddied at the recently opened Trevose Golf Club, and as I watched the flight of erratically hit golf balls by rich business men and their pampered wives, and trailed along with their heavy bags of clubs, my thoughts often turned back to Halligye; the halcyon days spent with my Uncle, Aunt, and their friendly old dog; and I longed to be back with them again.

St Martyn-in-Meneage Band, Simeon Norris second from the left in the back row.

The 'new' Post Office. Later Jack built Lyndale next door on the site of the cottage that he and his parents lived in at Shop.

St Merryn Garage

Part Three: Shop Village

20

Cob Walls, Cockroaches and Carnality

In the autumn of 1926 we moved from Lane End to a larger cottage on the crossroads in the village of Shop when Father left the golf course to drive a lorry for a haulier and garage owner.

Father's job was to deliver coal to many families in the parish; parcels from the Southern Railway Stations, feeding stuffs to outlying farms, and oil and other goods from Trinity House to Trevose Lighthouse.

Herbert Ingrey with the lorry he drove for H J Gridley.

In many ways our new cottage resembled the one at Lane End, but there were two bedrooms, and this enabled me to have a room of my own. The ground floor comprised a large, almost square living-room a long, narrow kitchen, and a larder-cum-store.

This cottage was very old, and was built entirely of cob, a mixture of mud, clay and straw walls almost three feet thick which made it cool in summer and warm in winter. Four small sliding sash windows peeped out from the roadside wall which was completely covered with scarlet Virginia creeper whose tendrils pushed their way into the cob and burst through the papered walls of the front rooms. The cob housed a variety of wild life and I often heard little ticking noises, squeaks and scurryings. Sparrows nested and roosted in the creeper; snails congregated under the slate window sills and spiders hung webs in the corners of windows.

Two gabled roofs, one spanning the living-room and the other the kitchen, with a lead valley between them, ran parallel with the walls facing the road.

A wide four-panelled front door led into the living- room via a minute, dark vestibule. A small unpredictable iron pump which coughed and sputtered out our water supply stood, with its granite trough by the boarded back door; and a two storied stone washhouse building of later vintage stood a few feet away from the cottage. A high stone boundary wall separated us from the Farmers Arms and the Post Office; and a low stone hedge from the small uncultivated field which I named my 'Summer Meadow.'

The front bedroom, occupied by my parents, had creaking floorboards which, with the thin match boarded partitions transmitted every sound and movement, often hilarious, sometimes embarrassing.

My bedroom, although fairly large, had only a small window which did not let in much light and, unfortunately, the ceiling was of whitewashed billowing calico identical to the one at Lane End. But, at last, I had gained some privacy.

Our long, narrow kitchen had small sliding sash windows with deep sloping reveals in the thick wall, and were positioned one on each side of the back door. An accumulation of bottles, brushes, combs, spanners and other articles of every day use rested on their internal sills because storage space was limited.

The white painted ceiling formed by the floorboards of my bedroom, were suspended over black varnished beams which sagged visibly when one walked about upstairs.

All floors of the cottage were made of large slate slabs laid on an uneven earth bed, and were no improvement to those at Lane End.

A black Cornish stove sat in a small recess, although small in size, Mother produced a prodigious amount of cooking from the oven. Roasts, pasties, saffron, seedy, currant, heavy cakes, and currant bobbins. 'Currany 'obbins' as we called them, were made from rolled out pastry sprinkled with currants and fashioned into a kind of thin Swiss roll which, after being baked, were cut into pieces about three inches long.

Mother made batches of small pasties for weekend consumption and sometimes left them in the oven overnight. One night after my parents had gone to bed, I arrived late after a visit to the Cinedrome at Padstow. A candlestick and box of matches were always kept on a chair inside the living room door. I lit the candle and, in its flickering light, I went into the kitchen where I noticed that the oven door was open and a number of pasties, tightly packed together, lying on the shelves.

I said to myself, "Mother won't miss one of these," and I extracted a pasty nearest to the front of the oven and carefully moved two others into the vacant space. I retired to the living-room, kicked off my shoes, stretched myself out on the sofa and relaxed. I took a slow bite into the end of this late night delicacy savouring the crispness of the pastry, the tender peppery flavour of meat, sliced potato and onion.

Suddenly I was aware of a slight movement in my mouth - something hard and it wasn't meat. Startled, I spat the contents out into my hand and a cockroach dropped to the floor; then two more emerged from the end I had just bitten and started to crawl up my arm. I let out a loud yell and flung pasty and

162

insects from me. Then there was movement upstairs and the sound of matches being struck.

"Is that you, Jack? What's going on down there?" shouted Father.

"It's cockroaches, the place is swarming with them!" I called, for I could now see more insects crawling across the floor. My parents came down and Mother knew immediately what I had been up to. She bent down, picked up the scattered pieces, looked into the oven and shouted, "The oven's full of them!" In the silence that followed, we could see, and hear the insects moving among the pasties.

In old houses, especially those with cob walls, there are invariably colonies of cockroaches, dormant by day and actively foraging by night. A small hole in the crimping of my pasty enabled them to enter it, when we examined the others, we found three pasties, each with small holes, and full of insects.

Thereafter Mother made sure the oven door was closed, and that all food in the larder was covered and secure against these nightly marauders. We often saw cockroaches after that incident, and crushed them underfoot but many scuttled away and escaped. We learned to live with them... and I discovered that cockroaches had been around for several million years, but I doubt if any of them had ever sampled a pasty supper before.

Our kitchen was dark and received no sunshine. We ate our meals on a small oilcloth-covered table placed against the wall between the back door and the window. Often the door was open to let in more light, but it made for cold dining.

In a built-up disused doorway recess hidden by a curtain were three shelves. The top shelf harboured an accumulation of old newspapers, below it sat Mother's workbasket and articles of clothing waiting to be darned. A mixture of culinary articles including tea caddies, cocoa tins, sauce and vinegar bottles stood beside a stack of cups, saucers and tea plates on the bottom shelf. On the floor below was a collection of assorted footwear in everyday use plus three pairs of Wellington boots. Our best shoes were kept upstairs in Mother's rickety wardrobe where they were free from mildew.

The area to the right of our backdoor constituted the scullery in which stood another large deal table with well-scrubbed top. On it stood a primus stove, sometimes temperamental when it caught fire and sent yellow flames shooting up to lick the low ceiling. But it supplemented the kitchen stove, and kettles boiled quicker on it when it was working properly.

Beneath the table were two baths - a small galvanized one in which Mother did the family washing, and a cumbersome white painted tin hip bath brought out each Friday night for our weekly bath in front of the kitchen stove. The bath water was heated in a large cast iron boiler on the stove alongside an equally large bucket. I bathed first and was sent off to bed because my parents were embarrassed for me to see them naked. Father added more water and

Mother had her bath. When she had finished she dried in front of the fire and Father, using the remainder of the water followed, lay soaking until the water was cold. I discovered a small crack in the flooring boards of my bedroom, and by lying flat on my stomach and squinting through, watched them scrub each others back, wipe each other dry, kiss and cuddle, etc, etc. If only they knew!

An all-purpose cupboard made by the local carpenter filled the end wall. The top half housed Mother's cheaper china for daily use. Two drawers were filled with trinkets, gadgets, gouges, spanners, hammers and miscellaneous junk, below them were two enclosed shelves which held bread bins, patty pans, mincing machine, rolling pin and earthen ware mixing bowls.

Our coal store under the stairs was sometimes visited by Jinny our tabby cat. Jinny left us in no doubt of her activities, for when a shovel full of coal was placed in the stove, the smell was nauseating. However, one morning Mother caught Jinny in the act, took her by the scruff of the neck, rubbed her nose in her efforts, and threw her out into the garden where she spent several hours cleansing herself. Mother's treatment was successful for never again did Jinny use the coalhouse as a toilet.

The larder shelves held an assortment of jars of pickled cabbage, bean chutney, blackberry and apple jam; boot brushes and polishes, stone hot water bottles and boxes of cartridges. Hams in calico bags jostled against braces of rabbits suspended on hooks from the beams. A large wooden meat safe with perforated zinc sides took up much of the floor space, and what was left was occupied by a kieve (wooden tub) filled with salted pork, and leaning against it was my bicycle and Father's double barrel gun.

Our living-room was similar to the one at Lane End, this enabled our furniture to be placed in identical positions, so we felt quite at home when we moved in.

Mother invested in a new dresser to display her best blue and white china dinner service. Our heavy iron-frame chiming clock sat on top of the dresser, flanked by two black china pug dogs whose ugly faces were set in perpetual sneers. The under cupboards were filled to bursting with assorted china and vases, mostly fairground prizes won by Father for rifle shooting.

The large Victorian style tiled fireplace consumed vast quantities of coal and logs in winter, and the brass fender and fire irons glinted yellow from its flames and were hot when one touched them.

Mother bought a hanging bookshelf unit to house my collection of much loved books: Six volumes of Cassells' 'Childrens' Book of Knowledge'; Arthur Mee's 'Childrens' Encyclopaedia' in fortnightly parts, each costing one shilling and three pence - a small fortune in those days. There was also the wonderful picture dictionary entitled 'I See All', and my Annuals – 'Chatterbox', 'Chums', 'Hobbie's, all carefully preserved. I had also acquired some sixpenny classics: 'The Old Curiosity Shop', 'Treasure Island', 'The Swiss Family Robinson' and

'*Ivanhoe*'. For my eleventh and twelfth birthdays my parents gave me '*The Moths of the British Isles Series I*', and '*Wayside and Woodland Blossoms*', both of which I still possess. As I turn their yellowing, much thumbed pages, fond memories of those wonderful nature rambles in fields, valleys and on cliff tops flash through my mind.

Every other year the uneven cob walls of the living room were re-papered, papering day was all hustle and bustle. Aunt Glad arrived early to help Mother, together they moved all the furniture towards the centre of the room to give them plenty of working space. Mother made a large bowl of flour and water paste and cut the paper into lengths, while Aunt applied the paste with a goose's wing saved from the previous Christmas and matched the pattern and hung the paper in a professional manner. During Spring 1939 when the cottage was demolished to make way for a modern house, I counted nine thicknesses of wallpaper, each with a different floral pattern.

I was encouraged to take up music and Father bought an old upright piano for two pounds. From the open cover its battered yellowed keys grinned at me like a mouthful of decayed teeth and challenged me to produce music from its twanging strings. Alas, Mother paid many hard earned shillings to Miss Francis Hicks who made vain attempts to produce harmony from my unwilling fingers. Music has always given me great joy and I cannot understand how, or why I was so stupid, for not one iota of her tuition bore fruit. I couldn't tell a quaver from a crotchet, and my rendering of '*The Robins' Return*' was as painful as Father's '*Humpty Dumpty*' when he was learning to play the cornet. If only I could have learned to play one instrument - even a tin whistle, I would be happy. But it is too late now.

Despite the lack of daylight, small windows and low ceilings, our higgledy-piggledy storage facilities and cockroaches, we were very comfortable within our cob walled cottage.

On two counts we were way ahead and more modern than most cottagers. We had cesspit sanitation and electric light, whereas others had bottom-of the-garden privies and oil lamps. When the new post office building next door was built, provision was made for our cottage to have an outside flushing lavatory. Gone were the days of one, two and three- hole seats; the emptying of over-filled buckets into pits in the garden. We were now provided with a fine lavatory with high level flushing cistern, chain and china pull, connected by a thick lead pipe to a white closet pan covered with a double flap imitation mahogany seat. And no more squares of cut-up newspaper, we now used rolls of soft pink toilet paper!

We all attended the inaugural ceremony with the plumber who demonstrated the flushing system. Later that day, when I put the closet to practical use, I stood in awe after pulling the chain and hearing the torrential roar as the pan emptied. Then came the hiss of the refilling cistern and I stayed listening until the last plops of falling water had ceased.

Father's employer installed a lighting plant to generate electricity for his garage and the post office building on the opposite side of the crossroads. As our cottage was next door and under the same ownership, we also were connected.

Our lighting was basic: Just a pendant with bulb under a white shade in each room which sometimes flickered alarmingly. It was wonderfully bright when the engine was running, but every bulge in the cob walls was accentuated; every flake of loose paintwork glistened; every speck of dust on furniture sent Mother running with a duster; and small holes in matting and curtains seemed twice as large.

We kept our discarded oil lamps in case of electrical failure, which happened several times during the winter months when too many lights were switched on at the same time which overloaded the system. Electricity was a delightful novelty and I never tired of turning the large bell-shaped switches on and off. Our cottage was the third property in the parish to have electric light, and it was several years before the Cornwall Electric Power Company brought supplies to the parish.

This is the cottage at Shop where Jack lived, it was previously the Old Post Office

21

Wireless with Witchard

THE VILLAGE PATRIARCH

Richard Parkyn

One evening in July 1927 I was reading in my bedroom and, hearing movement, I looked out of the window and saw Willy Quint the electrician climb to the top of a large elm tree in the back garden of the Farmers Arms. Willy held a roll of copper wire with two small white egg-shaped objects threaded to one end, which in turn was attached to a thin rope and tied to the topmost branch. He climbed down, crossed the garden, fixed a ladder against the wall of the unoccupied cottage which was part of the pub property and, still holding the end of the wire, proceeded to climb the ladder.

I leaned precariously out of my window, craned my neck until I could just see Willy who had now reached the top of the ladder and was climbing up the roof slope. Grunting with exertion and muttering to himself I heard him say, "Ahh! Got it first time!"

Willy did not move for several minutes, then I noticed that the wire was now horizontal, taut, and some twenty feet from the ground. What was its purpose? Surely not a clothes line?

Suddenly the coil of wire, now much smaller, dropped over the eaves, and I saw that Willy had attached the horizontal wire to the chimney with rope as he had done to the elm branch. Then I heard a shout, a loud bumping noise, and Willy sailed over the eaves pulling down a length of guttering and toppling the ladder. Horrified, I saw him collapse like a discarded spread-eagled puppet onto the ground; his hands twitched, reached out, and began to massage parts of his body grazed by his fall.

"Mr Quint, are you hurt?" I shouted.

Willy stood up, shook himself, disentangled the ladder from the wire-netting chicken run and said, "Bleddy 'ell, I could 'ave broke me neck; me arse is some sore, and old Dick'll make me pay for the gutter to be put back."

I drew away from the window so that Willy couldn't hear me laughing, and heard him place the ladder against the wall again. On the ground lay an assortment of carpenter's tools and, taking the brace and bit Willy mounted the ladder and bored two holes in the window frame, one at the top and one at the bottom. Through each hole he pushed a short length of black tube, and into the top tube some of the wire which he cut from the still dangling coil. Willy then descended slowly, gathered his tools together, shouldered his ladder and departed. I was completely baffled. What on earth was the purpose of this exercise?

About ten minutes later I heard sounds coming from within the linhay roof of the cottage and craning from my window, I saw another piece of wire come snaking through the lower tube. Willy reappeared carrying a piece of iron bar which he hammered into the ground below the window and secured the end of the wire to the bar. He then filled a bucket from the water butt, poured it over the bar, and muttered, "That'll make 'im go!" and he walked away. I carried on with my reading.

About ten minutes later a crackling noise came from the open linhay window of the cottage, followed by high pitched intermittent wails which rose and fell in the gathering dusk. My hair was ready to stand on end as I looked out and listened fearfully to these uncanny sounds. I thought I heard voices in between the waitings, but decided it was my imagination playing tricks. Then the noises ceased and Willy looked out of the window.

"What's making that noise, Mr Quint?" I asked.

"That's none of your business, sonny," he replied, and promptly closed the window. I waited a while but nothing further happened so undressed and finished my reading in bed, intending next morning to tell Father about the strange performance I had witnessed.

I completely forgot to do this and it was several weeks later when the evenings were drawing in that Father said: "Old Dick has got a wireless in the linhay. He listens to it after the pub is shut. But Mary Jane won't listen; she says it is the work of the Devil."

So it was Wireless. I had seen Marconi's great masts near Mullion when I stayed with my Aunt and Uncle at Halligye, and had heard vague references to 'wireless', but had no idea what it was all about. Suddenly I realised that what I had seen and heard that July evening was something to do with wireless, so I told Father the story.

"What you saw was Willy Quint fixing the aerial and earth wires, and the noise was the set oscillating," said Father.

"What's oscillating?" I asked.

"That squealing noise you heard. It comes when you tune in to a station. Anyway, you'll see it all tomorrow night - Old Dick has asked us in at half past seven to hear something special."

Mother and I were thrilled, for apart from the novelty of experiencing wireless for the first time, we were longing to see the interior of the cottage which had been unoccupied for so long.

168

At half past seven on a moonless Saturday night, after a devious, fumbling route through the Farmers Arms garden we stood waiting at the back door of the cottage. Father knocked loudly to announce our arrival. Nothing happened, so he gave the door three huge kicks. We heard a shuffling noise; a bolt being drawn back, and with a creak the door opened slowly outwards pushing aside a stack of empty beer bottles that danced and tinkled as they rolled over.

"Come in Herbert - and you Missus - and you Boy!" growled a voice, and Richard, holding a guttering candle, stood there with a grease-encrusted cap on his bald head, a woollen muffler around his neck and a dirty, striped shirt showing beneath his crumpled beer-stained jacket. His trousers were greasy and his heavy boots were unlaced.

Father winked at us as Richard stepped aside for us to enter. "Go straight upstairs," he said as he shuffled to bolt the door behind us.

The little vestibule was in darkness as we fumbled our way behind Father up the narrow, straight flight of stairs. Cobwebs brushed my face and dust from the handrail clung to my fingers. Mother whispered, "I don't like this one little bit."

I counted thirteen steps up and then I was standing in the linhay room which was bathed in weak yellow light from two hurricane lamps hanging from the purlin. The open rafters were festooned with ancient cobwebs, and one spider was still spinning furiously.

A tattered strip of coconut matting lay on the unevenly boarded floor from the head of the stairs to the far end of the room where it ended against a tea chest.

Upon the chest stood a strange object something like an open wooden box with two large black dials on its front. From within protruded a mass of wires which seemed to be connected to two large silvery electric light bulbs and two small tightly wound coils of wire. Other wires trailed down to the floor into a large car battery and beside it other wires connected into another oblong box from which sprouted a number of red and black plugs. Four pairs of what I assumed to be ear muffs were each connected by a leather band and more wires to the main contraption. Also on the tea chest stood a large black horn ending with a stem and pedestal.

The two wires which Willy Quint had pushed through the top and bottom of the window trailed across the floor, up the side of the tea chest and into the wireless.

A decrepit Windsor arm chair rested beside the tea chest and a tall fire-screen lurched at an angle between it and the first of three rickety kitchen chairs placed in a semi-circle facing the wireless. There was no other furniture in the room, old newspapers and rags were stuffed into the junction of the eaves with the floor to keep out draughts; a cheerless setting for an evening's entertainment.

Richard hobbled to the Windsor chair, sat down heavily, blew out the candle and waved us to sit down. I sat by the fire-screen and my parents sat with their feet on the matting.

"Are you comfortable then?" asked the old man.

"Yes, Cap'n," nodded Father. "Now, tell us all about it."

"This here is the Wireless," indicating the box of wires with his walking stick, "and the two batteries that work it are on the floor. Willy Quint made it up. Smart man, Willy."

Richard leaned over the instrument, turned a knob on the side and the two bulbs lit up. "They're the valves, and these are the coils." He pointed to the wire-covered articles, one standing upright, the other connected to it at right angles by a short metal rod with a knob on the end. "When I move one coil closer to the other, I make the sound louder, and when I turn it back it goes softer."

Pointing to the horn, Richard said: "That's the loud speaker. Willy tried it out, but the set's only got two valves and it isn't powerful enough to work it for very long. He's going to put in another valve soon, but tonight we've got to use the headphones."

Richard picked up two ear muffs and put them with their connecting band over his head.

"Put on your headphones like this, and make sure they're over your ears, and you're comfortable," he said, "and don't get up or you'll drag everything over. You understand Boy?" he said fiercely, frowning at me.

I nodded, and draped the things over my head and adjusted them to suit my ears. There wasn't much spare wire between me and the wireless, and I was afraid to jerk my head back. Father and Mother looked daft, I thought, sitting there with wires coming out from their heads.

"I'm going to tune in now", said Richard, and started moving the coils together.

My ears were filled with the same wailing noise I'd heard on the evening Willy Quint was in the linhay. He must have been trying out that loud speaker thing. Richard moved the coils apart, then together and the noise in my ears was like the sound of distant fighting cats. Father sat impassive; Mother's mouth gaped wide open and stayed that way. Richard grunted and continued fiddling with coils and dials. Suddenly - silence, a faint hissing then, miracle of miracles my ears were flooded with piano music.

"Tis tuned in now," said Richard, and sat back in his chair. A man's voice said –"This is 2LO calling," and went on to describe the forthcoming programme.

Several years later, when wireless was no longer a novelty, and we also owned a set, I discovered that what we heard on that memorable evening was the first of a series of broadcasts called Diversions - outside broadcasts which later evolved into the popular series 'In Town Tonight'.

170

That evening my ears were opened to a new world of sound: I sailed down the river Thames in a police launch - heard water lapping against the bows - the hooting of passing ships and voices of police and sailors. Then came a babble of foreign voices as the scene switched to Soho, London's Chinatown, over which was superimposed the voice of the commentator. The broadcast ended with a visit to the Tower of London for The Ceremony of The Keys. I sat riveted by the sound of footsteps echoing through ancient passages, and the challenging voice, "Who goes there?" "The keys! Whose keys?" "The King's keys" "Pass the King's keys!" Never had I experienced such entertainment.

The programme continued. The chimes of Big Ben thundered through my ears. Mother appeared to be in a trance. Another voice read a news bulletin of events, none of which I understood. Father shifted uneasily on his chair. Old Richard's chin was sunk on his chest and his eyes were closed.

The seat of my chair got harder and harder; my buttocks felt numb. Time passed...an orchestra played...

Idly I stroked the side of the fire screen and let my right hand creep behind the back of its tattered facade. I touched something large and round and made of china. Violins chirruped and flutes warbled in my ears as my fingers continued their exploration around the rim of the article. Fascinated, I leaned slightly sideways and lowered my hand inside - into something liquid, lukewarm and sticky. I fell backwards; my headphones came off with a jerk which made the wireless dance on the tea chest. The fire screen toppled forward. Mother screamed. Father stood up and the wire from his headphones pulled taut and almost dragged down the wireless. Richard sat up and blinked. The fire screen hit the floor, revealing and knocking over a disgusting, once-white brimming chamber pot whose contents enveloped the matting. Father laughed as though he would never stop. Mother lifted her feet and froze. Richard roared: "That boy of yours is a meddler! You can't trust the young ones anywhere!" He gave me a withering look. Involuntarily I brushed my dripping hand across my nose and almost vomited. I had forgotten to bring a handkerchief so had to wipe my fingers on my trouser leg.

Father said sharply, "Jack! You apologise to Mr Parkyn for being so clumsy," then to Richard, "I think he got a bit sore with sitting so long."

"Sorry, Mr Parkyn," I said, "my elbow got in the way." "Ummmh. It did, did it?" I could see he didn't believe me.

"It's getting late, and time we went," said Father. "That wireless is wonderful. Thank you Richard for letting us hear it." He put the fire screen back in position and took up the chamber pot. "I'll empty this on the way out."

Mother said, "I'll come in tomorrow morning and wash up the floor, Mr Parkyn."

"Don't bother about that, Missus, It'll be dry by morning," said Richard and, lighting his candle, hobbled down the stairs, unbolted the door and let us out into the night.

Father tossed away the remaining contents of the chamber pot and placed it by the door which Richard had already bolted, and we heard him plodding up the stairs again to his wireless.

Mary Jane, a wizened, black silhouette was standing in the back doorway of the now empty pub as we passed by. "Good night, Mrs Parkyn," we said.

"Where's Witchard? He should have been here to call 'Time'. It's not a woman's job! That old wireless is evil," and before Father could say a word, she slammed the door.

"Dad, why do they call it Wireless?" I asked when we were having supper that night. "I've never seen so many wires together before? They ought to call it Wiremore."

"I don't know. Jack, but I'll ask Willy Quint when I see him. And by the way - I hope you washed your hands before you sat down."

Richard Parkyn having a good old scratch.

22

Summer Meadow

I missed my visits to the valley when we moved up to the centre of the village, but a few weeks later I found a substitute - a meadow, only a stones throw from our new home. At weekends, or whenever the opportunity arose, I slipped away from the noise of the crossroads into its welcoming embrace and, as my visits were only seasonal, from June until early September, I named this haven my Summer Meadow.

Sometimes I took with me my weekly *'Boy's Magazine'* and, lying down in the tall, nodding grass, I would read adventure stories for a while, then, putting the book aside, I would watch billowing cloud armadas sailing slowly overhead until they passed from view below the metallic blue sky. Then after reading a few more pages, the magazine would slip from my fingers as I closed my eyes to the warmth of the sun and felt completely at peace with the world.

Here I heard sounds which I thought I would never hear again when I left the valley as I turned face down with limbs outstretched, my heart beating slowly as I listened to the flitter of butterfly wings as a Meadow Brown landed on a flower; the plop as a beetle as it landed on a dock leaf; the zzzzzing of a horse fly above my head, and a murmur of breeze through the few scarlet poppy heads.

As the sun poured down its warmth, I floated in and out of a dreamy oblivion. Once I awoke to the sounds of a cricket orchestra, I saw three little insects, only a few inches away from my face, playing a frenzied pastorale with the vibrating triangles of their saw-edged legs. I dared not blink, move or sneeze, as they played in harmony with the cello mumblings of a bumble bee which was seeking nectar from a clump of purple vetches who were dreaming the afternoon away. Mauve scabious heads nodded at each other in intimate conversation, their hairy stems standing translucent in the sun.

When my reading, daydreaming, and nature watching ended, I walked, if time permitted, around the four encircling hedges where honeysuckle poured out nectar-sweet scent which merged with the muskiness of meadowsweet. From the ditch, edged with loosestrife. Red Admiral and Peacock butterflies gorged themselves from the purple flower heads. As I moved, my shadow touched their wings, and they flew aloft like scraps of coloured paper, hovered for a moment, then fluttered down to feed again A small patch of self-sown oat and barley stalks, probably transported as seeds from the droppings of passing birds, grew in the western corner of the meadow. As they ripened the oat heads shivered in the breeze, and the barley swung in thin, undulating, golden waves.

A crumbling five-bar gate led to the roadway. It remained unopened for many years, and its woodwork was rotten and crusted with lichen; the bottom hinge was hung loose, and the gate leaned inwards to the meadow. If I pushed, I knew it would fall apart, so I had to bend down and clamber through the lower bars into the road, leaving my dreams and reveries behind me.

Each Christmas I made a single foray across the meadow, now shorn of all its seasonal beauty, where only sodden, grass, a few stumps of ragwort and brown stalks of dock rattled in the wind. I always headed for the centre of the western hedge to a large ivy bush which was always laden with clusters of berries hanging from glossy-leaved branches. As I tore them off, hibernating bluebottle flies angered at the disturbance, buzzed around my head and vanished in the winter gloom. With my arms full of greenery for decorating our cottage, I managed to negotiate the awkward gate and went home with sodden feet and legs.

I flecked the leaves and berries with silver paint, and on Christmas Eve morning. Mother and I mixed them with holly and paper-decorations and strung them around pictures, across the mantelpiece and the curtain poles where they remained until we took them down and burned them on Old Christmas Day.

As I grew older, my summertime visits to the meadow were less frequent; gradually consigned to the background for other attractions, and finally forgotten. At Christmas there were cleaner, manmade, artificial decorations, so I no longer plodded across wet grass to gather branches of ivy.

Many changes occurred as the village expanded during the next fifty years, but somehow the meadow remained intact and held its secrets. On a summer afternoon, ten years ago, I felt a sudden urge to walk in it again as I viewed it from my lounge window, and as with the valley I tried to recreate the atmosphere I experienced during my teenage years.

My Summer Meadow was much smaller; some of the flowers were there; loosestrife, vetch, and honeysuckle, but no meadowsweet, scabious or poppies, and the grass was only knee high.

I looked cautiously around to see if anyone was watching, and self-consciously, I lay on my back in the grass. Clouds floated overhead, but they weren't armadas - just shapeless straggles of vapour. The air vibrated with the roar of a Shackleton aircraft, tourist voices and the slamming of car doors. The ancient gate had vanished for that section of the meadow had been converted into a car park, and electric cables with transformers clinging to their poles, straddled two hedges. Three years later, an abortive attempt was made during the spring to turn the meadow into an instant allotment, by quickly ploughing it with a Rotivator and immediately planting seeds. Potatoes and beans sprouted in regimented rows; carrots, lettuce and potatoes appeared where once vetch and scabious had bloomed.

Nature quickly retaliated; ragwort, yarrow and sow-thistle sprouted and enveloped the whole of the attempted horticulture. The lettuces grew into spiked seed heads, vetches tangled with the beans, and the potatoes were never dug. The enthusiastic gardener gave up, having learned the hard way that an unbroken meadow needed careful clearance, preparation and fertilizing before a single vegetable seed could be sown. Many of the original wild flowers reappeared, but springtime cowslips and stars of Bethlehem were absent.

Another inroad followed when a Public Convenience was erected on the roadside boundary and the car park was again extended. When I returned from an autumn holiday in that same year, I found that every bush had vanished from the inner sides of the hedges; only hawthorn and blackthorn bushes on the roadside hedge remained. The elder and ivy bushes which had graced the western hedge, and a great heap of brambles, were piled high in the centre of the meadow where they were left to dry, to be consumed a few weeks later in a huge bonfire. The exposed faces of the stone hedges revealed beautiful herringbone stonework constructed by long dead craftsmen, and soon shoots of fern, previously stifled by overgrowth, began to sprout. I watched this change; disliked the barrenness, and hoped that the ejected, resident birds would find new roosts and nesting sites.

However, the new tenant of the meadow was competent, and during the winter and early spring, he ploughed, harrowed, rolled and spread fertilizer over the whole area.

Each day he arrived with one, or two of his three sons, and they worked with enthusiasm. Rows of vegetables were soon planted and, in contrast with the unlucky predecessor, no weeds grew, their vegetables flourished, and this mini market-garden was a pleasure to behold. We were never short of vegetables and merely shouted our requirements over the hedge and they were promptly uprooted and delivered. One of the boys owned prize bantams and installed them in a small house and run near the northern corner of the meadow, where once, long ago, I listened to the voice of the corncrake, I now heard the shrill crowing of bantams at five o'clock in the morning.

After three years, another change took place when the boys grew up and left home. Their father found it was too difficult to carry on alone, so he sub-let the meadow to a friend who cultivated it in a similar manner, except that after two years he filled the entire area with a potato crop, followed by a season of rape. The massed yellow flower heads delighted me, and I took many photographs. After the flowers had died, a small flock of sheep (the first animals to set foot in the meadow for at least sixty years) arrived to eat the green leaves, and remained there for several weeks.

The owners of the meadow then greatly enlarged their public house and found it necessary to once again increase the size of the car park. An even greater area was removed, and a high Cornish hedge was built along the entire length of the southern boundary, with no gateway for access, and so, and without this, the sub-tenancy of the meadow ended.

The following year a further crop of self sown rape appeared, much thinner of course, and with no sheep to eat it, a few flowers were still visible on Christmas Day.

That was not the end. Nature again moved in and produced a fine crop of grass, stimulated no doubt by fertilizer remaining in the soil. Brambles flourished in the ditches, hawthorn and blackthorn bushes again sprouted on he existing hedges, and the new stone hedge began to mature.

Last year, the transformation - or reversion - was complete. The assorted grasses grew to almost two feet in height, several clumps of purple vetch appeared together with yarrow, hawkweed, docks, buttercups, centuary, deary, purple loosestrife and ragwort.

This year, the prospects are even better and the old Summer Meadow of my youth is back on course again, less than half its original size, its magic diminished, and many of the original wild flowers are, so far, missing, but they are offset by the arrival of several new species. As there is no gateway, nobody enters the meadow, except me - for I can jump over the hedge, negotiate the ditch and its brambles, and lie in those tall waving grasses. During a lull in the passing traffic, I have heard a skylark trilling, and a cricket has jumped on my outstretched leg, but although I lay still in anticipation, he didn't bring his friends to chirp another Pastorale for my pleasure. Perhaps he is waiting for me to reach my second childhood.

The Grindley Family in the Harlyn Road Meadow.

23

A Vicious Vendetta

Richard Parkyn sitting on the wall of the Farmers Arms talking to Mr Geach, Mary Norris, Jack's Aunt, leaning in the doorway. Photo secretly snapped by Alex Old.

One morning after helping Dick move some beer barrels at the Farmers Arms, Father came in grinning like a Cheshire cat. "Dick is jumping mad! He's just opened an envelope with a photo of himself, and some rude verses inside," laughed Father. Dick said: "Tis that old devil across the road. I'll get even with him. You wait and see!"

Dick was referring to his neighbour and arch-enemy, Alex, the photographer, who lived in the ruinous, ivy-shrouded cottage opposite. Alongside was Alex' studio, a ramshackle mixture of wooden sheds with rusted iron roofs.

Alex had a spy-hole in the wall facing Dick's cottage doorway where he sat when the pub was closed. A large knot pushed out at eye level height, made an ideal viewing point for watching Dick's activities. By squinting through the hole, Alex watched Dick talking to passers-by, and manoeuvred his tripod and camera into position with lens aligned to the knot-hole. With his head under the black camera hood he watched, and at the appropriate moment, secured another interesting picture for circulation.

Alex was tall and thin; wispy grey hair straggled untidily beneath his crumbled trilby hat, and his dreamy grey eyes always seemed to be focussed on some distant object as he composed another photographic masterpiece. From his slightly pursed lips came sibilant whistles, interspersed with softly spoken long drawn out, "Poo-poo-poo-poo-poo's." He never heard one note of his impromptu compositions for, like Beethoven, he was stone deaf.

In dress Alex was, in some respects as untidy as Dick, his neighbour. His jacket, waistcoat and trousers hung from his sparse frame like a scarecrow's outfit, and were spotted with, and smelled of photographic chemicals. When he

Richard Parkyn with Gladys & Joy Brewer, Mary Norris and 'Jack'.

went out he invariably wore a shapeless light-brown mackintosh which flapped around his legs.

Despite his eccentric appearance, Alex possessed a shrewd, artistic brain; his landscapes, seascapes, and portraits won nationwide acclaim and appeared regularly in the press, guide-books and on postcards. In his declining years as Dick became more slovenly and unkempt, he would unconsciously scratch himself as he sat outside his door. Alex, watching through his knot-hole, photographed his victim when the scratching reached its climax, and later, when no-one was about, pushed the newly-taken photograph under Dick's front door. Sometimes Alex passed copies to his friends, knowing full well that one would end up in Dick's hands.

Dick invariably reciprocated by spreading half-truths and tittle-tattle regarding his enemy's affairs and libidinous activities. One involvement in his younger days with an apparently virtuous young lady found him clambering out of her bedroom window minus his trousers as her suspicious father, hearing noises above, mounted the stairs. As her seducer fled onto the road, he was seen by startled villagers, so to avoid them, he clambered over hedges into the fields, arriving home badly scratched. In the ensuing uproar both parties lost their jobs and effigies of the adulterers were burned on the village green. Many years later, Gran, related to me with great relish, her version of this rare spectacle.

Another lady whose brother was said to be surgeon to Queen Victoria, supposedly owed Alex a debt. After getting her tipsy, she posed for him, and the result was the famous Cornish Beauty photograph which became a best-seller. Another picture, taken with her large dog, is not so well known.

An extract from one of Alexander's poems to Dick reads;

> I've lived ninety years at the old Farmers Arms
> With my quaint little good-tempered wife,
> So with Mary Jane's cheer and a drop of our beer
> I jog along easy through life.
> So here's good health to St Merryn,
> I hope you will have a good time,
> And when you're at Shop try a glass of Dick's pop
> And you'll over all obstacles climb.

Alex was quick to celebrate any new event in the parish, and when a new garage was built on the crossroads he produced a poem of four six-line stanzas, with chorus. The owner was, of course, lampooned:

> Not far from our Dick's pub
> Our brand new garage stands
> Behind a row of petrol pumps
> With all the favourite brands,
> While I with oily talk and smiles
> Take money with each hand.

Chorus:
> For now I've started business on my own accord
> I'll soon scat Morris Cowley and Mr Henry Ford.
> And each week-day and Sundays too
> Your empty tanks I'll fill
> Or blow your tyres, or lend the pump,
> But all the same you'll later find
> 'Tis all down on the bill

After living in the village for a year, I made friends with Alex, and he allowed me into the mysterious interior of his domain. One room was filled with old bicycles propped against the walls, and others hung from the ceiling over a bench littered with spare parts and tools, for he loved tinkering with, and rebuilding old machines.

Another room had shelves stacked with books and magazines. He gave me copies of *'Popular Science'* sent to him by friends in America, and I found them interesting and easy to read; I also received copies of *'Amateur Photographer'* which sparked off my lifelong interest in photography. But there were magazines which I wasn't supposed to look at magazines which contained pictures of scantily dressed female film stars, which he quickly took from me saying, "What do you think of that lot, Ingrey? - What if we had a few of them here? Too young though, aren't you, eh?"

Once when his back was turned, I flipped through the pages of what I thought was a photographic magazine, and was amazed to find page after page of naked men and

Arthur May stands proudly in Alex Olds photographic studio at Shop. Arthur is Malcolm's Great Grandfather.

women with their bodies entwined. I knew what they were doing, and my excitement mounted. Then I heard him returning, and I put the book back but, on future visits, managed to have more surreptitious glimpses of this erotica which resulted in colourful dreams with embarrassing results when I awoke. Painted backdrops depicting balustrades, steps and foliage hung from the walls of the sheds, with two or three different styles of chairs placed in front of them, which gave his clients a choice of background for their portraits. A large bellows camera stood on a wooden tripod with lens pointing towards the backdrops, and on the wooden wall I saw the peephole from which so many clandestine pictures had been taken.

One afternoon Alex allowed me to watch him develop some glass plates. We entered the darkroom next to the studio and he locked the door. A red light shone over a narrow table on which stood three shallow dishes, each of which contained a clear liquid. There wasn't much room - our W.C. was far bigger, and I was already feeling claustrophobic. I didn't ask questions because he couldn't hear me anyway; but when he spoke it was in mono-syllables.

He took three glass plates from their casings.

"Developer...," pointing to the first dish.

"Three minutes...," as he consulted his pocket watch and eased the plates into the liquid.

"Agitate...," and he gently rocked the dish causing the liquid to ripple over the plates.

He pointed, and jogged me with his elbow. "Look...!" Faint faces appeared, and rapidly became clearer as he continued to rock the dish and consult his watch.

"Time's up!" He drew a plate from the dish with a pair of tongs and held it up to the red light. I saw a face, but it seemed to be inside out. Alex saw my puzzled expression.

"A Negative....," and he elbowed me aside and dropped all three plates into the second dish.

"Hypo...fixing...," the rocking motion continued and the smell of the liquid seemed stronger as he moved the dish. I felt very uncomfortable in the confined space, and hoped I wouldn't be sick. He looked at his watch, nodded, and plunged all three plates into the third dish. "Washing... takes longer...."

At last he unlocked the door, and I was out in a instant gulping down fresh air.

Meanwhile, he removed the three plates from the fixing dish and placed them carefully in an old earthenware sink outside, under a slowly dripping tap. Rubbing his chemical-stained hands together, he said, "Washing ...running water... half an hour..." I was glad the operation was not completed in his darkroom.

180

That was my first lesson in practical photography, but I did not pursue developing and printing; I decided it was too smelly and messy. Instead, I concentrated on taking better pictures with the Box Brownie camera given to me on my previous birthday, the local chemist processed my efforts, for I hadn't the nerve to ask Alex to do it, or see my results.

In front of Alex' cottage was a small courtyard enclosed by a low wall on which he sometimes sat with one hand cupped to his ear - listening. One evening, when riding my bicycle - a mongrel vehicle which, like Mother's first machine, was assembled from bits and pieces of discarded machines - Alex was talking with some cronies as I approached. Suddenly a loud grating noise came from the back wheel and I teetered to a halt. Despite his deafness he heard the noise, came to my aid, hoisted the bicycle over the wall, examined the wheel and passed judgement.

"Pooh-pooh-pooh-pooh-pooh! What a calamity!" he informed his audience, "Young Ingrey's been riding around the parish with his balls out!"

I blushed and, involuntarily looked down at my flies. They were intact. A roar of laughter erupted.

"They're not," I shouted.

"It's yer ball bearings wot's come out. Don't be so ignorant," said big Bill Hicks. "Sit here a minute; while he's looking at your wheel."

Alex carried my bike into his cottage. I sat on the wall and waited anxiously. Ten minutes later he wheeled it out and, lifting the back wheel off ground, he spun it and it revolved without a sound. "There you are, Ingrey - new balls."

"Please, Mr Old, how much do I owe you?" I asked. But he never heard, and was already deep in conversation; so I took my bike from him and rode away. Alex loved to play his banjo and often stood gazing through the cobweb-hung window as he plucked at the strings. After school was over, me and my mates sat on the wall listening with rapt attention to the non-stop, plinka-plonka, plinka-plonka recital. Sometimes he was joined by his friend Mr Pedlar, who played violin and piano accompaniments to silent films at the Cinedrome. These elderly men made a wonderful sound, oblivious of the ever-increasing audience outside.

Mr Pedlar also wrote poetry, and I recall a fragment dedicated to his musical friend:

> He's very find of music,
> In that we are akin,
> He plays the banjo beautifully
> With me the violin.
> I hope to have a run with him
> In his two-seater car,
> No matter where the journey is
> 'Twould never be too far.

Jenny Hicks wearing her finest hat for her portrait to be taken on the same day as her prospective husband Arthur May.

Many times I watched Alex embark on photographic expeditions in that ancient three-wheeler *Morgan* car. Clad in his shapeless mackintosh, with his black trilby hat pushed back from his forehead, he carefully placed his large bellows camera, box of glass plates, and wooden tripod on the spare seat. After several turns of the starting handle the engine juddered into life and, easing himself into the narrow confines of the vehicle, away he sped, leaving behind him a choking cloud of exhaust fumes.

One spring Saturday afternoon I was a privileged passenger, irritating though it was at being jammed in with his equipment. The chatter of the engine and the scented air was exhilarating as, with the canvas hood turned back, we drove slowly through lanes billowing with white May-blossom and cow parsley. Alex was a safe driver, but he always kept to the centre of the road and no following vehicle could overtake him. No honking horn or grating klaxon penetrated his silent world, and the absence of wing mirrors completed his isolation from an often increasing and angry entourage.

Today, however, we had only one follower - Reg Strongman going home from work on his motor bike. Try as he would, he had no hope of passing. He gave long blasts on his horn; he shouted and hooted; and shouted again: "Get over you silly old bugger. You're a menace on the roads!" I turned around. Reg saw me, "Tell him Jack! Tell him to pull over!" he pleaded. As I was a privileged passenger, I declined to disturb my host, and poor Reg, who worked with Father in the garage, sat fuming on his two stroke *Royal Enfield* until we passed through St Ervan.

Our first stop was at St Mawgan-in-Pydar, where I helped Alex set up his camera in the churchyard. I started asking questions; he never heard me but carried on his mono-syllabic narration as he had done in the darkroom. Then he beckoned me to put my head under the black-draped hood On the ground-glass screen I saw a picture of the church, but it was upside down. I never knew why for many months, and really wasn't very interested.

We stopped at Mawgan Porth and Bedruthan to take more photographs. I enjoyed my outing even though the conversation was one sided, but I think Alex enjoyed my company and assistance, so I told my parents he wasn't half as bad as old Dick had painted him.

But Reg Strongman had the last word. On the following Monday morning, he said to Father, "That boy of yours - is he deaf? If he isn't, he's just as bloody stupid as old Alex!"

Shop Crossroads, a photo taken by Alex Old. In the foreground is a pond the site of the present day garage, ahead is an ivy clad cottage, this is where Alex Old lived, his studio being at the rear and facing the Farmers Arms opposite where Richard Parkyn spent his days leaning on the pub wall. Jack's cottage is the crossroads side of the pub on the extreme right hand side of the picture.

Miss Alchin, the 'Cornish beauty' taken by Alex Old

Miss Alchin and her dog

24

Frolics at the 'Farmers Arms'

"Jack, you can bring in the parcels while I unload the coal," said Father one Saturday morning as he stopped his lorry outside The Farmers Arms.

Being free from school, I often rode with him on his Saturday round to and from Padstow, where he collected goods for distribution around the parish. My knowledge of the geography of the interior of the pub came after I dropped several packages of cigarettes and tobacco in the Bar. Then, as no one was looking, I tiptoed quietly into each of the five rooms which radiated from the passage, all of which reeked of stale beer and tobacco smoke.

The Bar contained an area dubbed by the locals as number Ten Downing Street, where discussions and heated arguments of rural, and political topics were generated, chewed over and finally buried when closing time arrived.

Behind the Bar was the Tap Room where beer barrels stood on wooden stocks, together with a clutter of smaller cider casks and crates of bottle beers.

To the left of the massive front entrance door was a larger room, rarely used except by the occasional visitor, and on Feast days and Xmas if the bar was overcrowded. Shutters, usually closed, blotted light from the small window under which stood an uncomfortable chapel pew, and against the opposite wall a large, high wooden settle was fixed. In the centre of the room two grubby, varnished tables stood uncertainly on the uneven floor which rarely saw broom or water. When the back door was open, chicken wandered inside, perched on chairs and fouled the floors.

During another morning delivery I saw something glinting in a heap of droppings in a corner of this room and, bending down, I plucked out a silver half-crown. Thus encouraged, I inspected every patch of dropping on future visits and gleaned many a coin from the excreta; my dishonesty, I am ashamed to say, was never discovered and punished.

An ugly tiled fireplace with chocolate-brown mantelpiece stood at the far end of this uninviting room. Beneath the hearthstone was a deep well which was occasionally pumped out when the water became polluted by dead rats...

A small, square back room whose only furniture was a few rickety kitchen chairs and a rickety baize-covered card table, was used occasionally by those customers who played cards or dominoes and for meetings of the parish Pig Club.

The Stock Room was stacked with cartons of cigarettes. pipe tobacco, and coils of twist tobacco which was both smoked and chewed.

The back door opened onto a vegetable garden, chicken run, crude Gent's urinal and cruder earth closet. The Farmers Arms originated as a Beer House under the 1830 Beer Act, and remained as such until the 1930s when a wine licence was granted, it was not until several years later that it became fully licensed for the sale of all intoxicating liquors

The landlord - Old Dick as he was dubbed locally, was a mason by trade. He built several houses in the parish which have stood the test of time but, like many others of that period, were built with mortar containing sea sand which, over the years produced vast patches of efflorescence on their internal walls, to the perpetual annoyance of their owners.

Old Dick's wife, Mary-Jane acted as landlady during daytime opening hours until he retired from his trade. Dick was tall, broad shouldered, and heavily built. He wore a cap which glistened with grease and dirt, and his clothing was equally soiled. He wore a muffler around his neck even in summer, and his down-at-heel unlaced boots gave him a shuffling walk.

Every drop of beer was drawn from the Tap Room to which Dick made endless journeys with a pint pot in each hand for the seated customers in Number Ten. Years later, after the death of Mary-Jane, Dick, now crippled with rheumatism, propelled himself with a walking stick, and his journeys doubled for now he could carry only one pint pot.

Mary-Jane was a small woman with piercing sloe-black eyes, her hair drawn back tightly into a bun on top of her head. Her face was often dirty, and the furrows which lined her brow were often ingrained with dirt - "grafted" was the Cornish word for her condition. She reminded me of a wrinkled chimpanzee. Mary-Jane wore a black blouse with leg o'mutton sleeves; a black skirt, lace-up black boots, and stockings which showed holes above her ankles. She addressed her spouse as 'Wichard'. "Wichard, you put a shovel of coal in the fire. Wichard - You do this...Wichard - you do that..." And Wichard always did as he was told.

Our cottage, being next door to The Farmers Arms, was an ideal place for both watching and listening to the varied activities next door when I sat in my bedroom window. Sometimes there was singing; on occasions swearing, and the exchange of blows in the back garden; in the darkness of winter nights, unsteady feet stumbled over our front door step after closing time.

When I was eighteen years of age, I entered The Farmers Arms as a customer, much to Grandmother's disgust. "The old beer won't do you any good! It breaks up families and brings rags to your backside!" she remarked, shaking her head when she learned of my visits which stirred memories of drunkenness we witnessed at Rose Cottage.

Saturday being pay-day, when men had money in their pockets, made The Farmers Arms a focal point in the evening for young and old alike. There in the smoke-filled, oil lamp atmosphere, oblivious of the dirt on walls and floors, they found crude comfort and companionship. Tongues loosened as the beer flowed; voices became louder and songs rang out. Sometimes a slurred solo was drowned in a beery tide of bass and tenor voices as other singers joined in. Being young and impressionable, I listened with ears cocked, and watched, as they unfolded hilarious tales.

The older men were a special breed and, as one by one, they died as the years passed, so died an era. Every pub had one distinctive character who sat in his self-appointed seat, and woe betide an unsuspecting stranger who usurped him. He was the first inside at opening time; usually the last one to leave after closing time; a teller of tales, a singer of songs, a gatherer and purveyor of the latest gossip, and a sponger of the first magnitude. Alas, such colourful personalities have long since vanished together with the grime and the gutting of the interior, to be replaced by younger birds of passage, social security gatherers, immigrants, and only a modicum of genuine locals.

There was Ern, his glass eye slightly askew, glittering in the lamplight; his hawk like face ruddy beneath his tipped-back trilby hat. As the singing increased in volume, Ern's voice also increased and, with elbows poised at right angles, he thumped them against the match boarded partition behind him. Ern's favourite song was:

O my darling Sarah Bell
She's a pretty little gel,
In her hat she wears
A pink and yellow feather.
She's very fond of fish
And pickles in a dish,
And sometimes she likes
A sweet potato...

Sometimes Ern lost both words and key when halfway through his ditty, but he made up for the deficiency by shouting, "Fire the rockets!" and punishing the partition with extra hard thumps.

Ern had the quaint habit of filling the pockets of his immaculate whipcord jacket with hen's eggs before he set out for his evening's entertainment. How they survived the mile and a half walk over hill and vale remains a mystery. At intervals during the evening, Ern took an egg (usually unwashed) from his pocket, cracked it with one hand on the rim of his pint pot, tossed back his head, opened his mouth and swallowed the contents in one gulp. His other hand co-ordinated his pint to mouth level and tipped the beer between his gaping, yoke-dripping lips. As the evening wore on a pile of broken shells crackled under foot.

But Ern's ritual ended abruptly one night when I happened, to be sitting opposite to him in Number Ten. Ern cracked an egg, threw back his head, his good eye focused on the beams. The contents of the egg entered his mouth - no yoke this time, but a well-developed downy chick. I watched, fascinated. For a moment a little yellow leg protruded from a corner of his mouth and, chewing noisily, Ern shouted, "Too late, my little beauty! Too late!" and the chick vanished in a great gulp of beer. A few minutes later Ern got up and went outside. When he returned there were no bulges in his pockets and he was strangely silent. He drank the remainder of his beer, and said, "I'm going to have an early night," and he went home.

That was the last time Ern enhanced his beer. When I asked him, "What did it feel like Ern, when you found you had a chick in your mouth?"

"Ugh! 'Twas all like snot and fluff - and one buggerin' claw scratched me throat on the way down, and I couldn't eat for days."

Ern's brother William, was a bright-eyed little hunchback, a painter by trade whose services were always in demand. He could match his brother in drinking and, when gently coerced would break forth into his favourite song:

"I'm Cocktail Joe, the Dandy O
The Dandy O, the Dando O.
Lightning and thunder
Jinny flip and brandy smash
Clip-clop, monkey-chop
And up she goes
Break a neck, dash a light,
Kee ki korum
Johnny there's none
Like Cocktail Joe-oe-oe-oe,
Johnny there's none like Cocktail Joe."

As he breathed forth the elongated chorus line, his bright eyes bulged, his little simian face turned towards the ceiling, and he reminded me of an Amazonian howler monkey in full cry.

Blind Charlie was another popular figure. Stout in build, moustached, thick lipped, ruddy faced with bulbous nose crowned by a pair of large black-lens spectacles, he sat in Number Ten holding his pint in one hand and his white walking stick in the other. As a young man, he often went shooting. One day his gun went off accidentally and blasted his face. Maimed and bleeding, he crawled around the field until found by a search party. Now, blinded in both eyes, and an empty life before him, he was persuaded to attend a training establishment for the blind.

He returned and earned a living by selling packets of tea, carrying his wares in a black portmanteau slung on a knobbed stick over his shoulders. Now, with sensitive hearing and an alert mind to cope with perpetual darkness, he tramped the lanes and stopped at each house and hamlet where he was welcomed and purchases made. Then he married, and with the help of a devoted wife, they opened a shop opposite the Council School. On many a pitch black night I have walked with Charlie from The Farmers Arms to a relative's bungalow near his house. Unerringly he strode through his self-made night, avoiding traffic and pedestrians, whilst I fumbled and stumbled in the blackness, occasion grasping his coat tails for guidance.

Charlie's favourite song, of which there were several verses, was *'Under the Parlour Stairs'*. He was by no means a good singer, but was word perfect, and the whole company roared heartily with him when he reached the tag line of every verse, "Under the parlour stairrrrs!"

Jack was another colourful character, a road mender who lived in one of a row of small dwellings known as Water Cottages. Jack was an expert at Skittles or Kales as they were known locally, and his drinking capacity was as large as his smile. His end was untimely, for he walked out of the front door of the pub one night into the path of an oncoming vehicle.

Tom and Frank were both small farmers from the hamlet of Towan who enjoyed their pint of beer and quid of tobacco. Two large spittoons stood one on each side of the stove, both men could, from a range of six feet, spit unerringly into the centre of either bowl. Many youngsters missed the target when attempting to emulate the skill of these elders. "You dirty devil! Go and get a floor cloth!" would be their concerted cry to the unfortunate one whose spit fell short. Billy Hicks from Trevear, curly headed, with cap tilted back, pipe dangling from mouth, pint pot resting on his knee, had his appointed chair near the stove. A confirmed bachelor who, it was rumoured sometimes joined his elderly landlady in bed; but it was never proved and Billy remained as inscrutable as the sphinx.

Percy, tall and broad, with a rolling gait who, when a young boy, left home one morning and walked to Mevagissey where he joined a ship and for many years sailed most of the world's seas. He fought in the Boer War, again at Gallipoli, and his tales were wondrous when we could get him to open up.

Harold, silent and expressionless, stood nightly in the passage, quaffing his beer, saying nothing, but observing everything. During his long life, he scarcely ventured beyond the parish boundary and had never ridden in a train. "I've got to be careful, I'm ruptured," was his cry when confronted with anything beyond the ordinary,

Thin-faced knowledgeable Arthur always had an excuse to argue. If it wasn't footpaths or parish rights of way, it was politics, and I delighted in watching him being goaded into verbal fury by acquaintances like Charles and Stan - two plumbers, who knew where he was most vulnerable.

Charles thrived on litigation, and must have been a godsend to the local solicitors.

Stan was also a brilliant mechanic who could take apart an engine and assemble it again with his eyes closed. He studied the occult; introduced me to that subject and lent me strange books, among them Eliphas Levi's *'Transcendental Magic'* and Emanuel Swedenbourg's *'Heaven and its Wonders'* and *'Hell'*, which scared the daylight out of me.

189

There were so many interesting personalities who frequented The Farmers Arms during my formative years, and if they were here today they would enjoy star rating during the tourist season. Guy Fawkes night was always a nightmare for Richard and Mary-Jane, for they suffered an annual bombardment of fireworks by the tearaway youths of the parish. The bar was always crowded on the night and, if one looked closely at the apparel of those assembled, it was obvious that Wellington boots, leggings and heavy coats were being worn as protection against what might happen during the evening.

From half past six onwards, bonfires blazed in back gardens where school children watched parents light carefully hoarded fireworks, bought from pocket-money saved over several previous weeks. When the Guys had been cremated, and the Catherine wheels, rockets and Roman candles had fizzled out, and the bonfires were dying embers, the younger children went home to bed; the teenagers, however, all hastened to the cross-roads to watch, and hopefully participate in the coming fun.

Kales at the Young Mens Green.

By half past eight The Farmers Arms was full of older men and a smattering of youths (including myself) all seemingly well-behaved and idly talking to one another. Yellow lamplight struggled to shine through the thick haze of tobacco smoke generated by the crowd, and the tabletop in Number Ten where I was sitting, was already awash with spilled beer.

I knew what was going on outside, and would later join the gathered crowd in the darkness, but this was the first Guy Fawkes night when I was old enough to be allowed in a licensed premises, and I wanted to experience at first hand the imminent bombardment.

Mary-Jane, her eyes glinting like little black beads, stood behind the counter, her head rocking from side to side like a metronome as she listened to distant explosions. Without warning, a hissing noise suddenly escalated from the front entrance door, a shower of sparks spat through the passage and caused a concerted inward rush by those unfortunates standing in the line of fire. Above the hubbub rose a wild banshee like shriek from Mary-Jane who, with the agility of a cat, jumped up on top of the counter yelling: "Wichard will fire! Wichard will fire!"

Richard had already disappeared from the bar and, in the electrically charged seconds which followed, all eyes were focussed on the massive door. With a thunderous boom the squib exploded, cracked the keyhole of the lock, and filled the bar with acrid grey smoke.

Mary-Jane's screams reached a new high, and from somewhere in the darkness outside I heard the sharp crack of a gun, followed by a cry of anguish. Amid coughing and swearing from the customers, Mary-Jane wriggled down from her perch and hissed: "The police'll catch 'em! They'll all be sent up the line!" referring, of course, to Exeter Gaol.

For a while some sort of normality returned; both front and back doors were opened to allow the smoke to disperse, until Mary-Jane ordered them to be closed again; but the front door had to be bolted as the lock was now damaged.

At the counter, unmoved by the recent activity, two farmers, Sydney, and Leadville, were deep in conversation. Leadville was standing with his feet apart, and his oilskin coat hanging down below his knees. Near him stood Bert, a youngster about my own age, smoking a cigarette and talking to John, his mate. I saw Bert wink, put a hand in his pocket and draw out a slim firework. John produced the largest jumping cracker I had ever seen. Bert then lit his firework from his cigarette, dropped it down on the floor and the touch paper glowed red. Leadville, still talking, stepped back a pace, and at the same moment John lit the cracker.

With a hiss and a swish the squib ignited simultaneously with the cracker which jumped up under Leadville's coat, and he let out a loud cry, punctuated by staccato oaths. Mary-Jane again leaped onto the counter screaming: "Wichard! Come here! Quickly! They're blowing up the house!"

The squib detonated with a violet flash, its concussion dousing the hanging lamp, while the cracker having exploded twice between Leadville's legs, fell to the floor and continued its gyrations. Pints slipped from hands and shattered; dense, choking smoke stifled a chorus of coughs, oaths and laughter in the darkness, and the cracker, on its last jump somehow reached the counter top (it might have been picked up and thrown) and dispensed its final spitting moments among a cluster of unwashed pint pots.

Someone switched on a torch and Leadville was revealed jumping up and down and flapping his coat like a grounded Batman. "I'm damaged! My bollocks are singed! I'm ruined for life!" he shouted, his cries were drowned in a surge of laughter. Ern, as usual thumped the partition and yelled, "Fire the rockets!" Someone in the crowd said, "You're too late Ern, they've just gone off!"

The lamp was again lit, and the ritual of opening the back door and the damaged front door was carried out until the smoke and fumes had dispersed. Leadville went out to examine his personal damage, and was seen standing over a hurricane lamp with his flies open with a look of relief on his face.

The hubbub decreased; no more fireworks were let off and I decided to leave. I pushed my way through the crowd and jumped over the boundary wall into our back garden. My intention was to conceal myself in the recess of our front door where I could watch and listen to the activities of the gang who were baiting old Dick. I knew Father and Mother would be upstairs watching from their bedroom window, but my plan was aborted for, as I landed, an arm reached out and grabbed me by the neck. The next moment I was enveloped under a policeman's cape.

"And where might you be going, my little man?" rumbled my captor. I had fallen foul of Sergeant Crocker.

"I'm going home," I said, "I was only taking a short cut, and you're not supposed to be in our garden."

The cape was lifted and I was released, but my captor was still treading firmly on one of my feet.

"Don't you be saucy to me," he growled.

"Eh? Whose garden did you say?" A torch was produced and shone in my face. I blinked like an owl in an ivy bush

"Well, if it isn't young Ingrey! I thought I'd got a better catch than you. Have you seen any Bennett's or Geaches around? They're mischief-makers and I'm going to get them tonight."

"No Sir, I havn't seen them, and I can't see very much, that squib that went off in..."

"Ah! That would be young Walters. He talks too much. I heard him say he was going to drop one. Now, you go indoors, and if you're wise, you'll keep out of this. And remember you havn't seen me!"

Sergeant Crocker moved his foot and released me. I stumbled through the darkness and grazed my ankle on the pump trough by our back door. I tiptoed through our cottage, to the front door, silently turning. The handle and drawing the door towards me,

Again I was startled. "Shhhh! Don't move Dick has got his gun loaded again," whispered a voice in my ear. It was Arnold Rabey.

"Come across the road and you'll not be seen when we light him up."

I crept across the road with Arnold and joined the huddle of youngsters among the maze of wooden scaffolding which surrounded the ivy-clad cob walls of the old cottage which was under reconstruction. I whispered that I had just seen Sergeant Crocker, who was, no doubt, watching us from across the road.

192

Silence for a moment. Then whispering, chuckling and little creaking noises from high up in the scaffolding. The unexpected hiss of a squib, as it landed smack in the doorway of the Farmers Arms cottage. In the shower of sparks I saw old Dick with shotgun raised to his shoulder. As the squib exploded I heard the intake of his breath as someone up on the scaffolding pinpointed him in the beam of a torch. Dick immediately fired into it, and an anguished howl rent the night, followed by the sound of the torch hitting the ground.

"Oh, my legs – they're bleeding!" moaned a voice, and the victim climbed down. A volley of squibs were lit by the other boys and hurled in the direction of Dick. Someone found the dropped torch and switched it on. The doorway was empty, the squibs were wasted; old Dick had gone.

"And now, my lads, what have you got to say?" Sergeant Crocker had tiptoed across the road and stood before us, his torch pinpointing us one by one.

"Same gang as last year - and the year before - and some new ones. I'll have you all for this. And what are you doing, young Roseveare! Licking your wounds, eh?"

There in the ring of light sat Roderick, his trousers rolled up to his thighs, his knees and calves dripping blood from several wounds.

"Lucky you're wearing a thick coat, eh? You'd have had some in your belly, wouldn't you?"

"The old sod," muttered Roderick, "he fired wheat grains, and they don't half sting. I shall be off work tomorrow."

"You'd better all go home," said Crocker, "and be quick about it. I've had enough of your antics. If I hear one more firework near the pub – that's your lot! And, for your information, a plain clothes policeman has been here all the evening, and he's taken your names. He'll call tomorrow and you'll be summoned to Wadebridge Court."

Sergeant Crocker switched off his torch and departed. We helped Roderick to his feet; his legs looked as though they had been bled by leeches. As he limped off home, he vowed he would get his own back, next year. Youth had had its fun, but this time old Dick was one up.

Next day several of the older lads were visited, questioned and handed summonses. They duly appeared at Wadebridge Petty Sessions and Inspector Norrish brought proceedings against them for letting off fireworks within fifty feet of the highway.

The 'Cornish Guardian' newspaper recorded the Inspector's speech:

"I have received considerable numbers of complaints of young men typical of the defendants letting off fireworks in St Merryn and frightening people there, and I have had to send constables out there in plain clothes in order to catch them. One man was so frightened that he would stand in his passage with a gun for fear that these young men would come along. At The Farmers Arms, the landlord and landlady are in bodily fear of those young men, who seem to make *a mark of them. In one case they put off such an amount of fireworks in the passage of the Inn that the lights in the bar were blown out."*

But I forgot to mention that I had seen sergeant Crocker's bicycle propped against the wall of the blacksmith's shop before I went to into the pub, and I let the air out of both tyres and threw away the valve rubbers. He had a long walk home that night, but he never admitted the fact to anyone - and neither did I - until now.

Jack Andrew of Trevethan Farm, Porthcothan, in his hunt regalia

25

The Week the Wine Came In

A ship was wrecked somewhere in the English Channel, perhaps on the Channel Islands themselves. She was said to be carrying a large consignment of wine for French troops in Algeria. Some weeks later barrels began washing ashore on our North Cornish coast. Word went around that some had been washed in at St Agnes, and some barrels had been seen floating past Newquay heading our way. Then came that memorable day that a barrel was left high and dry on Constantine Bay It was opened when found by the all year round beach combers and pronounced to be *vin rouge*; they said with proper bottling and maturing it would be ideal for festive occasions. Henceforth, curious little groups would huddle in the hollows of the marram grass covered sand dunes and scanned the restless seascape with binoculars and telescopes. Their patience was rewarded, and word spread around the parish that dozens of barrels were floating out to sea like a school of wooden whales. To add piquancy to the situation, a five gallon cask of pure alcohol was found early one morning and instantly removed. That cask lasted many years, and its contents were mixed with essences of various potent cocktails liqueurs, the potency of which I was privileged to sample on several occasions, the last time being in the late fifties.

I was a teenager when this harvest of the sea arrived. I jumped on my bicycle and pedalled away through Towan to Constantine village. The narrow, potholed road swarmed with people, all hastening seawards and carrying bottles and various other containers. At the mouth of the bay I parked my bicycle and observed the animated scene. The beach heaved with people across the wide stretch of sand to Booby's Bay. Dotted at random beyond the receding tide were several huge barrels, each surrounded by a bevy of locals. I decided to go home immediately and return to the scene again with as many bottles as I could muster, otherwise I might be too late. Father was away, and after I had imparted the news to Mother I asked her to give me some assistance.

In our wash-house we kept a store of empty bottles. Some were cobwebby, others contained long dead insects; some the dregs of ancient light ale, lemonade and vinegar. I hauled out my old four-wheeled trolley-butt which gave me much pleasure when I attended Board School, but which had lain neglected when I transferred to County School. It was made from an orange box mounted on an axle, with two large rubber-tyred pram wheels one on each side. From beneath the base, a flat board tightly nailed, protruded towards the front, and at its end - it was about eighteen inches long, - was loosely bolted another board about nine inches long to which was secured two smaller pram wheels.

Attached to this were two short lengths of rope by which I steered this contraption. A small seat fixed across the rear of the box enabled me to sit in comfort, and on level roads I draped my stomach over this, and with legs dangling behind, kicked myself along at considerable speed. Now I was too big to sit in or stretch over it, so it had to be pulled along.

Mother stood by the pump trough and washed out the bottles, these I stacked inside the butt. We gathered about eighteen bottles, all with corks or screw stoppers, and for good measure I added two large sweet bottles, a watering can, and a tin funnel through which I would pour the wine.

My legs moved at a steady trot as I pulled the butt with ropes taut and the vehicle swayed wildly behind me. Like Father, I was quite an athlete, and having not yet taken up smoking, reached the beach in just twenty minutes running time. Not without incident though; for rounding Cottie's Corner in a wide, unscheduled sweep, I failed to see portly Miss Roseveare until too late, and promptly scuppered her amidships with my bottle-rolling out-of-control contraption. She did not know me, but made me apologise, and when she asked me my name I gave her the name of one of my friends at Padstow. By coincidence she knew his mother, and later confronted her regarding the childlike way in which her son ran around St Merryn roads with a box on wheels. I heard him relating this some weeks later when travelling in the train to school, and with great delight told him what I had done. He had his revenge, for I kept my bicycle in a courtyard on Padstow Quay, and next evening found both tyres flat and the valves removed, so I had to walk the two and a half miles back to St Merryn that evening.

At the beach head I took stock of the situation and decided to go to one of the less crowded barrels. People were coming away with all manner of containers. One lady, who shall be nameless, manipulated a chamber pot under the bunghole from which the red nectar was flowing, and then emptied it into a galvanized bath. When the bath was full she gave the pot to her small daughter, who promptly put her head into it and wore it like a hat. Her two sons then took the bath by its handles and meandered away with wine slopping over their legs as they walked. At this stage everyone was patient, and took turns in tipping the barrel, and my funnel was welcomed. I filled several bottles, corked them, and moved on to another barrel from which white wine was flowing. Bill Jonas, who had been painting a house at Treyarnon, abandoned his task and had somehow acquired a leather bottle which the Arabs use when crossing deserts. He had evidently refilled it several times and was performing a sort of hornpipe when I arrived, and in between leaps thrust his head back and squirted wine from the bottle into his wide open mouth. At times he missed and squirted onlookers, and once temporarily halted his cavortings when he squirted himself in the eyes.

I watched the passing parade of bottle-filled sacks; two white enamel milk pans, thermos flasks, kettles, a black iron boiler which normally lurked on top of a Cornish stove, all brought to the light of day and manhandled with their brimming contents. Suddenly there was a commotion; consternation and people started running away, from behind the sand dunes appeared Constable Ede and Customs Officer 'Wiggy' Bennett intent on doing their duty. Wiggy was short in stature and broad of shoulder, with a pink complexion and pinker nose under greying hair surmounted by his braided peaked cap. Armed with brace and bit, and a mallet he proceeded to bore holes in the nearest barrel. "You aren't allowed to carry this stuff away," he yelled. "'Tis the King's property," and jets of wine spouted in glistening arcs and bubbled into the sand. "I've got all your names, so there's no need to run away, and you'll be notified of proceedings in due course." "Notified of what?" queried a small rat-faced woman who had been busy corking up a collection of medicine bottles. "'Tis wreck wine, 'tis come from the sea, and the rocks would have burst the barrels if we didn't open 'em!" she said. "Stealing – that's what it is - stealing from His Majesty's Customs and Excise," replied Wiggy. " I suppose you'll be taking a sip of that before you go to chapel next Sunday." From then on Wiggy and the Law moved from barrel to barrel, knocking in the bungs of two that were as yet unopened. He borrowed an enamel cup and sampled some of the contents, and passed judgement. "Bloody awful muck - French rot-gut, it'll go through you like a dose of salts, and serve you right!" Then moved off to mutilate the remaining barrels.

I came to a barrel of white wine which was not quite empty It tasted better than the red wine, so I emptied away two or three bottles and made a substitution, my butt was now laden with upright corked bottles, the sweet jars and watering can, all of which were full to the brim. I put the ropes across my shoulders and started the trek along the beach, but I had forgotten one important point. A butt containing empty bottles was far different to a butt containing full bottles, and I had not moved more than a few yards before I dragged to a halt. The wheels had sunk deeply into the sand and would not turn. I removed four bottles, and ran up the sand dunes where I scraped a shallow hole and concealed them. From the beach I noted the spot where I had buried them, and marked it by a tall spike of yellow ragwort which grew in the thick fields of marram grass.

I was now able to pull the butt, but made slow progress and by the time I had reached the beach entrance I was sweating like a pig, and sat down to get my breath back. The procession of wine collectors still straggled across, the beach, and. I was surprised to see the number of tea-tomalleys present. No doubt they would say they obtained it for medicinal reasons, two perambulators passed by, one was pushed and pulled by a family of four; the other manipulated by a childless couple. No bottles were visible, but they were hidden under a baby's coverlet, then came Reg and his mate from the garage struggling with a large glass carboy encased in a wicker cage, with handles on either side. As they ascended the short slope between beach and road there came a loud crack; the carboy disintegrated into several pieces and loosed a crimson flood, upon the sand. They looked at one another in horror, for they had borrowed it without the owner's knowledge. "We shall get hell", said Reg, "Twas full of distilled water and look what's happened!" I told him to collect all the pieces, wash them under our pump to get rid of the wine stains, and return it to its corner and forget it. He was grateful at this suggestion, put the remains on my butt and helped me pull it back to Towan Green. Here they removed casing and glass and hurried back through the meadows and were waiting by our garden hedge when I arrived, Mother was curious, so I had to tell her what they had done, but on no account must she tell Father for he too worked at the garage. Reg returned the broken carboy that night, and it was not until several days later when someone wanted distilled water for their wireless accumulator that his boss found it and thought it had broken through someone backing a car into it. I gave Reg and his mate a bottle each, and Father and I securely corked the remainder and put them up on the washhouse shelves to mature, together with the sweet bottles. The watering can, filled with red wine was taken indoors and we held a tasting session when Father returned from work. It proved to be as sour as vinegar, and no amount of sugar stirred into it would make it sweeter. The white wine was drinkable, and Father anticipated that in six months the red stuff would have fermented, and lost it sourness.

At each tide that week, more and more barrels arrived, and Wiggy had a busy time debunging them - at least those which he saw. Others were rolled away at night, and one enterprising farmer took a horse and chain-harrow to the beach and removed two barrels on it. Alas, when I returned with my butt some days later, I had forgotten where I had stood on the beach when I buried my bottles in the dunes. There were now scores of yellow ragwort plants in bloom. I dug until my fingers, were sore and never found my bottles I wonder how many years elapsed before they were exposed to the light of day again when the wind blew away their sand covering, and who finally found, and spat out their insidious contents.

My Father also had fun during this wine harvest, and one night I went with him and two of his friends in his employer's lorry, to Trevose Head. Someone told him that two barrels had washed up into the Round Hole an enormous crater caused by erosion of the sea into a cave, the roof of which had finally collapsed, Father and I sat on the cliff top and Bert and Harold, crept down to the entrance to the Round Hole. They discovered that somebody was already down there so they climbed back to discuss the next move with us. It was agreed that Father would let down two ropes into the hole, and in the meantime they would wait in the darkness of the cave entrance. Father would then shout loudly down into the hole, and switch on his torch, assuming that whoever was down there would take fright and run away.

In the near silky darkness, with a sickle moon over the bay, the Plough and Orion's Belt twinkling intermittently, and the scarlet sweep of the lighthouse beam to keep us company, we let down the rope and waited a few minutes. Then Father switched on the torch and swept the beam around, the bottom of the hole. There, transfixed, stood the village 'black sheep' and his friend beside two barrels, their mouths gaping open in surprise. "What are you up to? Stealin' wine after all the warnings you've had! You'll be for the high jump I've got your names!" yelled Father. They scuttled out of sight through the cave entrance and a few minutes later we heard them climbing up the cliff face. They did not see the parked lorry as they made their way to the boundary hedge where their bicycles were lying, and switched on their lamps and pedalled away into the night. Father yelled down the hole, "Hey! Are you there?" and there was a tug on the rope. We let out more rope and Bert shouted that one barrel was secured and ready for hauling to the top; he would, remain down there and Harold would help us pull it up. Harold duly arrived, and the barrel made its bumpy journey to the surface. The performance was repeated, with the second barrel, Bert rejoined us and we hoisted, them onto the lorry, together with a large coil of rope which they had found by the barrels. Both barrels were empty and in good condition. We learned that people were buying them at high prices to cut in half and make flower tubs for their gardens. Others were transforming them into seats. Next day, Father sold both barrels and split the proceeds with Bert and Reg. Being a junior, and not an active member of the operation I received two shillings for my efforts.

It was rumoured that the 'black sheep' when in his cups at the Cornish Arms, was heard to mutter that he had been robbed of his booty and his rope. But he did not mention that he had purloined the rope from his neighbour's barn, so when Father heard this through the grape vine, he quietly returned it to the farmer and explained what had happened. By way of grateful thanks - for the rope was worth several pounds he was given a bottle of brandy decanted from a cask which the farmer had found high and dry one morning, long before the wine had come ashore.

We never enjoyed that wine; several bottles fermented, burst and made a mess on the washhouse floor. In my eagerness to get to the scene, I had forgotten to pass all the bottles over to Mother for swilling out. Two contained dregs of methylated spirits, and when we opened them their contents burned our throats and made us gasp, so down the drain they went. The other bottles never matured; gradually gathered dust, and were, one by one, consigned to the dustbin until none remained. But strange to relate, there are still a few bottles to be found in the parish, and one I was told, was sampled only last month - nearly fifty years after it had washed ashore; and it tasted as bad as it did on the day it was bottled.

Images of the Late Jack Ingrey, Author.

26

Fun on the Fairways

Father gave up farm labouring during our latter years at Lane End and joined the staff of the new Golf Links at Constantine Bay where, under the supervision of the Course Architect and the owner, he helped to shape what is now one of the most popular golf courses in the West Country.

Father was a 'natural' sportsman: excellent footballer, keen on athletics, and thought nothing of a seven mile run 'just to warm up'; he was a good shot with a gun and we were never short of rabbits, partridges, wood pigeons and wild duck according to the season. Cricket did not interest him, but he became a first class golfer, playing to single figure handicaps and in later years at scratch.

During those early days Father and his mates cut branches from tamarisk bushes, shaped them into crude clubs and played their own version of golf on the embryonic course. Later the newly appointed professional sold them second-hand clubs and they learned from him the finer points of stance, swing, follow through and putting.

Father had high hopes that I would follow in his footsteps, and in due course bought me a small golf bag, two wood clubs, four irons and a putter. As the evenings lengthened during spring he took me to the course and we played a few holes. Father was a patient instructor; he placed my feet apart at the correct distance; he wrapped my fingers correctly around the shaft of the club, locked my little fingers together and pushed my elbows against my body.

"Now address the ball."

I concentrate on the small white object, feeling stiff and uncomfortable.

"Keep your head down and swing back - slowly."

I do this and my eyes start watering. I can see two balls.

"Hold it there a moment!"

The balls dance up and down.

"Swing down and through."

I feel like a clockwork toy. Click! At the moment of impact my eyes leave the shimmering balls to follow their flight.

"Your head was up too soon, but you hit the ball."

Fifty yards down the fairway on the left hand side I can see one ball.

"And you hooked it."

Father tees up another ball and smiles encouragingly.

"Now, have another go, and keep your head down after you've hit the ball. I'll watch where it goes."

The lesson continues. With luck, I hit the next ball further than its predecessor. Then I top the next two balls and they roll a few yards off the tee. Father's patience still holds. By chance I hit another good shot. I know this because the 'click' sounds right. The ball soars away; my head comes up just as the ball lands a good hundred and fifty yards down the centre of the fairway. Father is pleased.

"You can do that every time if you keep your head down," he says.

But I know that sport, including golf, doesn't run through my veins.

As I hit a ball into the rough and we tramp towards its position which I have marked by a flower stalk, as Father has taught me, my eyes wander from it to a skylark which takes flight before me and, forgetting the ball, I hasten to that spot and find a nest hidden in the grass.

"Look! Look Father! A lark's nest!" I cry and, bending down I pick up a warm greenish-brown egg. My lost ball is completely forgotten.

"You're learning to play golf; not looking for bird's nests." Father looks grim.

"Yes, Father."

"If I hadn't marked that ball, you'd never have found it. Now come over here and use the niblick. And put that egg back."

Reluctantly I replace the egg, withdraw the club, drop the bag and straddle the ball which Father has moved slightly to give me a better lie.

"Get the club head under the ball as you follow through, and use your wrists."

I do as I am told and, after three or four unsuccessful hacks, the ball reaches the fairway. My lesson continues, but out of the corner of my eye I watch the lark descend and run to her nest.

Sometimes during summer evenings wild flowers diverted my attention as I pursued my wayward ball in the rough, and I wandered off to examine spikes of yellow mullein, red stems of parasitic dodder entwining pink convolvulus, clumps of tall evening primrose and cushions of aromatic purple thyme.

Red and black winged cinnabar moths laying their eggs on stalks of yellow ragwort fluttered lazily before me as I disturbed them, and a few weeks later droves of the black and orange striped caterpillars emerged to eat the leaves and strip the plants bare until they dropped to the ground to pupate.

Father finally realised that I would never become a golfer, gave up his attempts to instruct me and left me to my own devices. His humiliation was complete on the evening of the annual caddies' competition when, after carrying my clubs for me, giving me advice on how to play every stroke, I made every possible mistake and received a special Booby prize for completing nine holes in the greatest number of strokes ever recorded. As I stepped forward to receive a handsome putter from the Club Secretary amid laughter and applause for my efforts. Father was heard to say, "He's far more interested in bloody larks' nests than golf."

I caddied because it was necessary for me to earn money to help pay for extras incurred each term after I transferred to Bodmin County School for, although I had won a free Scholarship and a minute grant towards expenses, there were such things as school dinners, bicycle upkeep, rail season tickets, and school clothing to be paid for, and Mother's caretaking and laundry work did not cover these extra items. So except for those weeks during the earlier years when I spent Easter and Summer Holidays with my Aunt and Uncle at Halligye, the remainder of the holidays were devoted to caddying.

Caddies reported to the professional's shop at eight o'clock each morning and he entered our names on a list. The higher ones name appeared on the list meant the greater the chance of one being engaged for two rounds on that day. Unfortunately I was not one of the professional's favourites who were detailed to carry clubs for the wealthy business men and their wives who were on holiday in the area. Those boys were automatically booked with the same golfers for the whole of their stay and generally received anything from five shillings (25p) to seven shillings and sixpence (37p) per round, whereas I and the other less favoured boys received the minimum two shillings (10p) to three shillings and sixpence (17p) per round from the less affluent golfers. However, on one occasion I struck big money for a whole fortnight.

Herr Sigmund Oskarhamm was a tall, overweight Swede, with a pink face, bald head and sagging lower lip. His wife was a petite lady with a china doll face, peaches and cream complexion and a permanently fixed smile. This late middle age couple played two rounds each day. The lady delivered each stroke with a slow, slow motion swing, and unerringly holed out with slow, slow motion putts. Each round took three and a half hours (the average time being two and a half hours) and Herr Oskarhamm, who was a long distance, but uncontrollable hitter was often the loser in each slow, slow motion marathon. His pink forehead dripped perspiration onto his gold-rimmed spectacles as he wiped his features with a king sized handkerchief. After pursuing most drives into the far rough with his caddy (one of the Pro's favourites) who staggered ahead under the weight of a massive leather golf bag containing thirteen clubs, he would call, "I will be with you soon, Mopsy darleeng." When his ball reached the fairway where I dawdled with Madame as she played her short, effective strokes straight to the pin, she would call to her spouse, "Oh Siggy darling, what a good shot you made!" Siggy, reciprocating, would call after she had played a further stroke, "Mopsy darleeng, you play like an Angel," and he would plant a blubbery kiss on her porcelain cheek and put an arm around her tiny waist, squeezing it gently as they processed towards the green.

Mopsy darleeng informed me during her husband's frequent excursions into the rough that they lived near Malrno on the southern tip of Sweden; were furniture manufacturers and employed five hundred workmen, and at the end of their holiday I was well briefed in the Swedish way of life, including the benefits of the Sauna, and all aspects of furniture manufacture.

At the end of each protracted round Herr Oskarhamm paid his caddy and myself with ten shilling notes, and Mopsy darleeng, unbeknown to her husband dipped into her handbag and presented me with another one. After their final round before their departure, the grateful Herr gave us each a crisp five pound note as a token of our efficiency, and Mopsy darleeng gave me a sly wink and another one. Such largesse was staggering and a great help towards my school expenses.

There were also eccentrics and tyrants. One left handed player was so quick and forceful in his actions that when addressing his ball on tee and fairway he almost mowed down anyone who had the misfortune to be on his wrong side.

Another elderly, plump, and very hairy gentleman was Mr James Henderson. He rarely had a partner and preferred to play the course on his own, he was aware that a single player had no status, but he always hired a caddy and, more often than not it was me. As soon as we were out of sight of the clubhouse windows he removed his clothing, stuffed it into a rucksack for me to carry, and then donned a minute pair of shorts which resembled a khaki Elizabethan codpiece. He said he was accustomed to be free of clothing when he played golf in Uganda, and the natives didn't wear much clothing either. The whole of Henderson's body was tanned a deep brown; he ambled with his head thrust forward and apart from his white Panama hat, he resembled a gorilla. He also carried his pipe, tobacco and matches in a little string bag which hung from his neck.

James Henderson paid only three shillings (15p) per round, but his good humour, and anecdotes made up for this deficiency.

"I ain't very well endowed with this world's goods," he said one afternoon when paying me on the seventeenth green before donning his clothes in order to look respectable on the eighteenth hole, but the considerable size of his codpiece belied this statement.

One day, however, Henderson who had played a round without a caddy, was summoned to the Secretary's office and given a sharp reprimand for playing golf in the nude, on totally inaccurate information supplied by a short sighted lady golfer, and poor old Henderson, taking umbrage for such an accusation, never played on the course again.

I dreaded one particular tyrant. This man had no favourite caddy and engaged whoever was next on the list and paid the minimum two shillings with one hand, and with the other proffered as a tip a silver threepenny bit. He expected to lose no balls, but if one was lost his caddy was forced to find a replacement. He rarely spoke to his partner or opponent and wore a permanent glowering expression. On the greens one stood to attention holding the pin with

204

the flag firmly between the fingers to prevent it flapping, and woe betide the unfortunate caddy who trod a heel mark in the line of the man's anticipated line of putt. His caddy was also expected to be psychic and draw each correct club from the bag without him asking. If he made a poor shot as a result of his caddy's choice he roared loudly, "You bloody idiot boy!"

I suffered this man's onslaughts for two trembling rounds, but one fearless caddy having also suffered enough, rose to the occasion, retorted, "Bollocks you bastard!" and was dismissed on the spot.

There were hilarious and sometimes embarrassing moments, one of which I experienced on the fourth hole. One summer evening I caddied for one of two brothers named Johnson. They were an energetic pair who played two rounds during the day with a break for tea and a short rest. Then they went out again for another nine holes. I had caddied for David the elder brother on several occasions. Daniel the younger brother carried his own clubs. Both men were erratic golfers, and the game was secondary to their gymnastic exercises, academic discussions and botanical sit-downs which occurred regularly.

The elder Johnson would, for no apparent reason, suddenly perform handstands, cartwheels and somersaults on green or fairway. His brother, whilst putting and playing fairway shots, would pay little regard to hole or direction but hold forth upon the glories of, Ancient Egypt, Queen Nefertiti, her pharaoh Akhenaton and the city of Tel el Amarna, all of which held me spellbound. Both men would squat on their haunches in the rough for minutes on end if one of them found an interesting flower in the vicinity of a ball. They were keen amateur naturalists, and I, who had studied our local flora and had learned to identify them, was able to assist; they lapped up this information and I was well rewarded.

On this particular evening when there was still lark song in the sky and the shouts of late holiday makers on the bay, we had progressed through the short third hole without incident and arrived at the fourth tee of that long and delightful dogleg hole whose green is set like a jewel against the backcloth of Dinas Head.

The brothers drove off, Daniel Johnson placing his drive straight down the centre of the fairway, whilst David pulled his drive into the rough on the left hand side.

I hastened to my man's ball, having marked its position by a clump of white Ox-eye daisies, and awaited his arrival. His next shot was a full blooded niblick disaster which flew into the marram grass dunes and disappeared over the lip of a little used and lesser known bunker. We climbed up the dune, reached the bunker together, and looked down - I gasped at what I saw.

In the lowest part of the bunker lay a nude couple, their clothing strewn at random and, oblivious of the world around them were engaged in energetic copulation. The ball was some three feet from the man's pulsating buttocks, and my unaccustomed teenage eyes were glued to the spectacle of what I knew a fair amount, but had never before witnessed or practiced.

David Johnson waved excitedly to his brother and beckoned him to join us, which he did after playing another long straight shot. In the bunker the activity momentarily subsided amid moaning and sighing and then recommenced as they shuffled into a different position. I watched with erotic fascination, the bulge in my trousers getting larger.

The brothers with heads together, conferred in whispers, then nodded in agreement at something I could not hear. Holding his niblick, David Johnson tiptoed stealthily over the edge of the bunker and into it. The copulators, oblivious of the intruder continued their lovemaking. Standing within a foot of the recumbent bodies he addressed the ball carefully, swung slowly and delivered a clean shot over our heads into a patch of less thick rough where I marked its position.

I looked back into the bunker and saw David Johnson turn, take the niblick by the head and, bending forward, deftly push the leather bound shaft between the man's convoluting buttocks. Then pulling it quickly away, he shouted, "Wake up, mate, and shove up an inch for me!" Then he ran up and out of the bunker.

The effect within was electric. The man, a stranger to me turned full frontal, open mouthed and speechless. His partner also sat up, speechless. And so was I - for she was a local lady of impeccable virtue, and for years afterwards, until her decease, she could never look me in the eye if we chanced to meet.

The Lake, Trevose Golf Links

27

Babes in the Wood

Musical Society's New Pantomime Success.

This year's pantomime by the St Merryn Musical Society is "Babes in the Wood"; Jack Ingrey has again written the script and given his cast a good story to work on. These Babes lived in the time of Robin Hood and they had an aunt, Maid Marion who promised to look after them when they were orphaned. But of course with a certain amount of topicality spivs kidnap the Babes and they are rescued by Friar Tuck, Little John and the rest of the merry men. So they come into their rightful inheritance. Robin Hood is pardoned so that he can marry Marion and the Bad Barons fate is to wed Lucrecia Loosebody, the children's unfortunate nurse.

The babes are played by Audrey Hawke and Ken Dingle. Every moment they are on the stage is a delight. They arrive in a pram and reward us with some slapstick that would be a credit to the Crazy Gang, yet they bring that touch of pathos to the scene when they are lost in the forest which is the sure mark of the true comedian.

Jean Curtis as Robin Hood is everything a principal boy should be. Her singing is much stronger and she moves with a swagger in real pantomime style. Stage duels are always a bit tricky but Jean has two and handles them well. With her is Mary Burke as Maid Marion who is singing just as well and looking just as attractive as she did last year, but still seems to be holding herself back a bit.

No restraint about the Baron

There is no question of restraint with the Baron of Richard Pitman, Anyone who contemplates a bit of villainy towards the Petrol Rationing Officer could not do better than get a few lessons from this Baron! Whether he is plotting with two spivs or wheedling his way into the Dames heart, he is equally convincing. The spivs played by Albert Dadswell and John Pitman are in all the fun and roguery, but perhaps they could have made rather more of their parts.

The St Merryn Dame has usually been given a part calling for a really boisterous performance, but this time Mr Ingrey has provided a part needing more acting and less slapstick. This suits Rex Trenouth who gives an all round excellent performance even though it is difficult to believe that this buxom, bouncing bodyguard is last years suave inscrutable Grand Vizier.

The classroom scene must surely make the biggest misery laugh. From the moment Ken Gray bounces in this is a riot. Ken Smith is the high spot as Ned the Nark, closely followed by a gem of comedy from Ruth Allen as Prunella. Bill Cheyney is a fearsome Jack the Ripper and Trixie Cowling sings far better than any of them. Jean Bennett also has a diverting part.

The Davy Crockett touch.

In their dream the Babes see Davy Crockett a part that gives Charles Pitman a chance to show us what a fine actor and singer he is. He is joined by some Black Feet Indians whose visit end with a first class war dance from Ken Smith. The dance of the Flame Goddess devised by Joan Prior is effectively done by Jean Bennett. This calls for a special word of praise for the lighting effect by Ernest Angell.

The Fair, based on an idea of Rosalind Thelwell, is a delightful scene with many sideshows and all the fun of the fair and complete with merry-go-round. Tarzani the strong man (Jim Harper), the bearded lady (Olive Daswell), the Crystal Gazer (Millie Trenouth) and the dancing bear and his keeper (Anthony Angell and Bill Cheyney) all do well, but the one who seizes his chances here is Frank Mc Key as senior Hoppo the Flea Circus proprietor. Elsie Gray brings off a delicious piece of comedy.

Singing and Dancing

Fine singing comes from Trixie Cowling as she dances with Jean Bennett and Julie Pate in the Robin Hood scene one of the best in the show. The Merry Men appear in several scenes with Frank Mc Key good as Friar Tuck and Charles Pitman as a lusty Little John and Dora Bray as Will Scarlett. Granny Grigg aged 95 pops in and out and is very nice work by Millie Trenouth. The company is completed by Jean Harvey, Elsie Paynter and Dorothy Ruff.

No fault is to be found with the production by Jack Ingrey and Ken Dingles stage scenes – his village green classroom and forest scenes – are a delight. The costumes are better than this company has had before and Joyce Hawken takes the credit for these. A feature of these shows is the lighting for which Ernest Angell and Royston Bell are responsible. Neil Burke is the stage manager and his helpers behind the scenes are Doris Angell, Jean Ayrton, Frances Hainsellin, Miriam Pitman, Marjorie Reynolds, Marion Smith, Raymond Allen, Jack Reynolds, and Cedwin Wills. The music is provided by Joy Dingle and Percy Keast.

Individual performances are nearly all good but the show as a whole does not move quite so slickly as "Aladdin" did last year. This is not a very serious criticism for "Aladdin" reached an unusually high standard.

Cornish Guardian 10th January 1957.

Babes in the Wood, Ken and Audrey as the Babes in the bedroom scene. The Indians are *L to R*: Ruth Allen, Julie Pate, Trixie Cowling, Ken Smith and Ken Gray, Davey Crockett played by Charles Pitman has just gone off stage.

Babes in the Wood, school room scene.

Babes in the Wood, Will Scarlet (Dora Bray), Ned (Ken Smith), Prunella (Ruth Allen), Little John (Charles Pitman), Robin Hood (Jean Curtis), Maid Marion Mary Burke), Little Nell (Trixie Cowling), Blackfoot Indian White Eagle (Bill Cheyney), Flame Goddess (Jean Bennett) and Blackfoot Indian Sitting Bull (Ken Grey).

28

Dick Whittington

Act I.   Prologue.   Good Fairy

   Scene 1. Mrs. Whittington's Cottage
   Scene 2. Mrs. Whittington's Cottage, late
             afternoon the following day

Act II.

   Scene 3. The Road to London
   Scene 4. A doorway in London, early morning
   Scene 5. The Kitchen of Sir Roger Fitzwarren's
             house, early morning
   Scene 6. The Kitchen of Sir Roger Fitzwarren's
             house, one hour later
   Scene 7. Cries of London
   Scene 8. The Kitchen of Sir Roger Fitzwarren's
             house, some months later

Act III.

   Scene 9. I'm in the Navy now!
   Scene 10. The Fires of Love ·
   Scene 11. By the Dockside
   Scene 12. What fun it would have been!
   Scene 13. The Road from London

INTERVAL

Act IV.

   Scene 14. The Harem of the Sultan of Barbary
   Scene 15. The Harem, later the same day

Act V.

   Scene 16. A Ship comes home
   Scene 17. A Garden by the River
   Scene 18. A Garden by the River, later same day

FINALE

THE PLAYERS

DICK WHITTINGTON	Jean Curtis
ALICE FITZWARREN	Rene Trenouth
PUSSKINS, the Cat	Audrey Hawke
THE MILESTONE	Albert Dadswell
SIR ROGER FITZWARREN	Charles Woodward
IDLE JACK	Gerald Harris
MRS. WHITTINGTON	Elsie Paynter
MARY, Dick's elder Sister	Betty Bray
JANE, Dick's younger Sister	Joy Gale
BUMBLECHOOK, the Bailiff	Horatio Pitman
MARTHA, the Cook	Gwen Keatt
TIMOTHY, a Scullion	Albert Dadswell
JANET, a Serving Maid	Lucy Threadgould
Captain CORNFLOWER	Richard Pitman
1st. SAILOR	Charles Pitman
2nd. SAILOR	John Prynn
3rd. SAILOR	Horatio Pitman
The SULTAN OF BARBARY	Frank Jewell
JUJUBE, The Sultan's chief wife	Millie Trenouth
SALOME, The Sultan's 2nd. wife	Lucy Threadgold
JASMIN, The Sultan's 3rd. wife	Dora Bray
MARIANA, keeper of the keys	Olive Dadswell
The GOOD FAIRY	Bromwyn Roseveare
The BAD FAIRY } and KING RAT }	Ruth Allen
A MESSENGER	Stanley Hesling

Pianist	Joy Dingle
Stage Management	Rita Adams and Neil Burke
Costumes and Wardrobe	Lucy Threadgould,
	Olive Dadswell and Louvaine Stead
Scenery	Jack Threadgould
Stage Carpenter	Raymond Allen
Curtains	Ken Gray
Lighting and Special Effects	Colin Cleave
Additional Dialogue and Lyrics	Lucy Threadgould

Devised and Produced from an original script

by JACK INGREY

in association with RITA ADAMS.

Dick Whittington, Alice Fitzwarren (Rene Trenouth) in her costume for the Finale.

Dick Whittington, Pusskins the cat played by Audrey Hawke.

Dick Whittington, in their Finale costumes are Sir Richard (Jean Curtis) and Lady Whittington with Sir Pusskins (Audrey Hawke).

Dick Whittington Act 3 Scene 9. *L to R*: 2ⁿᵈ Sailor (John Prynn), Idle Jack (Gerald Harris), and 1ˢᵗ Sailor (Charles Pitman).

Dick Whittington Act 2 Scene 6. Timothy (Albert Dadswell) and Martha the cook (Gwen Keatt).

Dick Whittington Act 2 Scene 8. The Good Fairy (Bromwyn Roseveare) and Dick (Jean Curtis).

Dick Whittington Act 4 Scene 15. The Messenger (Stanley Hesling) and the Sultan of Barbary (Frank Jewell), the Sultans wives (Millie Trenouth, Lucy Threadgold and Dora Bray) are in the background.

213

Dick Whittington Scene 2. *L to R*: **Mrs Whittington (Elsie Paynter), Jane (Joy Gale), Pusskins (Audrey Hawke), Dick (Jean Curtis) and Mary (Betty Bray).**

Dick Whittington's cast and producer Jack Ingrey taking their final bow.

29

Jack and the Beanstalk

St Merryn Musical Society's Success in Pantomime.

For the second year in succession the St Merryn Musical Society have hit the bulls-eye with their pantomime, which is being played at the Church Hall, St Merryn every evening this week.

Again written and produced by Jack Ingrey with some charming lyrics by Ken Dingle, "Jack and the Beanstalk" puts the accent on youth and beauty, but humour, spectacle, singing, dancing and a nice element of surprise are mingled into a lively and colourful production, a delight, from opening chorus to full stage finale.

There are 12 scenes ranging from Dame Dinah Doolittle's flower-hung cottage garden, with Annabelle, a wonderful cow, and a miraculous beanstalk via Shop Corner, the road to Wadebridge Market, the land of Nearly There, with its strange inhabitants to the kitchen of a giants castle itself, with a cannibal of a giant.

No fewer than 24 musical numbers are sung or danced, either as duet, trio, quartet or chorus, but the production lacks a really memorable number, and we sadly missed those charming solos from Charles Pitman, though he sang effectively in several numbers.

The Dame

As Dame Dinah Doolittle, with copper-red wig and "A1 copper-bottomed" humour. Horatio Pitman sings, dances and clowns with gusto and he made the "ballet lesson" one of the highlights of a grand performance.

Audrey Hawke and Gerald Harris made an incongruous comic couple with Creeping Jenny the predatory spinster, and Peter Piper, the man who gets hooked, bursting into song at the most appropriate and inappropriate moments with tremendous verve.

As principal boy and girl Jean Curtis and Rex Trenouth bring exactly the right touch of youthful romance and make an enchanting couple singing their duets enchantingly.

Richard Pitman's fine voice and sense of satire are again most effective and this time as Squire Grabem, Jenny's brother, Gwen Keatt as the Giants cook, shines with her usual ability and sings attractively, though we wished there might have been more opportunities for her splendid voice; and Frank Jewell, out-Simming Alistair, strides and roars his gigantic way through the part of Giant Colliewobble frightening and threatening most effectively. From the point of view of merit we would like to mention everyone concerned but in a team of nearly 40 this is obviously but regrettably impossible. We

215

must however mention the old lady Jill Hesling, and her transformation; the comic antics of Annabelle the cow – Albert Dadswell and Rex Trenouth; the enchanting ballet scene with its beautiful lighting effects, and the "school girl" and "school boy" numbers an excellent foil for each other.

Stage set and the "Etceteras"

No production however brilliant, can be colourful without a scene painter who knows his job, and once again Kenneth Dingle has proved this most effectively, with a nice sense of perspective, helped by Raymond Allen and Albert Dadswell were responsible for its construction. The many attractive costumes were made by Margery Reynolds and the lighting was in the capable hands of Colin Cleave.

To Rene Trenouth must go the credit for the clever and varied dance arrangements including the most charming scene of the whole show, "Dream dream dream." And the music was provided by Joy Dingle at the piano and Ken Smith and his trio, who added considerably to the success of the production. Jack Ingrey is again responsible for the excellent script which manages to be richly comic while being quite coherent – no mean feat. We could wish for more of several of the items, but would part with nothing. He has produced with professional efficiency, ably assisted by Rita Adams, and the whole show is one to see, enjoy, delight in, and remember. Well done St Merryn!

Jill (Rene Trenouth) and Jack (Jean Curtis).

From top to bottom: Creeping Jenny (Audrey Hawke), Peter Piper (Gerald Harris) and Squire Grabem (Richard Pitman).

Giant Colliwobble (Frank Jewell), Creeping Jenny (Audrey Hawke) and Hildegarde (Gwen Keatt).

The Ballet School: *L to R*: **Kenny Dingle, Rex Trenouth, Horace Pitman, Charlie Pitman and Albert Dadswell.**

Jack (Jean Curtis), the Cow (Rex Trenouth, front & Albert Dadswell, back),
Squire Grabem (Richard Pitman) and Creeping Jenny (Audrey Hawke).

30

Aladdin

Notable Production of Local Society.

With the successful launching of Aladdin at the Church Hall St Merryn on Thursday Jack Ingrey and the St Merryn Musical Society bring off the pantomime "hat trick".

The two previous productions have set a very high standard indeed but this is well maintained, and this year an even better balance has been achieved. There are four newcomers to the company – Mary Burke, Anona Holloway, Donald Weekes and Frank McKey – and all are distinct assets.

The comic element is well to the fore, as is to be expected with Horatio Pitman playing the Dame with verve, giving point to every line and singing and dancing with untiring zest. Widow Twankys version of the can-can danced with the Harem Fillies – Albert Dadswell, Donald Weekes and Ken Gray – is one of the highlights.
Richard Pitman reaches new heights as Abanazar the magician and uses his fine voice through the whole gamut of villainy including two amusing duets with Widow Twanky and a first class "death scene".

Grand Vizier and Genies

Another actor who has improved tremendously is Rex Trenouth who gives a most assured – and Chinese – performance as the Grand Vizier: and Charles Pitman and Kenneth Dingle as the two Genies appear and reappear with unflagging energy from the most unexpected places with every flash of lightning and clap of very realistic thunder. Their songs are a delight.

Gwen Keatt is an authoritative and buxom Empress of China and makes the most of the amusing scene in the Royal Bath blowing bubbles in the bathwater, and fishing out a strange assortment of submarine life, to the delight of the children and despair of her handmaidens Ruth Allen, Millie Trenouth and Trixie Cowling.

The romantic element is nicely emphasised by the excellent performances from Jean Curtis as the Principal Boy, and Mary Burke as Princess Boroda, their duets being especially Mary Burke is also particularly good in the difficult poisoning scene in the last act.

Frank Mc Key appears as the Emperor of China Audrey Hawke makes the most of an all-to-small part as Concubine 49 with amusing ambitions towards wifely status: Trixie Cowling sings most attractively and Donald Weekes gives a perfect cameo as a Jewish Merchant.

Pleasing Dances

The dancing throughout is very good most particularly that of the new little star Anona Holloway who's solo is delightful, and is also responsible for the excellent dance sequences.

There are 17 scenes including five full stage sets, ranging from Widow Twanky's Atomic Laundry – complete with old fashioned mangle and a wonderful whirling dryer – to the loveliest scene of all the cave of Jewels – a triumph for the scene painter, Kenneth Dingle.

The remainder of the large cast including Elsie Paynter, Olive Dadswell, Joan Harvey, Julie Porter, Albert Dadswell as a very amusing rickshaw man, Jean Bennett, Dora Bray, Millie Trenouth and Neil Burke – all do their share in providing a show full of fun and laughter, music and movement.

Writer and Producer

Jack Ingrey who has written the script, has produced with skill, assisted by Rita Adams, with Neil Burke in charge of the stage management. Marjorie Reynolds responsible for the wardrobe and Ken Gray for the curtains.

Equal credit must be given to the many helpers before and behind the footlights, including Raymond Allen, Leonard Buscombe, Jim Harper, Alex Bray, Louvaine Stead and Esther Trenouth, and a good measure of the success of the production is due to the untiring playing of Ken Smith and his trio, with Joy Dingle at the piano and the excellent lighting effects arranged by Ernest and Anthony Angell.

Nine performances are being given at the Church Hall St Merryn, up to and including Saturday followed by three performances at St Columb and three at Wadebridge.

The Guardian Thursday January 12th 1956

Dress rehearsal Aladdin, "Welcome to Our Pantomime". *L to R*: **Trixie Cowling, Donald Weekes, Julie Porter, Millie Trenouth, Audrey Hawke, Joan Harvey, Anona Holloway, Dora Bray, Olive Dadswell, Ruth Allen, Albert Dadswell and Elsie Paynter.**

Act 3 Scene 15. The Emperor (Frank McKey) and Empress (Gwen Keatt) in a moment of matrimonial bliss as they survey Aladdin's new palace.

Kenneth Dingle the Genie of the ring and Charles Pitman the Genie of the lamp reminisce on old times and sing Abracadabra.

Act 1 Scene 9. 'Twankey's Laundry': Yippee (Audrey Hawke), Yappee (Joan Harvey), Widow Twankey (Horatio Pitman), Kum-Kum (Jean Bennett) and Go-Go (Dora Bray), they are all busy disposing of the Empress's smalls!

221

The Genie of the ring has conjured the Harem Lillies to dance for the Emperor of China, Jean Bennett, Dora Bray, Anona Holloway and Millie Trenouth, the beautiful belles of Bagdad.

The Finale, all the cast is assembled with Jack, the producer, after the last Chorus.

31

'Sunshine Special'

Lively Show with an Unusual Theme

It may seem that summer has deserted this island but last week the people of St Merryn basked in brilliant "sunshine" fun and gaiety at the summer show of the St Merryn Musical Society – "Sunshine Special" an imaginary trip by motor-coach through France, Austria, Italy and Spain in four acts of laughter, music, singing and dancing.

It is always difficult to follow one good show by a second from the same pen, but Jack Ingrey has succeeded with honours and was rewarded with full houses at the Church Hall, St Merryn where a fourth and extra performance had to be given on Friday. Based on a good idea, given by a cleaver and enthusiastic cast, and played with verve "Sunshine Special" was a continental coach tour with never a dull moment.

Gerald Harris as the once Cornish and now cockney bus driver, took every opportunity whether humorous or musical, and as usual made the most of them all.

The "Tourists"

The four "Tourists" in the "bus" were Jenny and Fred Lee and their awful daughter Rosie, and the prim botany mistress from Penrose, Miss Dora Flora, know to her friends as Clottie.

Gwen Keatt was excellent as Jenny, whether gay and jovial or serious and seasick; with Albert Dodswell sleepily henpecked proving the perfect foil as her husband.

As their "owful child" Audrey Hawke gave a delightful performance, perfect from pigtails and Carmen Miranda! Millie Trenouth gave amusin' emphasis to the school teachers enjoyment of everything that came her way; Willies wooing cocktails, spaghetti, gondola trips in the moonlight and all.

Richard Pitman dispensed joy as he did the drinks with sure and liberal touch; dispatching the blues and the bull with high spirits.

As the wandering minstrel with the wandering eye, Stanley Hesling provided a romantic accompaniment and Frank Jewell's performance as the "ica creama" vendor was a gem in three countries.

Songs old and new

The vocal talents of the whole community were given full rein with songs old and new, serious and sentimental, droll and diverting, operatic and everyday. Almost every member of the cast sings with such infectious pleasure that several of the songs could have been encored if time and the plot had permitted.

From so many cleverly chosen songs it is invidious to chose favourites but special praise must go to Ruth Allen for her brief excerpts from opera, and to Charles Pitman for his charming and unassuming rendering of several not-so-highbrow songs.

With the vocal side of the entertainment so well represented. It might have been expected that the dancing talents of the community would have been relegated to the background,

223

but Jean Curtis and Rene Trenouth proved once again that singers can sometimes dance; a spirited can-can and lilting tango being two of the highlights. Smaller parts well played filled in the pattern of the whole, and included cameos by Elsie Paynter, Kenneth Dingle, Jill Hesling, Olive Daswell and Rex Trenouth the latter as a fine Ferdinand the Bull in the Spanish scene.

Helpers

Once again Mr Ingrey received unstinted help from Rita Adams as his co-producer; Olive Dadswell, Marjory Reynolds and Louvaine Stead who made the costumes and curtains; Kenneth Dingle who painted the splendid scenery, Colin Cleave in charge of lighting. Ray Allen and Ken Gray, stage and curtains.

The music was presented by Joy Dingle at the piano and Kenneth Smith with drums and their unflagging energy carried the show along.

Mr Ingreys "book" could with advantage have been a little stronger; the front cloth scenes, except in the bus, could have been longer and Millie should not have forgiven Willie quite so easily. More might also have been of the tourists imminent return home – back to gym and geometry the mobile fish and chippery, and driving the Padstow bus.

But these are very minor quibbles.

Guardian July 1st 1954

Mr. and Mrs. Lee, proprietors of the local Fish and Chip Shop, together with their awful child Rosie, aged twelve, are spending their holidays this year on a Continental Coach Cruise.

Accompanying them is Miss Dora Flora who is Games and Botany Mistress at a nearby Girl's School.

Their Driver and Conductor is Willy Nilly a hard boiled Londoner who was born in a small Cornish village.

Their tour takes them to France, Austria, Italy and Spain and we invite you to take part in their adventures.

━━━━━━━━━━━━━━━━━━━

Act I.	Scene 1.	Today's THE Day!
	2.	Over the Waves.
	3.	An Old French Custom.
	4.	GAY PAREE.
Act II.	Scene 5.	Coming down the Mountain
	6.	At "THE WHITE HORSE"
Act III	Scene 7.	Moonlight and Melody.
	8.	VENETIAN BLIND.

INTERVAL

| Act IV. | Scene 9. | Two in the front row. |
| | 10. | SPANISH OMELETTE. |

━━━━━━━━━━━━━━━━━━━

THE CASTE

The Coach Driver.

| Willy Nilly | ... | GERALD HARRIS |

The Tourists.

Mrs. Jenny Lee	...	GWEN KEATT
Mr. Fred Lee	...	ALBERT DADSWELL
Rosie, their daughter	...	AUDREY HAWKE
Miss Dora Flora	...	MILLIE TRENOUTH

The French People.

A Customs Official	...	RICHARD PITMAN
Alphonse, a Waiter	...	HORATIO PITMAN
A Street Musician	...	STANLEY HESLING
Yvonne }		RENE TRENOUTH
Frou Frou } two Folies Girls		JEAN CURTIS
Newspaper Seller	...	ELSIE PAYNTER
Monsieur Pierre }		KENNETH DINGLE
Monsieur Gaston } two Gendarmes		CHARLES PITMAN
Mimi, an Artist's Model	...	JILL HESLING

The Austrian People

Siegfried }		KENNETH DINGLE
Carl } two Tyrolean youths		CHARLES PITMAN
Herr Gruber, proprietor of the "White Horse"		RICHARD PITMAN
Frau Gruber, his wife	...	OLIVE DADSWELL
Gretel, their daughter	...	RENE TRENOUTH
Anna }		RITA ADAMS
Vikki } villagers		RUTH ALLEN
		JEAN CURTIS
Students		JILL HESLING

The Italian People.

Antonio, an Ice Cream Vendor		FRANK JEWELL
Pedro, a donkeyman	...	CHARLES PITMAN
Roma, Antonio's wife	...	JEAN CURTIS
Napoli, a Fruit Vendor	...	RENE TRENOUTH
Spaghetti, a cafe proprietor	...	HORATIO PITMAN
Gorgonzola, a Gondolier	...	STANLEY HESLING
Sicili, an Opera Singer	...	RUTH ALLEN
Cara Mia		OLIVE DADSWELL
Carioca } two Fishwives		ELSIE PAYNTER
Hurdy Gurdy Man	...	KENNETH DINGLE

The Spanish People.

Carlos, Ticket office attendant	...	CHARLES PITMAN
Don Alphonso, the great Matador		HORATIO PITMAN
Juanita, his wife	...	JEAN CURTIS
Rosita, a dancer	...	RENE TRENOUTH
Margo		ELSIE PAYNTER
Nita } peasants		OLIVE DADSWELL
Camillo, Master of Ceremonies	...	RICHARD PITMAN
Carlotta, a Gypsy Singer	...	RUTH ALLEN
Pablo, a Wandering Troubadour	...	STANLEY HESLING
Paloma, a Spanish girl		JILL HESLING
Ferdinand the King of Bulls,	...	REX TRENOUTH
Valentino	...	KENNETH DINGLE

Sunshine Special Act 1 Scene 1. *L to R*: Millie Trenouth as Dora Flora, Gwen Keatt as Mrs Lee, Audrey Hawke as Rosie Lee, Albert Dadswell as Mr Lee and Gerald Harris as Willy Nilly.

Sunshine Special Act 1 Scene 4. Jean Curtis and Rene Trenouth doing a dance routine as Frou Frou and Yvonne.

Horatio Pitman as Alphonse the waiter, with Jean Curtis & Rene Trenouth.

The chorus in the White Horse Inn.

Frank Jewell as Antonio the ice cream seller.

Sunshine Special Finale with Jack Ingrey the producer centre stage.

People and Places

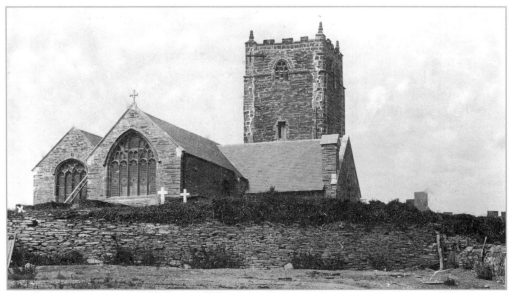

St Merryn Church

Reverend Olivey

Extension to the Wesleyan Chapel 1948

Map of St Merryn from the early 1930s, showing many of the places mentioned in the text.

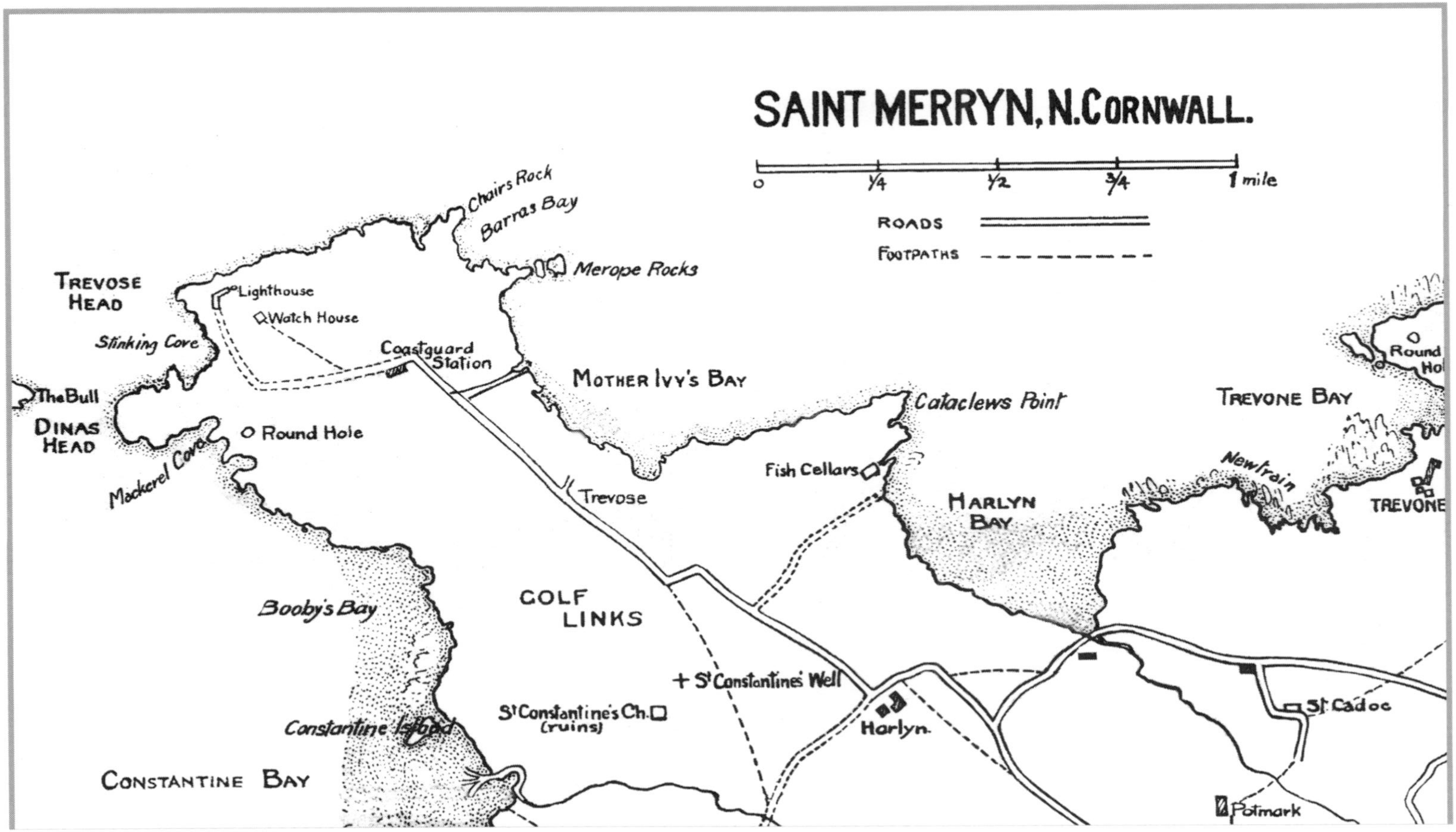

SAINT MERRYN, N.CORNWALL.

ROADS
FOOTPATHS

0   ¼   ½   ¾   1 mile

TREVONE

Round Hole

TREVONE BAY

St Cadoc

Newtrain

Potmark

Cataclews Point

HARLYN BAY

Chairs Rock

Barras Bay

Merope Rocks

MOTHER IVY'S BAY

Fish Cellars

Harlyn

+ St Constantine's Well

Trevose

GOLF LINKS

St Constantine's Ch.
(ruins)

Lighthouse

Watch House

Coastguard Station

Round Hole

Constantine Island

TREVOSE HEAD

Stinking Cove

The Bull

DINAS HEAD

Mackerel Cove

Booby's Bay

CONSTANTINE BAY

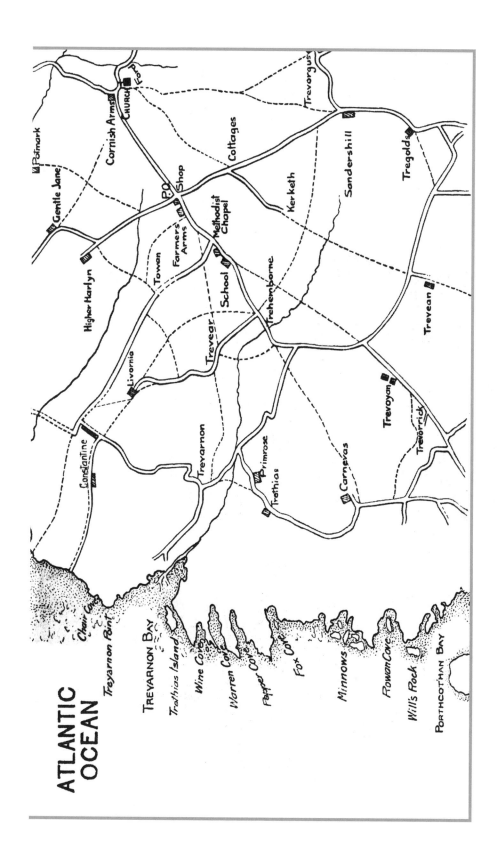

ATLANTIC OCEAN

Chair Cove

Trevarnon Point

TREVARNON BAY

Trethias Island

Wine Cove

Warren Cove

Pepper Cove

Fox Cove

Minnows

Rowan Cove

Will's Rock

PORTHCOTHAN BAY

Postmark

Gentle Jane

Higher Harlyn

Cornish Arms

CHURCH

Ford

Trevorgus

Cottages

Sandershill

Tregolds

Kerketh

P.O.

Shop

Methodist Chapel

Farmers' Arms

Towan

Trehemborne

Trevear

School

Trevean

Livornia

Trevoyan

Trevorrick

Trevarnon

Constantine

Primrose

Trethias

Carnevas

229

St Merryn School Pupils through the Years.

St Merryn School (1948)

Crigmorrick

St Merryn Churchtown from the Meadows

Porthcothan from the Meadows

Angling at Harlyn

Harlyn Bay by the fish cellars

232

Porthcothan

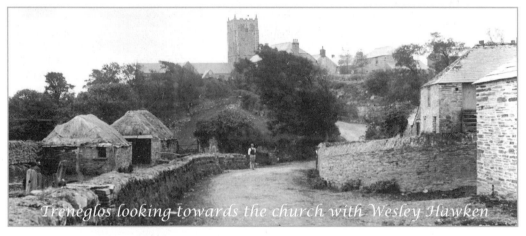

Treneglos looking towards the church with Wesley Hawken

Treyarnon Bay

233

St Merryn Ladies Red Cross, *'Penny a week for the war effort 1943'* . Back Row:
Mrs Wellsford, Miss M E Brenton, Mrs Bobby Darke, Mrs Audrey Rabey, Mrs
Doris Leverton. Front Row: Mrs Harry Parsons, Mrs Morcomb, Mrs Needham-
Cooper, Mrs Sam Brewer, Mrs Elizabeth Bellers.

The Cornish Arms, Stanley Curgenvens cottage adjacent and the vicarage barn on
the right. The band are marching to the Church for the evening service on Feast
week Sunday.

St Merryn Cricket teams from different eras.

Di Hawken at the St Merryn Carnival

**Edward Williams, Champion
Cornish Wrestler**

St Merryn Ladies

33

Work and Play

Photograph of the communal seining taking place at Mother Iveys. Without the help of so many people these seins would not have had the muscle power to bring in a good catch of mullet, bass or other delicacies caught in the net. The net would be taken out and rowed in a semicircle with the two ends then being pulled in from the shore. Sein netting was also carried out for pilchards having cellars at both Harlyn Bay and Mother Iveys.

The second picture shows the catch being shared-out between the volunteers.

Harvest Time at Higher Harlyn

Sheep at Harlyn Bay

Walking the horses at Polmark

238

Haymaking at Polmark

Seaweed Collecting

Shrimping at Porthcothan

Donkey ride on the Beach at Harlyn Bay

Treyarnon bathing pool where Jack spent many a happy hour. The cliff at this time was undeveloped, only one house is visible in this picture.

Paddling on the beach at Porthcothan

North Cornwall hounds first visit to St Merryn after being invited by Captain Percival Williams, Master of the Fourburrows Hunt. Leading the hunt is Percy West, Master ot the Hunt, with Jim Deacon, the whip behind him.

'Humpty Dumpty' at the St Merryn Carnival

Bill Thomas with parasol and Harvey Lobb (far right) at St Merryn Carnival

Red Cross Ladies at St Merryn Carnival

Early Cricket Match at Treyarnon

34

Warnings and Wrecks

Trevose Lighthouse

Trevose Fog Horn

Board of Trade Rocket Apparatus

'*Industry*' aground in Harlyn Bay (1912).

Firing a Rocket at Harlyn Bay

Recovering coal from the *'Industry'* at Harlyn Bay

Young Chris McCarthy providing a scale for the ribs of the Industry as they were in 1996.

Wrecks and Loss of Life on the Cornish Coast,

On the 3rd and 4th MARCH, 1897.

THE news that came to Padstow,
That was not of the best,
There was a Steamer below Trevose Head,
And she was in distress.

The Lifeboat men were summoned,
And to their post to stand,
They got the Rocket Apparatus ready
To run along the Land.

But the Steamer went to westward
In spite of all the wind and sea.
But they launched their Lifeboat at Newquay
And proceeded off to sea.

How fierce was the tempest !
How dark was the night !
Their oars were labouring heavily.
And the foam was glittering white.

It blew such a hurricane,
The tide, there was no slack,
But it blew such a heavy gale
That it forced the Lifeboat back.

Now the men they were exhausted
And that you could see.
That they had been labouring heavily
While they were on the sea.

Hark ! at twelve o'clock
There was another sound,
That they saw three quick flareups,
They thought the Steamer was gone down.

With twenty-four poor men they say,
All to be battered in the sea,
Some leaving their wives and children dear,
No matter if they were foreigners, their precious
lives were dear.

At three o'clock there was another sound,
It caused the people all to dress,
They said there was another vessel up in the bay,
And she was in distress.

The Lifeboat was got ready,
And away to her to steer,
And when they came so very close
It was the "Engineer."

No lives on board oh could they see,
They had to proceed right back to Newquay,
With four hour's hard pull they say,
Before they reached the Town of Newquay.

The men were worn out with fear,
To think they should hear tell the wreck of the
"Engineer."
When daylight came abroad, so they could see,
They saw great pieces of wreck washed in by
the sea.

The men, they walked along with fear,
At last they picked up a board
With the name of the "Engineer."

Three poor men were drowned,
They all three belonged to Newquay Town,
Some leaving their wives and children dear,
Someone lost her lover on board of the
"Engineer."

All you wives and children, and sweethearts dear,
Pray for all your friends to be on shore,
For in such a night, it never could be,
A little vessel to live in such a tremendous sea.

Now may the Lord have mercy on those poor men
that were drowned,
May their dear bodies be washed in and found,
And may their dear bodies be in a resting place
laid,
With a bunch of nice flowers to grow o'er their
heads.

And then their dear wives, and their children dear,
Be able to come down and say my dear father
lies here.
Oh ! what a blessing, a blessing that would be,
For the dear wife to come down and say,
My dear husband lies here instead of in the sea.

'Tis now my dear friends, 'tis God I must bless,
I can go home and die happy
Now I know my dear husband's body is at rest.

Now my dear friends, wherever you may be,
Pray for the dear sailors that go on the sea,
For without them we cannot do,
Pray, every storm, that they may ride through.

Now my dear friends
I have told you my song,
I hope you'll forgive me
If I've said anything wrong.

Composed by H. THOMAS, of Padstow.

Two photographs of the *'Jessie McClew'*, wrecked at Harlyn Bay

Wreck of the *'Petrel'* in 1886 and her cargo of marble

Wreck of the *'Hodbarrow Miner'* at Mawgan Porth, 1908

'Hemsley-1' on the rocks at Treyarnon in 1969

The *'Carl'* out of Hamburg, grounded in Booby's Bay in 1917

'Smiling Thro' of Lowestoft in Newtrain Bay, Trevone (1924)

Wreck of the *'Belt'* in Mother Ivey's Bay (1906)